Bloom's Modern Critical Interpretations

Bloom's Modern Critical Interpretations

Alice Walker's

The Color Purple
New Edition

Edited and with an introduction by
Harold Bloom
Sterling Professor of the Humanities
Yale University

BLOOM'S
LITERARY CRITICISM
An imprint of Infobase Publishing

Editorial Consultant, Brian L. Johnson

Bloom's Modern Critical Interpretations:
Alice Walker's *The Color Purple*—New Edition

Copyright © 2008 by Infobase Publishing

Introduction © 2008 by Harold Bloom

Bloom's Literary Criticism
An imprint of Infobase Publishing
132 West 31st Street
New York NY 10001

Library of Congress Cataloging-in-Publication Data
Alice Walker's The color purple / edited with an introduction by Harold Bloom.—New ed.
        p. cm. — (Modern critical interpretations)
Includes bibliographical references and index.
ISBN-13: 978-0-7910-9614-7 (hardcover : alk. paper)
  1. Walker, Alice, 1944- Color Purple. 2. African American Women in literature. I. Bloom, Harold. II. Title: Modern critical interpretations : Alice Walker's The color purple

PS3573.A425C6326 2008
813'.54—dc22   2008002775

Cover design by Ben Peterson

Printed in the United States of America

Bang BCL 10 9 8 7 6 5 4 3 2 1

This book is printed on acid-free paper.

Contents

Editor's Note

My Introduction ungallantly broods upon Alice Walker's agonistic struggle with the influence upon her of Zora Neale Hurston.

The essayists largely join Walker herself in denying any anxiety in literary relations between African American women authors. So deeply are most of them in amiable agreement that they differ only in emphases, not in judgment. Priscilla L. Watson finds a pathos of comedy in *The Color Purple*, after which Charles L. Proudfit bravely ventures a psychoanalysis of the heroine, Celie, while Linda Selzer centers upon black domestic ties.

Ethnic, gender, and black naturalist concerns are taken up by Daniel W. Ross and then by Lauren Berlant, after which Diane Gabrielsen Scholl praises Walker's novel as a stern parable.

Some of the controversies stirred up by Walker are sorted out by Jacqueline Bobo, while Martha J. Cutter invokes the myth of the ravished Philomela.

HAROLD BLOOM

Introduction

THE COLOR PURPLE (1982)

In my old age, as person and as literary critic, I am resolved to give up all polemic, and to limp off the battlefield, carrying my wounds with me, honorable and otherwise. Since I am (somewhat) at odds with nearly every essayist in this volume, as well as with their illustrious subject, a certain wariness necessarily informs my stance in what follows.

Alice Walker and her allied critics tend to idealize the influence-relationship between black women writers, indeed all women writers. Feminist ideology, at least in the academy, holds that rivalry, creative envy, and the sublime contest for the highest place among writers, are all masculine tendencies or anxieties. Either women do not beware other women and never compete with one another (or with their mothers), or else human nature is so purified by feminist discourse that all agonistic elements in literature subside.

Walker, whether in *The Color Purple* or *Meridian,* is very much Zora Neale Hurston's novelistic daughter. No book, she has affirmed, means more to her than *Their Eyes Were Watching God.* Though poignant, this affirmation is a touch redundant, since both Celie and Meridian are palpable revisions of Hurston's Janie. The literary issue then becomes (at least for old Brontosaurus Bloom) what is added to the representation of character and personality when we turn from rereading Hurston to rereading Walker. And since we are all mortal, whatever our idealisms or our ideologies, do we reread Walker, as I certainly go back to Hurston, or do we yield Walker up, since time is limited?

Walker's most glowing tribute to Hurston has the title: "On Refusing to Be Humbled by Second Place in a Contest You Did Not Design." I fear that all of literature is a contest that any new writer did not and could not design. Nietzsche wrote persuasively of "Hesiod's Contest with Homer," and Hemingway memorably boasted of being in training to take on Tolstoy himself. I grant you that Homer, Hesiod, Nietzsche, Tolstoy, and Hemingway were male, but George Eliot, Virginia Woolf, Edith Wharton, Willa Cather, and Iris Murdoch reveal intense agonistic relations between them. Ah, but these were none of them African-American. True. Toni Morrison's superb struggles with precursors involve Faulkner, Woolf, and Ralph Ellison, though Morrison, herself now highly ideological, also denies any share in the anxiety of influence. Perhaps we must wait another generation, and then we will see how younger black women novelists, of comparable gifts, resolve their struggle with Morrison.

The Color Purple, like *Meridian*, closely follows *Their Eyes Were Watching God* by giving us a heroine who has lived more than one revisionist moment in regard to her cultural context. If you repeat that moment, as Walker consciously does, then your imaginative gesture will not be one of origination. Hurston, who was anything but an ideologue, who was neither a feminist nor an African-American nationalist, wrote with the freedom of an original. Shadowed always by Hurston's achievement, Walker has shifted the agonistic ground to issues of feminism and political liberation, but at the high cost (at least for me) of speaking in a voice never altogether her own, the voice of Hurston's Janie.

DANIEL W. ROSS

Celie in the Looking Glass:
The Desire for Selfhood in The Color Purple

For many readers the turning point of Alice Walker's *The Color Purple* occurs when Celie, the principal character, asserts her freedom from her husband and proclaims her right to exist: "I'm pore, I'm black, I may be ugly, and can't cook. . . . But I'm here" (187). Celie's claim is startling because throughout her life she has been subjected to a cruel form of male dominance grounded in control over speech. The novel's very first words alert us to the prohibition against speech served on Celie by her father: "You'd better not never tell nobody but God. It'd kill your mammy." Thus, Celie writes, addressing her letters to God because she has no one else to write to and because she knows she must never tell no "body." But even then Celie addresses her letters to the orthodox Christian God, another version of the father. In short, Celie's language exists through much of the book without a body or audience, just as she exists without a self or identity.

Finding the courage to speak is a major theme of *The Color Purple*. But the novel also suggests that speech cannot come from the hollow shell of self-hood that Celie presents early on. Thus, I would like to focus on the discovery that must necessarily precede Celie's discovery of speech: the discovery of desire—for selfhood, for other, for community, and for a meaningful place in the Creation. The process of discovering or developing desire begins, for Celie, with the reappropriation of her own body, which was taken from her

Modern Fiction Studies, Volume 34, Number 1 (Spring 1988): pp. 69–84. Copyright © by Purdue Research Foundation. All rights to reproduction in any form reserved.

by men—first by her brutal stepfather and then passed on to her husband, Albert. The repossession of her body encourages Celie to seek selfhood and later to assert that selfhood through spoken language. During this process Celie learns to love herself and others and to address even her written language to a body, her sister Nettie, rather than to the disembodied God she has blindly inherited from white Christian mythology. The crucial scene, I will argue, in initiating this process is the mirror scene. In this scene Celie first comes to terms with her own body, thus changing her life forever.

I

One of the primary projects of modern feminism has been to restore women's bodies, appropriated long ago by a patriarchal culture, to them. Because the female body is the most exploited target of male aggression, women have learned to fear or even to hate their bodies. According to Adrienne Rich, women must overcome these negative attitudes if they are to achieve intellectual progress:

> But fear and hatred of our bodies had often crippled our brains. Some of the most brilliant women of our time are still trying to think from somewhere outside their female bodies—hence they are still merely reproducing old forms of intellection. (284)

Coming to terms with the body can be, for women, a painful experience. Alicia Ostriker, for example, notes that although among contemporary poets females are more likely to describe the body or to use it as a source of imagery than their male counterparts are, their images often focus on strangulation, cutting, mutilation, or depictions of "psychic hurt in somatic terms" (249). Consequently, women often think of their bodies as torn or fragmented, a pattern evident in Walker's Celie. To confront the body is to confront not only an individual's abuse but also the abuse of women's bodies throughout history; as the external symbol of women's enslavement, this abuse represents for woman a reminder of her degradation and her consignment to an inferior status. As the subject of repeated rapes and beatings, Celie tries alternately to ignore and to annihilate her body. The latter is her strategy for defense against her husband's assaults:

> He beat me like he beat the children. . . . It all I can do not to cry. I make myself wood. I say to myself, Celie, you a tree. That's how come I know trees fear man. (30)

But Celie's ignorance of her body is even more shocking than her desire to annihilate it, as her language makes clear. She describes her own hysterectomy in the words of a child: "A girl at church say you git big if you bleed every month. I don't bleed no more" (15). Even this knowledge, personal as it is, comes to Celie second hand.

Celie has no desire to get to know her body until the arrival of her husband's lover, Shug Avery. While serving Shug in the traditional female capacity of nurse, Celie feels her first erotic stirrings and associates them with a new spirituality: "I wash her body, it feel like I'm praying" (53). Celie's stirrings foreshadow her discovery, under Shug's guidance, of a new God that allows her to love sexual pleasure guiltlessly. Shug introduces Celie to the mysteries of the body and sexual experience, making possible both Celie's discovery of speech and her freedom from masculine brutality. But the introduction requires that Celie see her body and feel its components first. For this a hand-held mirror is necessary, as is Shug's encouragement that there is something worth seeing.

When Shug urges her to look at herself, Celie reacts much like a child who fears being caught by a parent: she giggles and feels "like us been doing something wrong" (80). Even Shug, for all her promiscuity, talks like a child in preparing Celie for what she will find:

> Listen, she say, right down there in your pussy is a little button that gits real hot *when you do you know what with somebody*. It gets hotter and hotter and then it melt. That the good part. (79; my emphasis)

The simplicity of Shug's language must certainly be designed in part to titillate Celie, but her uncharacteristic euphemism ("when you do you know what with somebody") suggests that even the free-spirited Shug has trouble speaking straightforwardly about sex or the body. While Celie looks in the mirror, Shug guards the door like a naughty schoolgirl, letting Celie know when the coast is clear.

Celie is astonished by what she sees in the mirror:

> Ugh. All that hair. Then my pussy lips be black. Then inside look like a wet rose. (79)

After her initial revulsion Celie sees in succession three things: the hair that shielded her vagina from view, her black lips, and, finally, her feminine beauty, symbolized as a rose. When Shug asks her what she thinks, Celie's immediate response abnegates her previous annihilation and ignorance of her body: "It mine, I say" (80). In discovering and accepting with pride her own body, Celie initiates a desire for selfhood. Next she begins to find an identity through a network of female relationships with Shug, Nettie (whose letters she soon discovers), Sofia, and Mary Agnes. With her newfound identity, Celie is able to break free from the masculine prohibition against speech and to join a community of women, thus freeing herself from dependence on and subjection to male brutality.

II

The hair, the lips, the rose. Each symbolizes an important aspect of Celie's attitude toward her body, an attitude that must change if she is ever to be free of male brutality. The hair represents Celie's old attitude of self-revulsion, evident in her spontaneous "Ugh." The pubic hair no doubt arouses Celie's memories of her stepfather's raping her; he came to her with scissors in hand, ostensibly to have her cut his hair. But inside herself Celie finds the wet rose, a symbol of her new attitude, which includes not only love but also an entirely different attitude toward God and Creation. Shug teaches Celie to find God in herself, in nature, and in her own feelings, including erotic ones: "God loves *all* them feelings," Shug tells her (178; my emphasis). In between are the lips, representing Celie's present ambivalence. Although she is gradually learning, under Shug's guidance, to discover her body, her lips are for the time being dry, indicative of her virginity (in Shug's sense of the word) and her silence. Both orifices, vagina and mouth, need moistening if Celie is to replace sexual abuse with sexual pleasure and then to assert her independence from Albert. When she and Shug make love for the first time, their pleasure is purely oral. They "kiss and kiss until [they] can't hardly kiss no more" (109). This scene culminates in an ecstasy that is both maternal and infantile for Celie:

> Then I feels something real soft and wet on my breast, feel like one of my little lost babies mouth.
> Way after while, I act like a lost baby too. (109)[1]

Infantilism and maternity can provoke negative memories for Celie: her stepfather raped her because her mother did not satisfy him, and her mother died screaming and cursing at Celie, who, pregnant with her first child, could not move fast enough to be an efficient nurse. But Celie does effectively nurse Shug's ills, and Shug, in turn, plays a maternal role by teaching Celie how to love. She sucks from Celie's breast as Celie's lost babies were never allowed to; we must recall here that Celie's children were taken from her before she could "nurse" them, leaving her with "breasts full of milk running down [her]self" (13). Celie's orgasm suggests a rebirth or perhaps an initial birth into a world of love, a reenactment of the primal pleasure of the child at the mother's breast. In psychoanalytic terms this scene presents the inauguration of primary narcissism that, "as a psychical reality, can only be the primal myth of a return to the maternal breast" (Laplanche 72). In essence, the story of Celie's life begins afresh here; as Terry Eagleton puts it, the desire to retrieve the mother's body drives "the narrative of our lives, impelling us to pursue substitutes for this lost paradise in the endless metonymic movement of desire" (185). I turn now to psychoanalysis to show how theories of infantile development can help explain just how far Celie comes in her development of an ego and love for another. Psychoanalysis demonstrates the crucial role Shug Avery plays in her development, especially in reconciling Celie with her own body.[2]

III

Modern psychoanalysis assigns great importance to mirror scenes. Such scenes are crucial in the development of an ego, for, as Freud noted, "the ego cannot exist in the individual from the start; the ego has to be developed" ("On Narcissism" 77). Jacques Lacan posited the beginning of that development in "the mirror stage," which normally occurs between six and eighteen months of age. The mirror stage, a metaphor for Lacan, is literally enacted by Celie and Shug in *The Color Purple.* Up until this stage a child has no perception of an external world, only of himself as, in Freud's famous phrase, "His Majesty the Baby" ("On Narcissism" 91).

Lacan believes that the mirror stage offers the child only an illusion of whole selfhood, when in fact the subject is always split. But Lacan's view of the unattainableness of whole selfhood finds a more optimistic revision in Walker's novel. *The Color Purple,* in fact, endorses another view prevalent in modern thought—that such illusions are not destructive but are positive accommodations that allow one to find meaning in life, far preferable to the desire for self-annihilation Celie voices early in the book. In Eagleton's words, if we analyze our situations in the world rationally, we are bound to conclude that we lack centering, but most of us interpret ourselves otherwise, to assure ourselves of our life's significance. Eagleton believes the relation of an individual to society, interpreted thus, resembles Lacan's view of the small child's image of itself in the mirror:

> In both cases, the human subject is supplied with a satisfying unified image of selfhood by identifying with an object which reflects this image back to it in a closed, narcissistic circle. In both cases, too, this image involves a *mis*recognition, since it idealizes the subject's real situation. (173)

But this *mis*recognition, Lacan's *meconnaissance,* says Eagleton, makes selfhood possible: "Duly enthralled by the image of myself I receive, I subject myself to it; and it is through this 'subjection' that I become a subject" (173).[3] To put it another way, the *mis*recognition fuels the desire to construct selfhood, because "the first Desire of any human is the absolute one for recognition (the Desire to be desired), itself linked to the Desire to *be* a unity"

(Ragland-Sullivan 58). Spurred by this desire, the subject begins looking to others for validation. The self is an imaginary construct; what the mirror offers, says Juliet Mitchell, is a chance for a child to grasp itself "for the first time as a perfect whole, not a mess of uncoordinated movements and feelings" (40). For Celie, the mirror opens the door of her imagination, helping her envision a world of new possibilities for herself.

The dangers of pursuing an illusory wholeness of selfhood are dwarfed by those of eliding the mirror stage. The child who experiences no normal passage through a mirror stage can be arrested, trapped in a very early stage of development. Such a child may become autistic, a sign of extreme disturbance in one's sense of identity (Mahler, Pine, and Bergrnan (11).[4] As I will show momentarily, this is Celie's condition early in the novel, when she is arrested in the pre-mirror stage of development. Without a positive sense of him/herself as a body, and without an imago to replace the parental one, the child who does not pass through the mirror stage is left without an awareness of externality or otherness. This lack of an other is extremely critical, for Lacan links the discovery of the other to our becoming social beings: without it we become overattached to early fixations of identity, unable to adapt them as necessary to life's demands (Ragland-Sullivan 43–44).

At least one other area of development is retarded if the mirror stage is elided: speech. For Lacan speech presupposes the existence of "the Other to whom it is addressed" (Sheridan viii).[5] Thus, Celie's inability to find a listening audience for herself is another sign of her autism, another result of her arrested development.[6] Only Shug Avery is able to draw Celie out of her autism; Sofia's early attempts to get Celie to speak for herself fail because Celie has developed no concept of otherness. Celie needs not only someone who will tell her how to act and what to say but also someone who will show her. She needs a sympathetic mentor and friend, a relationship that Sharon Hymer calls a "narcissistic friendship." In the earliest stage of such a friendship, the narcissistic friend serves as "the initiator of activities as well as the provider of a value system and lifestyle which the patient embraces as a germinating ego ideal" (433).[7] Shug does initiate such activities for Celie, helping her through the mirror stage to a discovery of her own body, her capacity for speech, and her ability to love an other.

The early portions of the novel illustrate Celie's arrested development. Many girls "regress" during adolescence, returning to preoedipal or pre-mirror stage fantasies of fusion with the mother; a close friend is often the key to helping them out of such regression (Dalsirner 25–26). But Celie, fourteen and friendless at the beginning of *The Color Purple*, seems trapped in this infantile stage throughout her teenage years.[8] In Lacanian psychoanalysis, says Ragland-Sullivan, the pre-mirror stage is "a period in which an infant experiences its body as fragmented parts and images." These images include "castration, mutilation, dismemberment, dislocation, evisceration, devouring, bursting open of the body, and . . . have a formative function in composing the human subject of identity and perception" (Ragland-Sullivan 18–19). Because of male brutality, Celie defines herself in terms of such images: her symbolic castration taking the form of her premature hysterectomy; her mutilation evident in her fear of the scissors her stepfather brings to her room with him; her dislocation symbolized in her being forced to take her mother's place; her feeling of dismemberment figured in the choking her father administers while raping her; the "bursting open of the body" imagined when Celie's "stomach started moving and then that little baby come out [her] pussy chewing on it fist" (Walker 12). Celie's fragmentation is most strongly reinforced by the way her stepfather presents her as less than a whole woman to her future husband, convincing him to marry her because "God done fixed her. You can do everything just like you want to and she ain't gonna make you feed it or clothe it" (18).

To make a desire for selfhood possible, Celie must take a new perspective on her own body. Rather than defining herself in terms of fragmentation or of lack, she must learn to define herself synecdochally, seeing *part* of her body, specifically her genitalia, as a sufficient symbol of herself as a whole. According to Ellen Forst Lowery, girls need a sublimation that "depends on the additional denial of the castrated state, or as some would protest, *their intuition of an equally valuable sex organ/identity*" (446; my emphasis). But such a radical reevaluation of the body is not likely for a woman living as Celie does. What she needs is the example of a woman who em-bodies sexual power; what she needs is Shug Avery.

Celie begins to fantasize about Shug before her own marriage. During the fantasy period Shug becomes Celie's ego ideal, an ideal self that "is aggrandized and exalted in the subject's mind" (Freud, "On Narcissism" 94), becoming "a model to which the subject attempts to conform" (Laplanche and Pontalis 144). Celie thinks of Shug while Albert rapes her on her wedding night, and, even though his lovemaking is as uncaring as her stepfather's, Celie begins to imagine the sexual act with some affection: "I know what he doing to me he done to Shug Avery and maybe she like it. I put my arm around him" (21). Even as an imaginary construct, Shug stirs Celie's first erotic feelings. When the real Shug steps into Celie's life, these feelings become activated.

Although Shug arrives ill and weak, she nonetheless exudes a sexual power that Celie has never before imagined in woman or man. Quickly, Celie reassesses Albert in light of Shug's sexuality:

> I look at his face. It tired and sad and I notice his chin weak. Not
> much chin there at all. I have more chin, I think. And his clothes
> dirty, dirty. When he pull them off, dust rise. (52)

Celie's three-sentence fixation on Albert's chin is revealing: by comparing her chin with his, Celie gets her first inkling of an anatomical superiority. Typical of "narcissistic friends," Celie and Shug take turns playing the supporting or, in this case, maternal role, and, interestingly enough, Celie goes first, nursing Shug through her illness. Here at last Celie is allowed the nursing role her stepfather deprived her of when he took away Celie's babies and left her with milk running from her breasts. During this nursing process Celie connects her feelings for Shug to her lost daughter and her mother: "I work on her like she a doll or like she Olivia—or like she mama" (57). The relation of the doll to the daughter and mother reflects a new development for Celie; as the psychoanalytic school of object relations would see it, the doll represents a transitional device that helps Celie come to grips with the complicated feelings of separation and ambivalence that characterize her thoughts of both Olivia and her mother. Celie, in other words, has begun to employ some typical mechanisms of psychic growth and development.

After Shug's recovery the roles shift, with Shug becoming Celie's nurse. Celie's illness, however, is not physical but psychological: Celie lacks an identity. Shug awakens Celie's desire for identity most explicitly when she sings a song she has written just for Celie. As Celie gratefully notes, "first time somebody made something and name it after me" (75). The act of naming something after Celie assures the integrity of Celie herself; she must be somebody to be a subject of a song. This act is also Celie's first clue that language need not come under the jurisdiction of male authority.

This is the background Walker gives to prepare us for the mirror scene and, after that, the first lovemaking scene between Celie and Shug. The mirror scene takes on particular meaning because the desire for ego-formation has already been sparked. From the Celie who thinks of her body as fragmented and who tries to make herself as unfeeling as a tree, Walker has taken us to a Celie whose passions allow her to begin to think about her body differently and to conceive of a relationship beyond the self, with an other. The mirror scene expedites Celie's development through the stage of primary narcissism, in which two love-objects exist—the self and the mother (Freud, "On Narcissism" 88–89)—to the onset of secondary narcissism, the stage in which self-love is "displaced onto an-other" (Ragland-Sullivan 37). In the scene, Shug teaches Celie first to perceive her genitals as whole and beautiful and then to masturbate.[9] That Celie and Shug act like children during this scene, giggling and running off to Celie's room "like two little prankish girls" (79), emphasizes the fact that they are engaged in an essentially juvenile drama that must be played through in order for Celie to reach a more mature stage of development.

This juvenile drama helps change Celie's perception of herself and her body. Celie's new appreciation for one part of her body allows her to revise her view of her entire body: to view her genitalia synecdochally rather than as a fragment. Celie's new synecdochal conception of her body allows her to regard her genitalia as "normal" symbols, appreciating the beauty of the part as symbol of the whole without allowing it to replace the whole completely (Laplanche 36–37). Celie's acceptance of her genitals ("It mine" [80]) clearly indicates that she no longer perceives her body as something to deny or annihilate but as a source of pleasure. Even if, as Lacan believes, the post-mirror stage forces the individual to confront again the fragmentation of the body and the self, this synecdochal process helps Celie adapt to that threat to her totality.

As part of the mirror-stage experience, the child should identify its unified image of self with the mother's body; this identification foregrounds the child's, especially the girl's, acceptance or nonacceptance of its sexual organs (Ragland-Sullivan 277–278). At the end of the mirror stage the father intervenes in the mother-child relationship, preventing total identification or fusion with the mother and thus establishing boundaries necessary to the child's individuation (Ragland-Sullivan 42, 55). This process seems clearly to have been aborted in Celie's childhood, leaving an important gap in her development that Shug Avery fills. Shug, then, not only plays the role of Celie's "narcissistic friend," but first and foremost she represents a mother-surrogate or, in Lacanian terms, a (m)Other. Under this formulation "a subject first becomes aware of itself by identification with a person (object), usually the mother," although the figure may be "any constant nurturer" (Ragland-Sullivan 16).

As (m)Other, Shug also plays a crucial role in resolving Celie's Oedipal conflict. All such conflicts are grounded in ambivalence, Celie's especially so, as Nettie's narrative of their early life reveals (160–162). Celie's father was hanged when she was two and her mother's health ruined. Celie's stepfather (whom she assumes to be her real "pa") married her mother when Celie was three to four years old, the age when the Oedipal phase begins. Every year thereafter, Celie's mother was pregnant, and her mental state gradually deteriorated. Celie's stepfather turned his lust on her when she had just passed puberty, at a time when the Oedipal drama is "internally staged for a second time," its outcome crucial in determining "adult sexuality and other vital activities and functions in later existence" (Marcus 313). Thus, Celie's early life proves to be a perverse rewriting of the Oedipal script, with Celie aware of her mother's ambivalence about yielding her wifely role to her daughter: "My mama fuss at me an look at me. She happy, cause he good to her now" (11). Celie's guilt is augmented by her mother's questioning her pregnancy and her cursing Celie on her deathbed. Given the profound guilt and confusion that Celie must have felt about replacing her mother, in addition to the disruption of her own psychic growth and the continued brutalization to follow, it is little wonder that Celie would seek to annihilate self. But the intervention of Shug as (m)Other and of Nettie's revelation that "pa is not our pa!" (162) allows Celie to reimagine the possibilities of selfhood. By taking her back to the mirror stage, Shug helps Celie identify with her more positive perceptions of selfhood, sexuality, and body.

Furthermore, as (m)Other, Shug gives Celie an unusual form of identification, at least for a woman. One of Freud's most controversial ideas is his suggestion that women tend to develop inferior object-choices to men's: where men transfer their narcissism to an other, women tend to rechannel love back into the self.[10] Such women love themselves more than anyone else, and they seek not to love but to be loved ("On Narcissism" 89). Man's "superior" object-choice is "anaclytic," in other words, based on the mother-imago; but, as we have seen, Celie also grounds her attachment in an other—Shug—who represents for her a mother-imago. As Laplanche notes, "even if one [anaclytic object-choice] is alleged to be more characteristic of men and the other [narcissistic object-choice] of women, they in fact represent two possibilities open to every human being" (77). Furthermore, if Celie's choice (both because it is based on the anaclytic model and because it is the choice of a woman) seems masculine, it is the first of several such choices she makes that help her to rise from passive submission and to develop independence and identity. Ultimately, Celie derives from her growth the power of speech that is crucial to her victory over male brutality.

IV

One sign of the mirror stage's end, for Lacan, is the coherent use of language (Ragland-Sullivan 29); another is the development of aggressivity (Lacan 19–20). Celie's progress toward gaining that coherent language in the form of speech is guided by Shug. As Elizabeth Fifer puts it, "each piece of Shug's advice changes Celie's language and becomes part of Celie's progress" (162). But aggressivity poses more sinister possibilities because Celie, once she develops her ego, cannot help but be driven to revenge against Albert. This drive peaks when she and Shug discover that Albert has been hiding Nettie's letters. Now sickened by Albert's cruelty to her, Celie believes she will feel better if she kills him. Celie gets her chance when Albert commands her to shave him, a command reminiscent of her stepfather's pretended desire for a haircut. Sharpening the razor, Celie contemplates murder, but Shug holds her back. Even after Shug takes the razor from her, Celie continues to fantasize her revenge:

> All day long I act just like Sofia. I stutter. I mutter to myself. I stumble bout the house crazy for Mr. _____ blood. In my mind, he falling dead every which a way. By time night come I can't even speak. Every time I open my mouth nothing come out but a little burp. (115)

What meager powers of speech Celie has at this time are overpowered by her desire for revenge.

Celie learns to take control over her aggressive desires by two means of sublimation: assertive speech and the substitution of one cutting instrument, the razor, for another, a needle.[11] Lowery believes that the process of acquiring language may be an early form of sublimation for children, the word standing for the desired object (443). By telling Albert that she, Nettie, and her children will "whup [his] ass" (181), Celie deflects the need to do so; speaking daggers, she need use none. Sofia has provided the lesson that only defeat can result from an attempt to quit violence with violence. Celie, in contrast, gains victory with speech. When she declares her independence from Albert, she feels almost possessed by a mysterious power: "Look like when I open my mouth the air rush in and shape words" (187). Through speech Celie establishes her freedom, breaking Albert's hold on her. She further recognizes the power of speech when her curse on Albert sinks him into a life-threatening depression. That curse is lifted and Albert's regeneration begun only when he does what Celie has demanded—return Nettie's letters to her.

Celie has previously seen the power a woman's voice has to break male domination in the example of Mary Agnes. Here too is an example of the kind of sacrifice women must make in order to bind themselves together in a community that resists the pressure of male domination. Mary Agnes, once beaten up by Sofia, her rival for Harpo, helps free Sofia from prison by submitting to rape by the warden, her illegitimate father. This act of submission gives Mary Agnes a power of guilt over the warden that expedites Sofia's release. Ironically, Mary Agnes the victim emerges from this encounter with a new power over men in general. Though she comes home with a limp, her dress torn, a heel from her shoe missing, she repudiates her derogatory nickname ("Squeak") and demands that she be called by her real name (95). Not only does Mary Agnes no longer "squeak," but she also begins to sing. Although Celie reports that "she got the kind of voice you never think of trying to sing a song" (96), Mary Agnes soon emulates Shug's success, using her voice to give her a new freedom from, and power over, men. She begins to travel, choosing when to move in and out of Harpo's life. Thus her story foreshadows the story of Celie's freedom, both stories validating the theme that strength can come from enduring oppression with as much dignity as possible and then rising to denounce it. Ultimately, the victim gains moral power over the oppressor.

Celie's aggressivity is further sublimated in the development of her own form of art: sewing. Freud of course maintained that artistic creation was a major source of sublimation. It is no small irony that Celie adopts a traditionally feminine form of art to complete her separation from the violent masculine world. By sewing, Celie narrows the gap between the sexes, making pants for both men and women. More important, sewing links Celie to woman's primordial power that predates patriarchy. As Adrienne Rich describes it, sewing or weaving emphasizes woman's "transformative power":[12]

> the conversion of raw fibers into thread was connected with the power over life and death; the spider who spins thread out of her own body, Ariadne providing the clue to the labyrinth, the figures of the Fates or Norns or old spinning-women who cut the thread of life or spin it further, are all associated with this process. (101)

Freud's interpretation of this process is more fantastical and more sexist, [13] but it also can be instructive. He regarded sewing or weaving as evidence of woman's shame, caused by her castrated genitals. Weaving, thus, is motivated by a desire to follow the pattern of Nature, who

> would seem to have given the model which this achievement imitates by causing the growth at maturity of the pubic hair that conceals the genitals. The step that remained to be taken lay in making the threads adhere to one another, while on the body they stick into the skin and are only matted together. ("Femininity" 132)

For Celie sewing represents not a means of covering up her castrated genitals but of binding together the sexes so that both male and female can "wear the pants." Furthermore, Celie's sewing associates her with a select group of female characters in American literature who use their art not to reveal their shame, as Freud suggests, but to transplant it, placing it where it really belongs—on their male oppressors. The most prominent member of this set is Hawthorne's Hester Prynne. Forced by the patriarchs of Salem to wear the scarlet letter as an emblem of shame, Hester uses her art to create a letter that represents, to the narrator who discovers it two centuries later, a "mystic symbol" (28), giving evidence "of a now forgotten art" (27). Inspired by this symbol, Hawthorne creates a story in which the bearers of shame are the Puritan patriarchs who try to dehumanize and defeminize Hester for her refusal to submit to their code. Celie's art has a similar, although more immediate, effect. Rather than revealing the source of shame to a later generation, Celie's success in sewing helps Albert face his own shame and even begin a process of self-regeneration. At the end of the book Albert is a new man, capable of loving and sharing. The change in him is symbolized by his partaking, with Celie, in the traditionally feminine activity, sewing. Having had his lifelong view that "men spose to wear the pants" (238) corrected, Albert joins Celie in a communal act that, as Celie describes it, helps eradicate the differences that make for sexual domination: "Now us sit sewing and talking and smoking our pipes" (238).

V

Very late in *The Color Purple* Celie stands before a mirror, full-length this time, again. At this time Shug has left her for a nineteen-year-old fling. This scene provides the test that proves Celie's psychic growth has continued unchecked, that she will not regress in a crisis. Standing naked before the glass, Celie asks herself, "What would she love? ... Nothing special here for nobody to love" (229). That Celie comes through this depression signifies that she has broken free of Shug, further establishing her independence and identity. Ultimately, says Hymer, a person who relies on a narcissistic friend must "develop an identity apart from the friend" (433), just as one must split oneself from the (m)Other. Celie does develop her identity and, in the process, finds a network of friends "matrifocal" in structure but open to men who can put aside their desire to dominate.[14]

Matrifocality dissolves the hierarchies that perpetuate dominance and oppression. The loss of such hierarchies changes one's perception of the self in society and even in relation to God. Thus, it is only a short step from a belief in woman's independence from man to Shug's concept of a nonracial, genderless God: "People think pleasing God is all God care about. But any fool living in the world can see it always trying to please us back" (178). Shug carefully notes here that one must live in the world to get to know God; merely surviving and waiting for a reward in heaven, as Celie did earlier, is the patriarchal way. Shug's version of God deconstructs the fountainhead of patriarchy, the Lacanian Name-of-the-Father who is the source of law and power, replacing it with a belief that one must become engaged in the Creation as Celie does, creating one's own self, art, and community. Demonstrating a parallel commitment to matrifocality, Sofia and Mary Agnes, former rivals, learn to share Harpo and the responsibility of raising each other's children as a means of maintaining freedom while avoiding the permanent dependence on one man that perpetuates masculine power. And, in Africa, Nettie first assists Corinne in raising Adam and Olivia and, after Corrine's death, replaces her as wife and mother before yielding the children to their true mother, Celie.[15]

As I have shown, one of the climaxes in the novel is Celie's first love-making scene, when she and Shug reexperience the primal pleasure of the child at the mother's breast. *The Color Purple* suggests that for one who develops a sense of self and then of other, similar kinds of primal experiences can be recaptured at points throughout life and not just in sexual encounters. One kind is recaptured again at novel's end when Celie and Nettie are reunited (with Celie's children) in a fairy-tale ending:[16]

Then us both start to moan and cry. Us totter toward one nother like us use to do when us was babies. Then us feel so weak when we

touch, us knock each other down. But what us care? Us sit and lay
there on the porch inside each other's arms. (250)

Such childlike joy depends on staying alive, constructing one's ego, and
learning to invest love in the other. Only after that process has been completed can we, in the words of Harpo (a man), "spend the day celebrating
each other" (250).

NOTES

1. Lesbianism is an attempt to recapture or reexperience the mother-daughter
bond. Sue Silver-marie describes the process as follows: "In loving another I discovered the deep urge to both be a mother and to find a mother in my mother. . . .
When I kiss and stroke and enter my lover, I am also a child re-entering my mother"
(quoted in Rich 232–233).

2. The subject of the construction of selfhood or ego has a very complicated,
uneven history in psychoanalysis. Depending on the theoretical model one adopts,
many views are possible. As Steven Marcus says, "the notion of the self that we can
construct out of contemporary psychoanalysis contains a new enlarged admixture in
it of archaic, pre-Oedipal, prephallic, and preverbal components, pieces of psychic life
that remain unintegrated, and of a self that is neither stable nor coherent in its earliest
vital and formative phases" (318). This being the state of things, I must draw on a wide
range of theorists whose ideas are not always compatible. In seeking to describe Celie's
construction of a self, I am concerned not with establishing the superiority of any
school of psychoanalysis but with accurately tracing the development of her selfhood
as Alice Walker dramatizes it. The terminology of psychoanalysis is extremely useful
for this process, although the theorists I cite might not always agree with each other.

3. For arguments that illusions such as the type constructed here are necessary
in modern life, see Ernest Becker and my own "*Lord Jim* and the Saving Illusion,"
forthcoming in *Conradiana*.

4. I follow Mahler, Pine, and Bergman here in distinguishing Celie's severe
autism from the "normal autism" every child evinces during the early months of
life. "Normal autism," a stage of primary narcissism, gives way to an awareness that
"need satisfaction cannot be provided by oneself, but comes from somewhere outside
the self" (42).

5. The distinction between the other (*objet petit a*) and the Other (*grand Autre*)
is very complicated in Lacan. They represent algebraic signs that Lacan refused to
translate. In particular, the Other does not represent, as some wrongly assume, a
specific person who becomes an object of desire; Ragland-Sullivan comes closest
to a definition when she says it designates "various external forces that structure a
primary and secondary unconscious" (15–16). Because the lower case "other" more
nearly represents a single imago or object of desire, I use it to refer to Shug's relationship with Celie. See Lacan (19).

6. Behind the principal neuroses people suffer from, Freud found unresolved
conflicts traceable to one's early development. Lack of resolution leads to a point
where one's development becomes arrested or fixated. See Eagleton (158).

7. Hymer finds similarities between the "narcissistic friendship" and many
ancient views of friendship as described by Aristotle, Plato, Cicero, and Zeno (423).

Also relevant here is Heinz Kohut's theory of "alter-ego transference" or "twinship" (115).

8. In his forthcoming book on narcissism and the novel, Jeffrey Berman notes that developmental arrest can be the result of "parental empathic failure." This sort of arrest can produce "feelings of emptiness, depression, or dehumanization." I am grateful to Professor Berman for sharing the manuscript of his book with me.

9. Freud believed that clitoral masturbation was a necessary response to penis envy. Without it the girl is likely to remain dissatisfied "with her inferior clitoris" ("Femininity" 127). Whether or not one thinks Freud is right, it seems clear that in *The Color Purple* Celie must come to accept her body as it is before she can share it with another. Masturbation is a natural means of coming to this acceptance.

10. For a harsh critique of this view, see Kate Millett (196–197).

11. The latter strategy has also been identified by Teresa M. Tavormina (222). Her article promises intriguing parallels between language and sewing, but it finally says rather little about language. Tavormina's best point is that *The Color Purple* is itself a kind of quilt, a mosaic of patches from everyday life and memory "brought together so as to make a whole meaning from Celie's and Nettie's seemingly separate lives" (225).

12. The ultimate symbol of such power, of course, is menstrual blood, "which was believed to be transformed into the infant" (Rich 101). In this light it is interesting that Walker parallels Celie's development with the story of her daughter's coming of age in Africa. In the latter story Nettie recounts how the Olinka patriarchs make menstruating women stay out of sight and how they initiate girls undergoing menarche with a ritual "so bloody and painful, I forbid Olivia to even think about it" (172).

13. *The Color Purple* strongly reinforces the feminist complaint against Freud's belief that girls resolve their Oedipal crises through a fantasy of having the father's child. Celie lives out this fantasy (until her rapist's true identity is revealed), and it proves to be a nightmare.

14. Dianne Sadoff, who calls such matrifocal structures "adaptive strategies," gives a superb account of how they grew out of slavery (10–11). Nancy Tanner explains that although matrifocal structures tend to center on the mother, they also promote sexual egalitarianism: in matrifocal societies men and women share important economic and emotional roles. Flexibility, which is assured by the "network" of kinships, is the great advantage of matrifocality, allowing its members to live together and take turns caring for each others' children (Tanner 131, 151). Although less happy with the term "matrifocality," Carol B. Stack describes the structure similarly, adding that the network may be composed of kin or non-kin, as Celie's are. Because of great social, economic, and other hardships, Stack notes, black women turn to such networks to strengthen the family, even if they threaten "any particular male-female tie" (115).

15. Corinne's suspicions of Nettie indicate her own inability to accept matrifocality. Besides reflecting her guilt for not having borne her own children, this auspiciousness seems to be a critique of Corrinne's education at Spelman, which has indoctrinated her in the white, patriarchal set of mind. Walker further exploits this theme by portraying the limitations of the patriarchal perspective in Africa.

16. On the Cinderella parallels to *The Color Purple* see Margaret Walsh'a article. The weakness of her reading is its reduction of Shug Avery to a "fairy godmother" or "magic helper."

Works Cited

Becker, Ernest. *The Denial of Death*. New York: Free, 1973.

Berman, Jeffrey. *Narcissism and the Novel*. New York: New York University Press, forthcoming.

Dalsimer, Katharine. *Female Adolescence: Psychoanalytic Reflections on Literature*. New Haven: Yale University Press, 1986.

Eagleton, Terry. *Literary Theory: An Introduction*. Minneapolis: University of Minnesota Press, 1983.

Fifer, Elizabeth. "The Dialect & Letters of *The Color Purple*." *Contemporary American Women Writers: Narrative Strategies*. Eds. Catherine Rainwater and William J. Scheick. Lexington: University of Kentucky Press, 1985: pp. 155–171.

Freud, Sigmund. "Femininity." *The Standard Edition of the Comph Works of Sigmund Freud*. Vol. 22. Trans. and ed. James Strachey. London: Hogarth, 1957: 24 vols., pp. 112–135.

———. "On Narcissism: An Introduction." *SE*. Vol. 14. pp. 73–102.

Hawthorne, Nathaniel. *The Scarlet Letter*. Eds. Sculley Bradley, Richmond Croom Beatty, and E. Hudson Long. New York: Norton, 1961.

Hymer, Sharon. "Narcissistic Friendships. " *Psychoanalytic Review* 71 (1984): pp. 423–439.

Kohut, Heinz. The *Analysis of the Self: A Systematic Approach to the Psychoanalytic Treatment of Narcissistic Personality Disorders*. New York: International Universities Press, 1971.

Lacan, Jacques. *Écrits: A Selection*. Trans. Alan Sheridan. New York: Norton, 1977.

Laplanche, Jean. *Life and Death in Psychoanalysis*. Trans. Jeffrey Mehlman. Baltimore: Johns Hopkins University Press, 1976.

Laplanche, Jean, and J. B. Pontalis. *The Language of Psychoanalysis*. Trans. Donald Nicholson-Smith. New York: Norton, 1973.

Lowery, Ellen Forst. "Sublimation and Female Identity." *Psychoanalytic Review* 72 (1985): pp. 441–455.

Marcus, Steven. "The Psychoanalytic Self." *Southern Review* 22 (1986): pp. 308–325.

Mahler, Margaret, Fred Pine, and Anni Bergman. *The Psychological Birth of the Human Infant*. New York: Basic, 1975.

Millett, Kate. *Sexual Politics*. Garden City: Doubleday, 1970.

Mitchell, Juliet. *Psychoanalysis and Feminism: Freud, Reich, Laing, and Women*. New York: Pantheon, 1974.

Ostriker, Alicia. "Body Language: Imagery of the Body in Women's Poetry." *The State of the Language*. Eds. Leonard Michaels and Christopher Rick. Berkeley: University of California Press, 1980: pp. 247–263.

Ragland-Sullivan, Ellie. *Jacques Lacan and the Philosophy of Psychoanalysis*. Urbana: University of Illinois Press, 1986.

Rich, Adrienne. *Of Women Born: Motherhood as Experience and Institution*. New York: Norton, 1976.

Sadoff, Dianne F. "Black Matrilineage: The Case of Alice Walker and Zora Neale Hurston." *Signs* 11 (1985): pp. 4–26.

Sheridan, Alan. "Translator's Note." Lacan. vii-xii.

Stack, Carol B. "Sex Roles and Survival Strategies in an Urban Black Community." *Women, Culture, and Society*. Eds. Michelle Zimbalist Rosaldo and Louise Lamphere. Stanford: Stanford University Press, 1974: pp. 113–128.

Tanner, Nancy. "Matrifocality in Indonesia and Africa and among Black Americans." *Women, Culture, and Society*. Eds. Michelle Zimbalist Rosaldo and Louise Lamphere. Stanford: Stanford University Press, 1974: pp. 129–156.

Tavormina, M. Teresa. "Dressing the Spirit: Clothworking and Language in *The Color Purple*." *Journal of Narrative Technique* 16 (1986): pp. 220–230.

Walker, Alice. *The Color Purple*. New York: Washington Square, 1982.

Walsh, Margaret. "The Enchanted World of *The Color Purple*." *Southern Quarterly* 25 (1987): pp. 89–101.

LAUREN BERLANT

Race, Gender, and Nation in The Color Purple

The passion with which native intellectuals defend the existence of their
national culture may be a source of amazement; but those who condemn
this exaggerated passion are strangely apt to forget that their own psyche
and their own selves are conveniently sheltered behind a French or
German culture which has given full proof of its existence and which is
uncontested.

> —Frantz Fanon, "On National Culture"

Ask anyone up Harlem way
who that guy Bojangles is.
They may not know who's President
But they'll tell you who Bojangles is.

> —"Bojangles of Harlem," *Swing Time*

"Dear God, I am fourteen years old. I—am I have always been a good
girl. Maybe you can give me a sign letting me know what is happening to
me."[1] *The Color Purple* begins with the striking out—but not the erasure—of
"I am." Celie's crisis of subjectivity has both textual and historical implications: her status as a subject is clarified, in the course of the novel, by her
emergence from the enforced privacy of a prayer-letter to God sometime
in her fourteenth year, to public speaking, of a sort, during a community

Critical Inquiry, Volume 14, Issue 4 (Summer 1988): pp. 831–859. © 1988 by The University
of Chicago.

21

celebration on the Fourth of July, during the 1940s. The appearance of the Fourth of July in the novel's final moments appears to be a ratification of Celie's own personal liberation at the nation's mythicopolitical origin, the birth of the American "people." But what Independence Day resolves for the identity of Anglo-Americans it has raised as a question for Afro-Americans:[2] along with narrating Celie's history, *The Color Purple* stages, in its journey to this final day, an instance of black America's struggle to clarify its own national identity[3] from the point of view of American populism.[4]

The Color Purple problematizes tradition-bound origin myths and political discourse in the hope of creating and addressing an Afro-American nation constituted by a rich, complex, and ambiguous culture. But rather than using patriarchal languages and logics of power to describe the emergence of a postpatriarchal Afro-American national consciousness, Celie's narrative radically resituates the subject's national identity within a mode of aesthetic, not political, representation. These discursive modes are not "naturally" separate, but *The Color Purple* deliberately fashions such a separation in its attempt to represent a national culture that operates according to "womanist" values rather than patriarchal forms.[5] While political language is laden with the historical values and associations of patriarchal power, aesthetic discourse here carries with it a utopian force that comes to be associated with the spirit of everyday life relations among women.

Alice Walker has said that her intent with *The Color Purple* was to supplant the typically patriarchal concerns of the historical novel—"the taking of lands, or the births, battles, and deaths of Great Men"—with the scene of "one woman asking another for her underwear."[6] Walker manipulates the horizon of expectations of the historical novel[7] by situating the text within the traditionally confessional, local, privatized concerns of the autobiographical epistolary novel and, from this point of view, expanding to include the broader institutional affiliations and experiences of Afro-American women.[8] This is why the reemergence of nationalism at the end of the novel is puzzling: Celie's New World aesthetic and the celebration of the American revolution seems a contradictory alliance in the postpatriarchal culture set up by the novel.

Unlike *The Color Purple*, Walker's early novel *Meridian* explicitly addresses the *paradoxes* of Afro-American identity. Suffering a "hybrid"[9] affiliation to both sides of the hyphen, the Afro-American citizen learns not of the inalienable rights but of the a priori inferiority and cultural marginality of Afro-Americans—as if the "Afro" in the complex term were a syntactical negation of "American." Meridian, the woman whose political biography is told in the novel, learns of her contested relation to the rights of full American citizens as Celie and many Americans do: in public school, where the ideology of American identity is transmitted as if a part of the very air students inhale. On one important occasion, Meridian participates in an oratorical competition at her high school,

> reciting a speech that extolled the virtues of the Constitution and praised the superiority of The American Way of Life. The audience cared little for what she was saying, and of course they didn't believe any of it, but they were rapt, listening to her speak so passionately and with such sad valor in her eyes.[10]

Suddenly the meaning of what she says pierces Meridian's awareness; she almost faints, simultaneously gaining and losing "consciousness" on comprehending the horrible joke American national ideology has played on her, reproducing itself in her mind like a kind of vague dream or baby talk. On awakening to the hypocrisy behind the discourse of "inalienable rights," Meridian opposes the American assertion that it is a privilege just to be able to utter these phonemes unconsciously. To Meridian, black nationalism must dedicate itself to constructing a political and cultural context in which one might, indeed, enjoy a positive relation to national identity, rather than a negative relation to a race always already marked by its status as a social "problem."

> For she understood, finally, that the respect she owed her life was to continue . . . to live it. . . . And that this existence extended beyond herself to those around her because, in fact, the years in America had created them One Life.[11]

The movement in these phrases from the solipsism of everyday life to the symbolic unity of "One Life" takes place under the symbolic and political force of "years in America." Despite its crucially oppressive role in the historical formation of racial consciousness, America in this novel remains the sign and utopian paradigm of national identity. Meridian's new selflessness, born of an American-inspired melding of individual self-interest with populist social concerns, serves as a model for the future nation Afro-Americans can construct, founded on a transformation of their atomized historical experience into a mass of resources and a spirit of courage and survival.

Meridian is Walker's most explicitly and narrowly "political" novel.[12] It exposes the gap between the official claims of American democracy and the state's exploitative and repressive practices, and views "personal" relationships as symptoms of the strained political situation. The novel is critical of the sexism within the civil rights movement, for example. Nonetheless *Meridian* subordinates the struggle within gender to the "larger" questions raised by the imminent exhaustion or depletion of the movement itself. Meridian's theory of "One Life" dissolves the barriers of class and education between herself and the black community at large and effectively depoliticizes the struggle with the movement's patriarchal values and practices by locating the "personal" problems of sexism within the nationalist project.

In contrast, *The Color Purple* problematizes nationalism itself, in both its Anglo- and Afro-American incarnations. Most strikingly, the Anglo-American brand of national pride is lampooned. Like Meridian, Celie and Nettie first encounter the concept and the myth of American national identity as a fundamental element of basic literacy disseminated by public schools. But unlike Meridian, Celie is never fooled or impressed by the nation's self-mythification. She reports:

> The way you know who discover America, Nettie say, is think bout cucumbers. That what Columbus sound like. I learned all about Columbus in first grade, but look like he the first thing I forgot. She say Columbus come here in boats call the Neater, the Peter, and the Santomareater. Indians so nice to him he force a bunch of 'em back home with him to wait on the queen. [P. 19]

The Color Purple opens its discourse on the problematics of Afro-American national-historical identity by revealing the manifest irrelevancy of the classic American myth to Celie. Her comic reduction of the American origin tale to a matter of garden-variety phonetics not only indicates the vital importance of oral and folk transmission to less literate communities like the one in which Celie lives, but also suggests the crucial role oral transmission plays in the reproduction of the nation itself, from generation to generation. Elsewhere, for instance, Shug and Celie's rambling discussion of the world during World War II—which ranges among subjects such as the war, U.S. Government theft of land from an "Indian tribe," Hollywood, national and local scandals (pp. 189–90)—represents the haphazard, ad hoc fashion with which the nation disseminates and perpetuates itself among its citizens, even in everyday life.[13]

To maintain power among the people—indeed, to maintain "the people"—America must maintain a presence as accessible and intimate as the familial name and tradition.[14] Celie must gain agency within her immediate, "subjective" environment before she can come to terms with her "impersonal" or institutional relations.

•••

The Color Purple opens with Celie falling through the cracks of a language she can barely use. Her own limited understanding, her technical insecurity, and her plain sense of powerlessness are constructed in contrast to the powerful discourses that share the space with her stuttered utterances. The epigraph of *The Color Purple*, for example, is Stevie Wonder's imperious exhortation, *"Show me how to do like you/Show me how to do it."* Clearly this quotation is a direction as well as a request to the muses, contemporary and historical: *imitatio* is the graphic mode of this novel. Showing me something that is an action you *do* is not only intimately pedagogical, teaching me how to repeat the component gestures of the "doing" that is uniquely like "you"; the epigraph can also be read as the novel's most explicit political directive, deployed to turn individuals into self-conscious and literate users/readers of a cultural semiotic.[15]

For example, Shug is the novel's professor of desire and self-fulfillment, and as such her "example" is not only symbolic but technical, practical. Her first gift of knowledge to Celie is transmitted through a picture Celie and her stepmother see that has fallen out of Mr. _____'s wallet. The answer to Celie's question "What it is?" is: "The most beautiful woman I ever saw. . . . I see her there in furs. Her face rouge. Her hair like somethin tail. She grinning . . ." (p. 16). On the very next page Celie dresses exactly like Shug to keep her father from raping Nettie. Even before Celie possesses technical language about sex, pregnancy, and her body, she "learns" from what Shug "does" in the picture about the standard connection between male sexual desire and the desire to degrade women: "He beat me for dressing trampy but he do it to me anyway" (p. 17). In this regime there is no such thing as "mere" or passive reading: reading is an act of cultural self-assertion, an engagement in the mimesis of social relations.

The crucial intertwining of private and public acts and consciousness signified by the ambiguity of the epigraph's "you" is answered by another ambiguously placed line, hovering above the text proper, also in italics: *"You better not never tell nobody but God. It'd kill your mammy"* (p. 11). This unsigned, double-negative message marks the contested ground on which Celie's negative relation to discourse is established. The disembodied voice pronounces a death threat against Celie's mother, and holds Celie hostage; it is never directly attributed to "Pa," but we learn through linguistic repetition that it must be his. By the end of the third paragraph of Celie's first letter, he repeats the advisory locution "You better" with a similar but different message: "shut up and git used to it."

Lost in a wilderness of unnamed effects, Celie is nonetheless able to resist her silencing by embodying for God's (and the reader's) benefit the generic scene of female humiliation. "Sister Celie" (p. 48) is raised to the level of female exemplum when every woman who sees her tells her, in effect, "You got to fight" (pp. 25, 28, 47). Stripped of any right to the privacy of her body, and sentenced to vocal exile, she manages to "speak" in public by becoming a talking book, taking on her body the rape, incest, slave labor, and beating that would otherwise be addressed to other women, her "sisters." Celie's response to these incursions into her autonomy is to enter history for the first time—not really by "asking another woman for her underwear," but by crossing out "I am" and situating herself squarely on the ground of negation.

Celie's particular negation arises not only from the (f)act of rape, effecting her bifurcation into a subject and a subject-made-object-to-itself. Rape here only intensifies the negation that grows from the ongoing patriarchal subjugation of women. Her oppression, as represented early in the novel, circulates around the vulnerabilities that grow from her gender, as constructed within the social space which her "Pa" respectably occupies.

But gender oppression is neither the only nor the main factor operating in the oppressive paternal ideology: behind the story Celie thinks she knows, in which the father's control of the family's "private" resources effectively gives him license to violate "his" women, is a story that reveals not the family's private or internal structure but its social and historical placement. Behind "Pa"'s story, as Celie discovers, is the story of her biological father's lynching and murder.

The Color Purple telegraphs the traumatic transformation of Celie's family history by emphasizing Nettie's generic departure from standard epistolary form to the fairy tale. Nettie writes her, "Once upon a time, there was a well-to-do farmer who owned his own property near town. Our town, Celie." Celie's biological father, who, like her mother, is never named in the book (not even by a _____), has been lynched. We receive no eyewitness reports of this event, and no spot or discursive mark verifies the father's life or death. "And so, one night, the man's store was burned down, his smithy destroyed, and the man and his two brothers dragged out of their homes in the middle of the night and hanged" (p. 160). Unlike Celie after her rape, the lynched father cannot speak, act, desire for himself. Moreover, as "Pa" tells Celie, "Lynched people don't git no marker" (p. 167). How does this lynching, and its resistance to representation, transform the cultural politics of this novel, no longer confined to witnessing violence deployed on women by men?

The surprising emergence of racial violence, the murder of three black men by an indeterminate group Nettie calls "the white merchants," induces Celie's second semiotic collapse. The first collapse, which opens the novel, emerges from Celie's confusion about what is "happening" to her in the present tense. Celie's second collapse under the weight of painful knowledge is unconnected to the facts of her contemporary situation: rather, its effects reach back to her origin, and in so doing completely destabilize her identity. This crisis is evident in Celie's almost catatonic announcement—in which, uncharacteristically, all of her verbs are disrupted—"My daddy lynch. My mama crazy. All my little half-brothers and sisters no kin to me. My children not my sister and brother. Pa not pa" (p. 163).

In this revised autobiographical tale, racism succeeds sexism as the cause of social violence in the narrative. The switch from a sexual to a racial code, each of which provides a distinct language and a distinct logic of social relations, releases into the text different kinds of questions about Celie's identity: the new information challenges what Celie (and her readers) mistakenly thought they already knew about the horrific systematic sexual violence that seemed to be the distinguishing mark of family life for women.

For Celie and Nettie's biological father, race functions much as gender functions for the sisters: not as a site of positive identification for the victim, but as an excuse for the oppressor's intricate *style* of cultural persecution. Lynching, in his narrative, has a structural equivalence to Celie's rape, in its violent reduction of the victim to a "biological" sign, an exemplum of subhumanity. This mode of vigilante white justice was a common threat to Southern blacks through the 1930s: Angela Davis, and Frederick Douglass long before her, record the reign of terror propagated by white men ostensibly on behalf of white women's vulnerability to the constant danger of being raped—by black men.[16]

In the narrative of *The Color Purple* the first violation, rape, is succeeded by the second and prior act, lynching: a "logic of equivalence[17] is installed in the narrative that in effect makes race a synonym for scandalous, transgressive Afro-American sexuality.[18] Both in the conventional link between racial and sexual violence, and in the novel, gender difference takes on the pressure of justifying and representing racial oppression. The (unrepresented) act of lynching effects a transfer at the moment of brutal contact from one (the racial) system of oppression to another (the sexual)—precisely the scandalous code that terrorizes Celie at the beginning of the novel.

This complex substitution of paternal tales effectively frees Celie to reclassify her early experience of sexual violence as a *misunderstanding*. Incest, the collapse of structural taboos that ensure the sexual and economic dissemination of the family, is also a figure for the primal illiteracy with which she has been afflicted. The perversion that marked Celie's entry into consciousness had circumscribed her understanding of the world: fundamentally negated by father and husband, in the church and in the marketplace she would also stay as invisible as possible to avoid provoking further violation. Thus it is understandable that the new tale of paternal origins empowers Celie—because Pa is not pa. Having eliminated the perversion from her memory of being raped by her stepfather, the rapes themselves seem to disappear. Celie then recovers from the guilt and shame that had stood in the way of her "right" to control her body and her pleasure.

But this paternal plot twist also short-circuits whatever legitimate understanding of power's institutional operations Celie might have gained from knowing the complicated motives behind these familial events. If one effect

of the second origin tale is to revise Celie's comprehension of the paternal
conditions of her production, another simultaneous effect is to repress the
scene of history insofar as the extrafamilial elements of social relations are
concerned. She understands that people hurt people; but she has no curiosity
about the larger, situational motives of what appears to be personal behavior.

For instance, the new origin tale reveals yet a third factor driving the
transformation of social life and of signification: it reveals the white men's
economic aim to liquidate the father and his two brothers.

> And as [the father] did so well farming and everything he turned
> his hand to prospered, he decided to open a store, and try his
> luck selling dry goods as well. Well, his store did so well that he
> talked his two brothers into helping him run it. . . . Then the white
> merchants began to get together and complain that this store was
> taking all the black business away from them. . . . This would not
> do." [P. 160]

The store the black men owned took business away from the white men,
who then interfered with the free market by lynching their black competi-
tors. Thus class relations, in this instance, are shown to motivate lynching.
Lynching was the act of violence white men performed to *racialize*—to invoke
the context of black inferiority and subhumanity—the victim; the aura of
sexual transgression is also always produced around the lynched by the lynch-
ers, white men guarding the turf of their racial and sexual hegemony.

But Celie never understands it this way, for a number of different reasons. First, the language of Nettie's fairy tale encourages the substitution of
family discourse for the language of capital relations. Rather than naming
names—her own father's, her mother's, her stepfather's—Nettie emphasizes
abstract kinship terms like "the man and his two brothers," "the wife," "the
widow," "the stranger" to describe their positions in the tale. Because the importance of the story to Celie lies in its transmission of new information
about her family history, the tale brackets class issues within the context of
family relations, as if the capitalist economy is generated by the operations of
family ideology.

Second, Nettie's fairy tale reflects—without really reflecting on—the
historical proximity of racial and sexual oppression to the class struggle that
marks Afro-American experience.[19] Yet because her fairy-tale rhetoric emphasizes the personal over the institutional or political components of social
relations, the nonbiologized abstraction of class relations virtually disappears
from the text.

Third, Celie's disregard of the class issues available in this narrative also
serves Walker's desire to effect a shift within the historical novel. The fairy-

tale paradigm Nettie provides replaces the "realist" *mise en scène* that had previously governed the novel's representations of intimate familial violence; in so diminishing the centrality of Alfonso's/the stepfather's rapes of Celie, the text abandons its demystification of male behavior in the family to focus on a reconstruction of the "family"—this time under the care of women. This suggests that Celie and Nettie's feminist fairy tale (the "womanist" historical novel) absorbs and transforms the traditional functions of patrifocal-realist mimesis; and that this transformation makes possible the movement of *The Color Purple* into its communal model of utopian representation, in which a partnership of capitalism and sisterhood plays a central role.

In *The Color Purple*, then, the identity crisis that grows from the violence within the family during Celie's childhood is "explained," traced to its origin, in two significantly different ways. The first narrative installs the greed of patriarchal sexual practice in the unflattering mirror of the "private" family; the injustices manifested in the world outside that central core—for example, in Mr. _____'s sadistic treatment of Harpo—appear from the initial point of view to extend, in a vast synchronicity, from the father's private example.

In contrast, the second family fairy tale represents Celie's crisis of self-comprehension—now an inheritance from her mother—as an effect not of sexual abuse but of a relatively noncoagulated set of practices that have escaped full representation within the mainstream culture: class relations filtered through racial animosity, sexual relations resulting from economic domination. Whereas the first representation of family life located evil forces in the most personal of bodies and intentions, the second tale reveals a more general dispersion of responsibility among unnamed and alien subjects and institutions. Still, reflected in the realm of social theatrics that includes but is not contained within the family scene, sexism and racism provide privatizing images for class struggle, making the lynching appear to Celie a personal and "natural"—but not political—event that takes place on "the father's" so-called private body. This set of textual associations, in which class relations become absorbed by personal histories, forms a paradigm in *The Color Purple*: capitalism becomes the sign of "political" history's repression, both in the everyday life consciousness of the subject and in the narrative at large.

Finally, the very *unreality* to the sisters of the new originary fairy tale extends in part from their alienation from the political and historical context within which these acts took place. Neither woman has ever lived outside of the family in the public sphere of American racism. The story of Celie's original parentage marks the first time in her represented life that specifically racist practices come close to hurting her. In *The Color Purple* the burden of operating within a racist social context, which includes working through the oppressive collaboration of racism and sexism, is generally deflected from Celie's tale onto events in the economic and cultural marketplace.

•••

The trial of thinking and making it through the "racial problem" in *The Color Purple* falls mainly to Sofia Butler, the "amazon" (pp. 69, 198) who enters Mr. _____'s extended family as Harpo's first wife. The voice of sexual and racial *ressentiment*—for instance, she twice expresses a desire to "kill" her sexual and racial oppressors (pp. 68, 98)—Sofia is the first woman Celie knows who refuses to accede to both the patriarchal and the racist demand that the black woman demonstrate her abjection to her oppressors. But the mythic test of Sofia's strength takes place in her refusal to enter the servitude of double discourse demanded of blacks by white culture. She says "Hell no" (p. 86) to the mayor's wife's "complimentary" suggestion that Sofia come to work as her maid; next Sofia answers the mayor's scolding slap of her face with her own powerful punch. For her effort to stay honest in the face of the white demand for black hypocrisy, Sofia gains incarceration in a set of penal institutions that work by a logic similar to that of lynching: to racialize the scene of class struggle in the public sphere and to deploy prejudice against "woman" once behind the walls of the prison and the household. As Sofia tells Celie about her stay in prison: "Every time they ast me to do something, Miss Celie, I act like I'm you. I jump up and do just what they say" (p. 88).

The social coercion of Afro-Americans to participate in a discourse that proclaims their unworthiness is resisted by Sofia, and then performed on Sofia's behalf by Squeak. Squeak's telltale name, in its expression of her distorted, subvocalized voice, describes her original purpose in this text: she enters the narrative as Harpo's dutiful replacement for Sofia, who had refused to allow Harpo to dominate and to beat her.

Squeak knows well how to be properly submissive. But faced with Sofia's crisis Squeak subversively uses her expertise in "proper" feminine self-negating hypocrisy in her supplication for special treatment to the warden of Sofia's prison. The warden is conventionally known as her "cousin," since he is the "illegitimate" father of three of Squeak's siblings. This sloppy familial euphemism leads to a comedy of double- and quadruple-talk that includes Squeak asking for (and getting) the *opposite* of what the warden incorrectly *thinks* she wants. (She wants Sofia released from the prison to serve the rest of her sentence as the mayor's maid; she tells the warden that Sofia is not suffering enough in prison, and that to Sofia the most exquisite torture would be being a white woman's maid; he "fornicates" with Squeak and releases Sofia to the mayor's household.)

The warden's "liberties" with Squeak, so different in representational mode than the young Celie's rapes, also serve as the diacritical mark that organizes Squeak's insertion into the "womanist" order. Having exposed herself to sexual, racial, and political abuse in the name of communal solidarity, Squeak assumes the right to her given name, Mary Agnes. She also earns the right to "sing." She wins these privileges by learning to lie and to produce wordplay while seeming to be an unconscious speaker of the enslaved tongue: Squeak attains social mastery in learning to ironize the already-doubled double-talk that marks the discursive situation of the female Afro-American subject in the white patriarchal public sphere.

•••

The degree of discursive self-alienation expressed in the multiple inversions of language that become the violated ground of both rape and humor in *The Color Purple* in part reflects W. E. B. Du Bois' classic observation, in *The Souls of Black Folk,* that his "people" is marked by a "double consciousness."[20] For American blacks, according to Du Bois, irony takes on an almost allegorical charge as the split or "colonized" subject shuttles between subjectivity and his or her cultural, "racial" status as Object. Henry Louis Gates, Jr. has further elaborated on the cultural machinery of Afro-American "double consciousness" by employing Mikhail Bakhtin's reading of class discourses. Gates suggests that colonized discourse is twisted simultaneously in opposite directions: toward an internal polemic and an external irony.[21] Crucially, each of these discursive modes requires the subject's internalized awareness of a hostile audience. This is the context of a priori negation that results in the inevitable production of double consciousness for socially marginalized citizens.[22]

Frantz Fanon complicates the classic model of colonized double consciousness by characterizing the body that houses the different modes of self-alienation he feels (Blackness and Objectness) as yet another unsutured site of identity. Rather than reading his fragmentation as the fragmentation of a whole, Fanon observes that the inscription of the white parody of black culture—"I was battered down by tom-toms, cannibalism, intellectual deficiency, fetishism, racial defects, slave-ships, and above all else, above all: 'Sho' good eatin'"—on the colonized black body creates a metonymic paradox. On his body the parts do not stand in for a whole; nor do they add up to a whole. "What else could it be for me but an amputation, an excision, a hemorrhage, that spattered my whole body with black blood? But I did not want this revision, this thematization. All I wanted was to be a man among other men."[23] Body parts erupting blood—not red human blood but the black blood of a race and the indelible ink of cultural textuality—constitute him a priori as a mass of part-objects with no relation to a whole.

Fanon here uses the sensation of dismemberment as an allegory for the effects of racist discourse: the fractured body stands in for the fragmented relation to identity suffered by subjects of a culture who have learned the message of their negation before they had a chance to imagine otherwise. This process of part-identification is different from that of the subject described by post-structuralism, who shuttles between the ruse of self-presence and its dissolution.[24] By definition, the colonized subject is unable to produce even the mirage of his or her own totality. Fanon's catalogue of the society's names for him identifies the surplus naming of the marginalized subject as the crucial incision of history into the subject's self-consciousness.

Fanon speaks within the racist discursive context *already reproducing* the white parody of black culture: this is surely the spirit in which Walker represents Harpo, the black parody of a white man (Harpo Marx) who compensates for his voicelessness with music, whose character is expressed in his "feminine" pathos as well as his pathetic aping of masculine pretensions. The tragic aphonia of Celie's mother and the witty, ironic repartee about "uncle Tomming" (p. 93) by Shug, Squeak, and Sofia reveal the even more complex negotiation required of women who aspire to legitimacy in the face of both sexism and racism. Celie's youthful masquerade as Shug in order to deflect her father's sexual greed can also be read as a complex and contradictory message growing out of this kind of negating context. So what looks like simple irony or sarcasm already contains the negating effects of cultural delegitimation. Blackness does not signify except from inside the negative space prepared for it by the history of white culture's relation to black; the same general idea operates in gender relations as well for the Afro-American woman making her way in the context of a double erasure.

The only relief from such torturous negotiating exists in conversation among women. Speaking as a "woman" among women in *The Color Purple* also involves countering the delegitimating pressure of specifically female marginality by finding expression and refuge in wordplay, in the masterful and courageous deployment of language in irony, in rage, in fun, in lies, in song, and in deadly silences. In the racially and sexually fractured situation, back talk resulted in punishment; among women in a man's world, the back talk produces pleasure.

The singers Shug and Mary Agnes articulate professionally the fact and the privileges (current and imminent) of female speech in the liberatory distinction between words and music in, for example, "Miss Celie's Blues." As Celie says, "It all about some no count man doing her wrong, again. But I don't listen to that part. I look at her [Shug] and I hum along a little with the tune" (p. 75). All the speaking women in the novel learn to turn a phrase in acts of defiance and self-expression.[25] They "fight" for the right to take an *attitude:* style itself, apart from content and reference, becomes the first pure note of female signifying.

Celie first displays the pleasure of speech within a female context in her complex response to Corinne, whom Celie sees in town carrying her stolen child, Olivia. Celie invites Corinne to escape the racist glares of the white men in the marketplace by sitting in her wagon; Corinne expresses her gratitude to Celie with a pun on the word "hospitality." Celie demonstrates the power of the joke: "*Horse*pitality, she say. And I git it and laugh. It feel like to split my face." When Mr. ＿＿＿ comes out, he realizes immediately that this shared joke, such as it is, threatens his control over the discursive space in which Celie lives. "What you setting here laughing like a fool fer?" he says (p. 24). Her split face all too graphically refers to the scars she bears, the mask of dumbness she hides behind, and also refers to an object posed, but not yet constituted, the split face that produces plurivocal discourse, not a muted utterance from a victimized shadow.

•••

The implicit context of a priori negation for Afro-Americans that obtains in American culture undergoes a dramatic shift when Nettie's African letters are read into the record. Nettie's letters from Africa at first seem to provide an indigenous alternative history for black consciousness that reverses its traditional invisibility or debasement in the racist American context. To the missionaries, the mission to convert the Africans to Christianity seems specially authorized by a providential and historical allegiance of all "Africans." Aware of a potential problem arising from cultural differences between missionaries and the objects of their attention, Samuel articulates the special privilege he, Corinne, and Nettie will enjoy in Africa:

> Samuel . . . reminded us that there is one big advantage we have. We are not white. We are not Europeans. We are black like the Africans themselves. And that we and the Africans will be working for a common goal: the uplift of black people everywhere. [P. 127]

Nettie records with awe how different the world looks to her from the point of view of African/racial dominance: "Something struck in me, in my soul, Celie, like a large bell, and I just vibrated" (p. 132). With amazement she witnesses Americans in Harlem who worship Africa, not America. She reports with pride about an Afro-American church in which God is black. And there's the great text of racial *ressentiment:* in the Olinka origin narrative, white men are secondary productions of African culture expelled into the nakedness and vulnerability of Otherness (p. 239). The pure pleasure Nettie derives from reading Blackness from a proper and sanctified point of view is the affective origin of the specifically nationalist politics previously repressed in *The Color Purple:* what hope and uplift can Africans all over the world take from their common field of history?

The missionaries' attempt to forge a response to this question produces ambiguous answers. Their version of pan-African consciousness forges a strong sense of world-historical identity within the Afro-American community that in part derives from the greatness of African culture in the centuries before European imperialism. The Afro-American church also sees the spiritual power of the African other-world inhabiting its own driving spirit to convert and to empower the masses of Africans, now disenfranchised from power and progress, economic, cultural, and spiritual.

The white, Western-identified missionaries who sponsor Samuel's particular mission tend, on the other hand, to keep the contemporaneous tribal cultures at arm's length: a white female missionary, for example, "says an African daisy and an English daisy are both flowers, but totally different kinds. The man at the Society says she is successful because she doesn't 'coddle' her charges" (p. 127). The values that lead the missionary society to think it has a progressive message to deliver to the heathen brethren are shown to be well-intentioned, patronizing, misguided, and culturally destructive. While Samuel clearly identifies his destiny with that of the African people, he also unintentionally aims to reproduce the normative social relations of Western culture in the midst of his attempt to reform their spirit.

The primary site of cultural contact between the missionaries and the Africans is pedagogical: the connection between cultural literacy and power established early in the novel is reiterated in the missionaries' retraining of the tribal peoples in the "superior" and Christian practices and materials of Western culture. The issue that brings to the surface the contradictions inherent in the missionaries' creation of a pan-African consciousness is in the sphere of gender relations. Samuel feels compelled to lecture the Olinka women on the virtues of monogamy over polygamy, even though the alliances made among the wives of individual men render the polygamous women far more powerful than Corinne, for example, feels in her ambiguous relation to Nettie. Nettie, in turn, smugly offers to reveal to the Olinka women the movement among women in civilized nations toward liberation from patriarchal oppression in the public and private spheres. But there too the Olinka women see the limitations of Nettie's apparent freedom of movement and knowledge: she is "the missionary's drudge," an "object of pity and contempt" (pp. 145, 149). In short, as Samuel later painfully realizes, what passed for racial identification across borders and historical differences was really a system of cultural hegemony disguised as support and uplift.

The event that clarifies how politically useful the missions are to the European imperialists, standing as agents or prophets of spiritual progress, is the coming of the big road. Generous in their estimation of human nature, the Olinka refuse to understand that the theory of property and propriety under which they live is irrelevant to the Western juridical code. Most natives assume (as American white people always do, notes Nettie [p. 155]) that the superpower force that cuts through the jungle builds a road to the tribe, for the tribe; they admire Western technology, viewing it as they view roofleaf, something nature makes in abundance for the well-being of its devoted people.

But Samuel, Corinne, and Nettie are no more sophisticated in their understanding of the ways of "civilized" culture than are the "natives": this is one instance where the pan-national racial identification between American and African blacks proves sadly accurate. Too late, the missionaries realize that the road threatens their mission; desperately, they exhaust their resources trying to protect the tribe. The only survivors are the tribal citizens who can read well enough to see their death sentence in Western culture and join the *mbeles*, the underground group of radicalized Olinka.

Samuel could have foreseen the failure of his mission. His life story, the only male autobiographical narrative in *The Color Purple* privileged to replace (temporarily) the reigning female subjectivity, reveals the shallowness with which he understood his own cultural privilege. He tells Nettie of the time in his youth that he encountered W. E. B. Du Bois, whose impatience with the pretensions of missionary culture could have taught Samuel that Pan-Africanism requires material transformations of the techniques of power before a new spirit would have any place to grasp:

> Madame, he said, when Aunt Theodosia finished her story and flashed her famous medal around the room, do you realize King Leopold cut the hands off workers who, in the opinion of his plantation overseers, did not fulfill their rubber quota? Rather than cherish that medal, Madame, you should regard it as a symbol of your unwitting complicity with this despot who worked to death and brutalized and eventually exterminated thousands and thousands of African peoples. [P. 210]

Like the lynched body, the black hand here not only serves as a figure of racial "justice" for whites, but also becomes a kind of rebus for the metonymic "hand" of capitalism, in which the worker is an economic appendage reduced to the (dis)embodiment of his or her alienation.[26] This kind of symbolism was on Du Bois' mind in the period after World War I, when "lying treaties, rivers of rum, murder, assassination, mutilation, rape, and torture have marked the progress of Englishman, German, Frenchman, and Belgian on the Dark Continent" ("AR," p. 361). The Pan-African movement, organized by Du Bois to counter the European exploitation of Africa's plentiful resources, took up the question of Belgium in 1919 and 1921 much as these hands "take up" the question of slavery.[27] Du Bois saw in the capitalist infiltration of Africa the origins of world racism against blacks: "'Color' became in the world's thought synonymous with inferiority, 'Negro' lost its capitalization, and Africa was another name for bestiality and barbarism" ("AR," p. 362).

The ramifications of the peculiar kind of racism produced by capitalism led Du Bois to try to organize all of the African nations of the world: to create a "people" that would fight for its right to national self-determination, for the (he would say, inevitable) democratization of capital, and for the eradication of the racist representations that have masked the capitalist pilfering of Pan-African resources. But Samuel does not go as far as Du Bois did in attacking the origin of contemporary racism in Western relations of capital, even though Nettie's letters register the information that local traditions of land and cultural ownership are completely subsumed to the absentee ownership of the non-African nations feeding off the continent's wealth (p. 132). Instead, Samuel sees his failure to understand his unwitting complicity with colonialist practices as a flaw in his theory of spirit. The mission's total powerlessness to prevent the destruction of the culture they had come to "save" provokes Samuel and Nettie to redefine what it means to serve God.

> God is different to us now, after all these years in Africa. More spirit than ever before, and more internal. Most people think he has to look like something or someone—a roofleaf or Christ—but we don't. And not being tied to what God looks like, frees us. [P. 227]

The link between the theory and practices of "capitalism" and of "religion" or spirit is the key to the novel's reformulation of mainstream Afro-American nationalist politics and consciousness. Having spent the first part of the novel tracing the pernicious effects of the national-patriarchal-capitalist domination of personal and natural resources, Walker opens the second part with Nettie's moving tributes to the fabulous richness of African culture, read as a pan-national phenomenon. Nettie unconsciously quotes "America, the Beautiful" in her report of it: "And we kneeled down right on deck and gave thanks to God for letting us see the land for which our mothers and fathers cried—and lived and died—to see again" (pp. 132–133).

The missionaries' disillusioned removal to the United States signals a transformation of their relation to both African and American nationalism. By viewing America as the place of the new redeemed church shorn of idols, Samuel and Nettie repeat seventeenth-century Puritan religious and civil representations of America as the only site where a sanctified and defetishized church might have a chance for survival. In so embracing the theory of an idol-free America, the missionaries refute their initial intention to enrich their historical affiliation with Africa—Africa seen as a body of land with a distinctive history—and with the problem of Afro-American political disenfranchisement to which Pan-Africanism had been a response. And to replace the cultural and political solution Pan-African nationalism had offered to the missionaries, a religion free from boundaries and margins emerges based on unmediated relations of Being to Being.

The last half of the novel, after Nettie's letters are discovered, traces how the characters' departure from formal alliances—based on race, organized religion, politics—takes the form of a nationalist aesthetic that places essences (human and inhuman) in their proper social relation regardless of apparent material conditions and contradictions. Capitalism, as we shall see, is no longer a hegemonic and mystified mode of exploitation; rather, it becomes an extension of the subject's spiritual *choices*. And the hybrid, fractured status of Afro-American signification reemerges in its earliest form: instead of infusing the African side of the compound term with the positive historical identification usually denied in the American context, the last half of the novel returns "Africa" to the space of disappointment and insufficiency, finally overwhelmed by the power of "America" to give form to the utopian impulse.

•••

Every transformation of belief that marks Samuel and Nettie's return "home" to America has a correlate in a change of Celie's worldview—sexual, social, and spiritual. For Celie, like Nettie, sexual awakening not only transforms her relation to her body and to pleasure in general, but also leads to a major shift in her understanding and mastery of power in the world. It is Shug Avery who saves Celie from being paralyzed by rage at Mr. _____'s concealment of Nettie's letters; Shug also channels Celie's confusion at the collapse of her original way of understanding the world into a radical revision of that understanding—starting with God, the prime Author and Audience of her tortured inner life.

This shift in Celie's mode of belief reveals to her a world saturated by a sensual beauty that signifies God's work. "Admiration" is Shug's word for worship: Celie's religion, like Nettie's, is transformed from a social, institutional enterprise to an aestheticized and surprisingly solitary sexual practice. Admiring the color purple is equated with what Celie calls "making love to God," an act she performs with the aid of a reefer.

Celie adopts a mode of sensual pleasure and power beyond the body that effectively displaces the injustices that have marked her tenure in the quotidian. She heralds her glorious transformation into self-presence by shedding her scarred historical body as she leaves Mr. _____ : "I'm pore, I'm black, I may be ugly and can't cook, a *voice say to everything listening*. But I'm here" (p. 187; my emphasis). This pure and disembodied voice speaks of its liberation from the disfigured body and enacts, through disembodiment, the utopian scene of self-expression from Celie's point of view. In this scene, the negated, poor, black, female body—created for Mr. _____'s pleasure, profit, and scorn—is replaced by a voice that voids the vulnerability of the bodied historical subject. To Mr. _____'s prophecy that Celie will fail in the world because she has neither talent, beauty, nor courage "to open your mouth to people" (p. 186), Celie performs her triumphant Being—"I'm here"—and asserts the supremacy of speech over the physical, material despotism characteristic of patriarchy. Her new mode of counteropposition also deploys the supernatural power of language, turning Mr. _____'s negativity back on himself: "Until you do right by me, I say, everything you even dream about will fail." The authority of this curse comes from nature: "I give it to him straight, just like it come to me. And it seem to come to me from the trees" (p. 187). Speech here becomes the primary arena of action: the natural world lends not its material resources but a spiritual vitality that can always assert itself while the body is threatened and battered. And writing, as the fact of the letters suggests, is the place where the voice is held in trust for the absent subject who might be seeking a way of countering the patriarchal and racist practices of the social world.

This revision of Celie's point of view frees her from her imprisonment in stoic passivity. But if Celie's body has taken a beating, it also carries the traces of her violently inscribed history: multiple rape, incest, disenfranchisement through a marriage trade made between two men (in which Celie and her cow have equivalent status), as well as through her stepfather's repression of her mother's will, and, finally, sexual, economic, and psychological exploitation and abuse by Mr. _____ and his family. Celie's ascension to speech, a new realm of "bodiless" happiness, does not include coming to terms with these events as she leaves them behind: she is completely reborn, without bearing witness to the scars left in knowledge and memory.

Indeed, in her new domestic regime Celie first occupies her "old" social powerlessness like a natural skin. According to Shug, Celie would have been happy to devote her life to being Shug's maid (p. 190); but Shug insists that Celie find meaningful work for herself. And the rest, as they say, is history: the letter Celie writes to Nettie describing Shug's capitalization of her production of "perfect pants" is signed "Your Sister, Celie / Folkpants, Unlimited. / Sugar Avery Drive / Memphis, Tennessee" (p. 192). Through Shug, both a sexual and economic provider, Celie gains the *nom du père* of capitalism: a trademark, which becomes a part of Celie's new signature, itself a reflection of Shug's own nominal dissemination on the road map of her culture.

Celie's Folkpants provides such a service for the woman or man who purchases them as well. The simple message Folkpants advertises is that the pants truly are for "the people," marketed for all genders. The unisexuality of the pants deemphasizes the importance of fashion in the social context in which the pants are worn: following the ethical and aesthetic shift from worshipping the white male God to appreciating the presence of spirit and color, Celie emphasizes fabric, print, and color in their conception and distribution.

A mode of ontological mimesis governs the specifications of each pair of pants, tailoring each to embody the essential person but not his or her physical body: one size, one cut fits all. Each pair of Folkpants is shown to release the wearer into authentic self-expression. At the book's end this semiotic democracy, based on the authenticity of all speaking subjects, reflected in and enacted by their commodity relations, replaces the sexism and racism of "natural" languages of the body and consciousness.

In addition, when grammar enters the realm of manifest struggle, the essence of the expression reigns over its historical or conventional usage. Darlene, who works in Celie's factory, tries to teach Celie "proper" English.

> You say US where most folks say WE, she say, and peoples think you dumb. Colored peoples think you a hick and white folks be amuse.
>   What I care? I ast. I'm happy. [P. 193]

Shug settles the argument by asserting that Celie can "talk in sign language for all I care" (p. 194): in Shug's revisionary semiotic, the medium of transmission is proclaimed as transparent while "the message" is everything. She embraces an aesthetic of live performance: a mode of discourse that can only be activated in the performance of a speech act between a living speaker and a co-present receiver. As a result, all speech acts become intersubjective and are therefore authentic within the speech context created by the confluence of subjectivities. Shug here produces the "theory" of the everyday life language practiced by Celie: the populist elements of such an ethic are vital to the formation of the Folkpants industry.

The vestments of "the people" quickly become the ligaments of a new family as the workshop where the Folkpants are made moves from Shug's house to the house of Celie's birth. Celie's return to this house, however, is not represented as a confrontation with long-buried memories of sexual violation or personal danger. On this go-round, the house comes with yet a third new prehistoric origin myth, in which the Mother has protected her daughters from the deadliest penetration of patriarchy by preserving her property for the girls. The wicked stepfather, trespassing on their property as he has on Celie's body, had wrested it from the sisters; his death sets them free from their exile and they return, one at a time.

This move does more than to bring them back to the Mother: it also provides closure to the narrative genealogy of racism and class struggle inscribed in Celie's family history. Celie now situates herself firmly in her family's entrepreneurial tradition; she runs her business from the store tragically occupied by her stepfather, and her father before him. Where her father and uncles were lynched for presuming the rights of full American citizens to participate in a free market, and where her stepfather survived by doing business exclusively for and with whites (p. 167), Celie's business is as perfectly biracial as it is unisexual, employing both Sofia and a white worker to sell her goods so that *everyone* will be well served (p. 245).

Thus it would seem that capitalism, figured as a small (but infinitely expandable) family-style business, provides for the socially marginalized characters in *The Color Purple* the motivating drive for forging a positive relation to social life. The family-as-business has the power and the resources to absorb adversity while providing the ground for social relations based on cooperation rather than on coercion. Not socialist-style cooperation, of course—Shug, Celie's financial backer, specifically orders her to hire "women . . . to cut and sew, while you sit back and design" (p. 192).

To join the closely knit family of female capitalists, one must simply identify with the "female world of love and ritual" that includes the everyday working relations among women that center on the home.[28] A woman can assert her allegiance to other women simply by joining the business: for men who admit a childhood/natural desire to engage in the housekeeping practices of their mothers (Harpo, p. 63; Mr. _____, p. 238), the franchise is conferred.

United around these activities, Celie's new family emerges from the gender and racial fractures that had threatened to destroy it. Yet it is finally not family discourse that organizes the life of the redeemed community: the last event of the novel, after Nettie and the children's return to Celie, not only fulfills the familial model of utopian capitalism that dominates the last third of the narrative, but also reinstates nationalist discourse as the proper context for Celie's autobiography.

•••

"Dear God. Dear stars, dear trees, dear sky, dear peoples. Dear Everything. Dear God" (p. 249). With this lyric, the end of *The Color Purple* proclaims the ascendancy of a new mode of national and personal identity. In a letter Celie addresses not to the God who is everything but to the everything that incorporates godly spirit, she writes of the fulfillment of the womanist promise, as the community turns toward the future in expectation of more profit, pleasure, and satisfaction from their labor and from each other. Shug speaks of retiring. "Albert" / Mr. _____ prattles about the new shirt he's made. Celie speaks about "how things doing generally" while she compulsively stitches "up a bunch of scraps, try to see what [she] can make" (p. 249). As in the rest of the novel, the idiom of Celie's victory is deliberately apolitical: while she might have used the new formation of the utopian community as an opportunity for metacommentary about the revolutionary conditions of its production, Celie continues to favor the materials of the common language in the construction of the new social space.

And yet it is precisely at this protonationalist moment, when the changes sought within the family have been realized in the woman-identified community and extended to the outside world through the garment business, that *The Color Purple* turns back toward the kinds of explications of social life that Celie has previously rejected. In the novel's final pages, conventional mythopoetic political discourse about American culture, about "the births, battles, and deaths of Great Men" previously exiled from the text's concerns and representations, surfaces for adoption. In so doing, this radically revised and "womanized" historical novel calls into question its own carefully established social and textual metamorphosis.

Celie's rapprochement with Mr. _____, for example, is significantly sealed when he personally places a letter in her hand—not from Nettie, but from America: the Department of Defense telegram notifying Celie of Nettie's apparent death (p. 225). But this gesture comments more on the symbolic relations of patriarchal to state forms than it does on changes in the experiences or consciousness of the characters. The redemption of America is linked with the redemption of Mr. _____, forecasting the novel's imminent refranchising of patriarchal modes of analysis and representation.

On this occasion we also witness Celie's startling use of the narrowly "political" language which, I have argued, has been absent from her practice throughout the rest of the novel. Celie's fear of Nettie's death suggests to her that, in this time of crisis, America confers on American blacks the cultural status of lynched subjects like Celie's father: "Plus," she says, "colored don't count to those people" (p. 245). There is nothing contradictory or insidious in this particular observation of Celie's, but it too heralds the revalorization of a mode of heretofore exiled cultural analysis.

The final day of the narrative telegraphs the novel's turn to American nationalism at its most blatant and filiopietistic: it is July 4, Independence Day. It is the first and only day narrated in the novel that takes place after Nettie's return to the fold. It is uniquely positioned to provide textual commentary about the relation between its limited set of "characters" and the operation of dominant and contested cultures that has marked Afro-American experience.

The dialogue that constitutes explicit comment on the subject of the holiday ranges from personal "complaint" to epic recognition:

> Why us always have family reunion on July 4th, say Henrietta, mouth poke out, full of complaint. It so hot.
>
> White people busy celebrating independence from England July 4th, say Harpo, so most black folks don't have to work. Us can spend the day celebrating each other.

Ah, Harpo, say Mary Agnes, . . . I didn't know you knowed
history. [P. 250]

We didn't know that Harpo knew history either: he never seemed to need to
know it. With the single, special exception of Sofia's fifteen minutes of freedom on Christmas while indentured to the mayor's wife, at no other time in
the novel has work on the farm or anywhere else within the black community depended on or referred to the demands of white American hegemonic
culture for its work timetable or its mode of leisure. Mary Agnes' surprise
at Harpo is appropriate, for this consciousness of "history" is imported specially for the novel's closing moments.

But what does the rearticulation of Celie's family within a specifically
American scene do to the politics of history in *The Color Purple?* In this late
moment, Celie's early assertion of her autonomy from American national
identity is silently answered by the next generation's commentary: Harpo's
"history" suggests instead that Afro-American culture exists confidently in
the interstices of Anglo-American historical time. He characterizes the relation between Anglo- and Afro-American culture as structured around an opposition and a hierarchy that discriminates racially, and yet implies that blacks
have all the room they need for full cultural self-articulation.

Possibly this shift represents a historical change—a change in the
modes of cultural reproduction. Whereas the home life Celie experienced
as a child and a young woman mainly involved the black community, the
life she leads with Shug overlaps the circulation of blues culture throughout
both black and white urban communities. Perhaps, as a result of her wider
experience, a traditionally national language was the only discourse available to describe this variegated cultural landscape. If this multiracial cultural
articulation, commonly known as the American "melting pot," is the main
motive behind the resurgence of American consciousness, then the final images of *The Color Purple* might be said to abandon the project of specifically
representing an Afro-American national culture for a less racially delimited,
more pluralist model.

But if the image of the reconstituted family in the text's final letter suggests the American melting pot, it also represents the clearly Jeffersonian cast
of Celie's family. Rural, abstracted from the mainly urban scene of consumption, this "matrician" homestead remains the symbolic and actual seat of the
production of Folkpants. Folkpants, in turn (no doubt soon to be joined by
a line of Folkshirts designed by Mr. _____), retain their capacity to express
the consumer's unique and unmarked soul, along with embodying the ideal
conditions of social relations.

From this point of view, the novel's resuscitation of American national
discourse can be explained by the way Celie's "family," in the final instance,

can be said to mark its own separate, specifically Afro-American recoloniza-
tion of American time, American property, and mythic American self-help
ideology by casually ironizing it. Harpo's droll analysis of the reason behind
their July Fourth gathering minimizes the melting-pot aspect of American
Independence Day, reducing the holiday to a racial and not a national celebration. Mary Agnes' uncontested depiction of Harpo's statement as history
might suggest that this final event is meant to illuminate the real poverty of
a politically established Anglo-American national identity when set next to
that of the Afro-American community that has fought on all grounds for the
right to have everything—life, dignity, love, family, nation.

But to enter, as the novel does, into a mode of political analysis that em-
ploys the ideological myths of hegemonic culture to define Afro-American
culture raises questions about the oppositional status of the novel. Such an alliance severely problematizes the critique of conventional historical "memory"
and cultural self-transmission that Walker intended to make in this "historical novel." It implicitly represents American racism as a condition of Afro-
American self-celebration.

The novel's apparent amnesia about the conditions of its own production is symbolized in the denial or reversal of age heralded in the novel's and
Celie's closing sentence: "Matter of fact, I think this the youngest us ever felt"
(p. 251). As if deliberately replacing her very first utterance, "I am fourteen
years old," with an assertion of victorious subjectivity and a control over the
context in which she speaks, Celie commits herself to the production of a
new age but ascribes no value to the influence of the past on the subject or
on the culture.

Such a model for the reformulation of Afro-American national identity
threatens to lose certain historical events in the rush to create the perfect
relations of a perfect moment. That the text might use the repression of certain kinds of memory as a strategy for representing its new, utopian mode of
production was signaled in the narrative repression of the class element in
Celie's father's lynching. The profit motive killed her father and, indirectly, her
mother; it made Celie vulnerable to her stepfather's sexual imperialism and
almost resulted in her disenfranchisement from her property. But the novel's
progressive saturation with capitalism and its fruits, along with its insistence
on the significance of the product in the consumer's self-knowledge and self-
expression, marks the relative cleansing of violence from its class and capital
relations. The Afro-American nationalism imaged in the new familial system
can be said to use the American tradition of autonomy through property to
imagine the new social epoch.

The Color Purple's strategy of inversion, represented in its elevation of
female experience over great patriarchal events, had indeed aimed to critique
the unjust practices of racism and sexism that violate the subject's complex-

ity, reducing her to a generic biological sign. But the model of personal and national identity with which the novel leaves us uses fairytale explanations of social relations to represent itself: this fairy tale embraces America for providing the Afro-American nation with the right and the opportunity to own land, to participate in the free market, and to profit from it. In the novel's own terms, American capitalism thus has contradictory effects. On one hand, capitalism veils its operations by employing racism, using the pseudonatural discourse of race to reduce the economic competitor to a subhuman object. In Celie's parental history, *The Color Purple* portrays the system of representation characteristic of capital relations that *creates* the situation of nationlessness for Afro-Americans.

But the novel also represents the mythic spirit of American capitalism as the vehicle for the production of an Afro-American utopia. Folkpants, Unlimited is an industry dedicated to the reproduction and consumption of a certain system of representation central to the version of Afro-American "cultural nationalism" enacted by *The Color Purple*. But Folkpants, Unlimited also participates in the profit motive: the image of the commodity as the subject's most perfect self-expression is the classic fantasy bribe of capitalism.[29] The illogic of a textual system in which the very force that disenfranchises Afro-Americans provides the material for their national reconstruction is neither "solved" by the novel nor raised as a paradox. The system simply stands suspended in the heat of the family reunion on Independence Day.

What saves Celie and Nettie from disenfranchisement is their lifelong determination to learn, to become literate: Nettie's sense that knowledge was the only route to freedom from the repressive family scene gave her the confidence to escape, to seek "employment" with Samuel's family, to record the alternative and positive truth of Pan-African identity, to face the truth about her own history, to write it down, and to send it to Celie, against all odds. Writing was not only the repository of personal and national hope; it became a record of lies and violences that ultimately produced truth.

The Color Purple nonetheless ultimately rejects writing for an ethic of voice—from Shug's advocacy of self-present, performative discourse to Walker's own postscriptural description of herself as the book's "medium." The fantasy of the novel is that these voices might be preserved as pure "text," cleansed of the residues of historical oppression. Celie herself embraces a mode of cultural nationalism unable to transmit objective knowledge—knowledge that does not derive from experience and intimacy—about the way institutional forms of power devolve on "private" individuals, alone and in their various social relations. Such an emphasis on individual essence, in a false opposition to institutional history, seems inadequate to the construction of any national consciousness, especially one developing in a hostile, negating context. Mythic American political discourse is precisely unable to account for the uneven devolvement of legitimacy on citizens obfuscated within the nation's rhetoric of identity. And if *The Color Purple* clearly represents anything, it is the unreliability of "text" under the historical pressure to interpret, to predict, and to determine the cultural politics of the colonized signifier.

NOTES

Much thanks to Houston Baker, Laura Brown, W. J. T. Mitchell, and Tom Stillinger for their tremendous help with this essay.

1. Alice Walker, *The Color Purple* (New York, 1982), p. 11; hereafter cited by page number.

2. The Fourth of July has been a politically charged holiday for Afro-Americans as well as for other marginalized groups. See Philip S. Foner, ed., *We, the Other People: Alternative Declarations of Independence by Labor Groups, Farmers, Woman's Rights Advocates, Socialists, and Blacks, 1829–1975* (Urbana, Ill., 1976), pp. 14–15.

> As long as slavery existed, most blacks refused to participate in celebrations on the Fourth of July, setting aside July 5 for that purpose. In his July 5, 1832, speech in the African Church, New Haven, Connecticut, Peter Osborne declared: "Fellow Citizens: On account of the misfortune of our color, our fourth of July comes on the fifth; but I hope and trust that when the Declaration of Independence is fully executed, which declares that all men, without respect to person, were born free and equal, we may then have our fourth of July on the fourth." Frederick Douglass, the ex-slave and black abolitionist, summed it up succinctly in his great speech, "The Meaning of July Fourth for the American Negro," delivered in Rochester, New York, on July 5, 1852: "I am not included within the pale of this glorious anniversary! . . . This Fourth of July is *yours*, not mine. You may rejoice, but I must mourn. . . ."

3. Afro-American nationalism has generated too many important primary and secondary works to be documented in one contextualizing footnote. The anthology *Black Nationalism in America*, ed. John H. Bracey, Jr., August Meier, and Elliott Rudwick (Indianapolis and New York, 1970) contains many of these primary polemical documents. For the purposes of this essay, the most important work on the growth of and struggles within the black nationalist movement have been the complete works of W. E. B. Du Bois (his fiction, his autobiography, his book-length essays, and his journalism), now available in the Library of America collection *W. E. B. Du Bois: Writings*, ed. Nathan Huggins (New York, 1986); Frantz Fanon, *The Wretched of the Earth*, trans. Constance Farrington (New York, 1963); Fanon, *Black Skin, White Masks*, trans. Charles Lam Markmann (New York, 1967); Fanon, *Toward the African Revolution: Political Essays*, trans. Haakon Chevalier (New York, 1967); Houston A. Baker, Jr., *The Journey Back: Issues in Black Literature and Criticism* (Chicago, 1980); and Manning Marable, "The Third Reconstruction: Black Nationalism and Race in a Revolutionary America," *Social Text* (Fall 1981): 3–27.

4. The historically unique characteristics of American populist movements require the critic to take nothing for granted in evaluating the "franchising" of membership in the American national community. This is the lesson of Michel de

Certeau in "The Politics of Silence: The Long March of the Indians," *Heterologies: Discourse on the Other, Theory and History of Literature*, vol. 17, trans. Brian Massumi (Minneapolis, 1986), pp. 225–233. Important work on the politics of "indigenous" or populist movements has been done by Ernesto Laclau and Chantal Mouffe in *Hegemony and Socialist Strategy: Towards a Radical Democratic Politics*, trans. Winston Moore and Paul Cammack (London, 1985), as well as in Laclau's earlier genealogy of the category "populism" in "Towards a Theory of Populism," *Politics and Ideology in Marxist Theory: Capitalism—Fascism—Populism* (London, 1977), pp. 143–198.

     5. Walker, *In Search of Our Mothers' Gardens* (San Diego, 1983), p. xi. "Womanist" is a neologism of Walker's invention. Much more than an idiosyncratic translation of "feminist" into a black/third-world female tradition, the term describes the "woman" in a range of personal and social identities: "Usually referring to outrageous, audacious, courageous or *willful* behavior. Wanting to know more and in greater depth than is considered 'good' for one. . . . *Also:* A woman who loves other women, sexually and/or nonsexually. . . . Sometimes loves individual men, sexually and/or nonsexually. . . . Traditionally universalist, as in 'the colored race is just like a flower garden, with every color flower represented.'" In calling the new nationalist epistemology imaged and advocated in *The Color Purple* an "aesthetic/symbolic" logic, I mean to honor the careful historical and categorical distinctions that operate in the novel and in Walker's critical work around it. Central to her practice is a delegitimation of traditionally patriarchal-racist political practices, institutions, and language.

     6. Walker, "Writing *The Color Purple*," *In Search of Our Mothers' Gardens*, p. 356.

     7. The *locus classicus* of discussion about the political uses of the historical novel is Georg Lukács, *The Historical Novel*, trans. Hannah and Stanley Mitchell (London, 1962). My description of Walker's method of refunctioning the historical novel departs very little from Lukács' own valorization of Walter Scott's method in *The Heart of Midlothian*, especially the use of woman to reconstitute the national spirit. Walker's real departure from the conventions of the historical novel is located in her refusal to reinvest the "revised" national consciousness in the legitimation of patriarchal forms of authority. After Lukács, the most significant theorist of the national implications of the historical novel is Benedict Anderson, *Imagined Communities: Reflections on the Origin and Spread of Nationalism* (London, 1983).

     8. *The Color Purple* repeats in practice *Meridian*'s revelation that "One Life" always contains multiple voices (see below). Celie's autobiography is firmly in the Afro-American tradition of cultural self-exemplification epitomized in and theorized by Du Bois in *The Souls of Black Folk* (1903) and *Dusk of Dawn: An Essay Toward an Autobiography of a Race Concept* (1940). See also William L. Andrews, *To Tell a Free Story: The First Century of Afro-American Autobiography, 1760–1865* (Urbana, Ill. 1986).

     9. Homi K. Bhabha, "Signs Taken for Wonders: Questions of Ambivalence and Authority under a Tree Outside Delhi, May 1817," *Critical Inquiry* 12 (Autumn 1985): 156.

     10. Walker, *Meridian* (New York, 1976), p. 121.

     11. Ibid., p. 200.

     12. Walker has written much fiction and many essays addressing black nationalism in its recent embodiment in the civil rights movement, and contrasting it to other liberated nationalisms, notably Cuban, in *In Search of Our Mothers' Gardens*. *Meridian* addresses directly the need for national identity among Afro-

Americans. Short stories from Walker's *In Love and Trouble* (San Diego, 1973), such as "Her Sweet Jerome" and "Everyday Use," see black nationalism not as an expression of Afro-American historical and political solidarity but as a way for "cultured" blacks to oppress noneducated or unsophisticated blacks. *The Color Purple* retains the positivity of *Meridian* toward national identity but also reproduces the negative, antipatriarchal, and antielitist tone of the stories by rejecting, or so it seems, a specifically political (in the narrow sense: discourse that takes place about power) articulation of Afro-American identity for an aesthetic or symbolic construction of the new national subject. In stories written between *In Love and Trouble* and *The Color Purple*, Walker also addresses the *problem* of representing the complex of racial, sexual, and national issues also at the forefront of *The Color Purple*. See especially the remarkable "Advancing Luna—and Ida B. Wells" in *You Can't Keep a Good Woman Down* (New York, 1981), pp. 85–104.

13. It is perhaps to show with clarity the erasing or negating effects of American racism on a contested subculture that *The Color Purple* contains a number of brief narratives about the fate of native Americans. These tales exhibit the American ability to absorb symbolically a set of cultural differences it claims to honor; they also provide a stunning warning about what happens to cultures that neglect to witness their history. The result, in Samuel's simple words, is that "it became harder to think about Indians because there were none around" (p. 209).

Unconsciousness of the history of racial displacements that distinguishes the colonization of America means, at least in *The Color Purple*, that the subculture in question has lost its ability to read its own history, registered in the genetic traces of its dispersal among the American and Afro-American population. Nettie transcribes Samuel's narration of Corinne's life story:

> Sixty years or so before the founding of the school [Spelman], the Cherokee Indians who lived in Georgia were forced to leave their homes and walk, through the snow, to resettlement camps in Oklahoma. A third of them died on the way. But many of them refused to leave Georgia. They hid out as colored people and eventually blended with us. Many of these mixed-race people were at Spelman. Some remembered who they actually were, but most did not. If they thought about it at all . . . they thought they were yellow or reddish brown and wavy haired because of white ancestors, not Indian. [P. 209]

Even in a community of blood-related readers, the bodily text of the native American descendant seems more like the blank sheet of a stucco wall than it does like the crucial petroglyphs of a fading culture. This means that the cultural framework that would have made these signs legible to a "people" has vanished, and that this people is culturally illiterate—with respect to itself. Even memories passed down orally, through the family or within a community, are not strong enough to keep the meaning of national signs alive.

Furthermore, in place of the positive identity that native American culture might have maintained had it constructed ways to protect and preserve itself, American Indians are represented here as having developed a way of life that takes its cultural negation as a given. Shug's son, working on an Indian reservation in Arizona, not only experiences racist treatment by the Indians but witnesses with sadness the Indians' reproduction of their cultural disempowerment: "But even if he [Shug's son] try to tell them how he feel [about their racism], they don't seem to care. They so far gone nothing strangers say mean nothing. Everybody not an Indian they got no use for" (p. 235).

14. Benedict Anderson writes eloquently of the way the citizen's "political love" of country partakes of the affect and the libidinal charge traditionally invested in other institutional relations of love—especially through the family. But while the family has conventionally been a signifier of disinterested, uncorrupted love (love "no matter what"), the feminist/"womanist" critique of the family aims to unveil the modes of coercion and exploitation behind the apparently objective and dispassionate quality of the Fathers' love and guidance. See Anderson, *Imagined Communities*, p. 131.

15. Houston Baker describes this mode of mass address as characteristic of the Afro-American text:

> The text, transmitted as performance, is a public occasion . . . rather than a private act of literacy. It is a ritual statement of the solidarity and continuity of a culture; it takes its place among other transmissions and elaborations of culture such as weddings, festivals, funerals, and so on. As such, it has a register different from the ones traditionally specified for literary texts.

See Baker, *The Journey Back*, p. 128. Robert B. Stepto has also addressed the political and aesthetic motivations of the reader reading "as" an Afro-American. See Stepto, "Distrust of the Reader in Afro-American Narratives," in *Reconstructing American Literary History*, ed. Sacvan Bercovitch, Harvard English Studies 13 (Cambridge, Mass. 1986), pp. 300–322.

16. Angela Y. Davis, "Rape, Racism and the Myth of the Black Rapist," *Women, Race and Class* (New York, 1981), pp. 172–201; Frederick Douglass, "Why Is the Negro Lynched?" *The Life and Writings of Frederick Douglass*, ed. Foner, 5 vols. (New York, 1950–1975), 4: pp. 491–523.

17. The notion of the "logic of equivalence" is important to Laclau and Mouffe's arguments about the discursive texture of social relations. See Laclau and Mouffe, *Hegemony and Socialist Strategy*, p. 129.

18. Eve Sedgwick has identified a similar strategy of displacement in *Gone With the Wind*, although she sees the transference among discourses as operating more symmetrically than I see it working here. See Eve Kosofsky Sedgwick, *Between Men: English Literature and Male Homosocial Desire* (New York, 1985), p. 9.

19. Anderson points out that class struggle is often the hidden interface of racist practices. See Anderson, *Imagined Communities*, p. 137; see also Marable, "The Third Reconstruction."

20. "The Negro is a sort of seventh son, born with a veil, and gifted with second-sight in this American world,—a world which yields him no true self-consciousness, but only lets him see himself through the revelation of the other world. It is a peculiar sensation, this double-consciousness, this sense of always looking at one's self through the eyes of others, of measuring one's soul by the tape of a world that looks on in amused contempt and pity. One ever feels his twoness,—an American, a Negro; two souls, two thoughts, two unreconciled strivings; two warring ideals in one dark body, whose dogged strength alone keeps it from being torn asunder" (Du Bois, *The Souls of Black Folk*, reprinted in *Three Negro Classics* [New York, 1965], pp. 214–215).

21. Henry Louis Gates, Jr., "The Blackness of Blackness: A Critique of the Sign and the Signifying Monkey," in *Black Literature and Literary Theory*, ed. Gates (New York and London, 1984), pp. 285–321.

22. For a more extended discussion of the effects of political oppression on the construction of public discourse and of the subject's consciousness, see Lauren Berlant, "The Female Complaint," forthcoming in *Social Text*.

23. Fanon, *Black Skin, White Masks*, p. 112.

24. See Gates, "The Blackness of Blackness," pp. 297–305.

25. Nettie is an exception to this; but she has full control over the space of writing and thus from the beginning is able to use the letter as the utopian, liberated site of expression.

26. See, for example, Du Bois, "The African Roots of War," in *W. E. B. Du Bois: A Reader*, ed. Meyer Weinberg (New York, 1970), pp. 362–363; hereafter abbreviated "AR."

> Thus, the world began to invest in color prejudice. The "color line" began to pay dividends. For, indeed, while the exploration of the valley of the Congo was the occasion of the scramble for Africa, the cause lay deeper. [England, France, Germany, Portugal, Italy, and Turkey, among others, all spend the last quarter of the nineteenth and the early twentieth centuries in a "scramble" for Africa.] . . .
>
> Why was this? What was the new call for dominion? . . .
>
> The answer to this riddle we shall find in the economic changes in Europe. Remember what the nineteenth and twentieth centuries have meant to organized industry in European civilization. Slowly the divine right of the few to determine economic income and distribute the goods and services of the world has been questioned and curtailed. We called the process Revolution in the eighteenth century, advancing Democracy in the nineteenth, and Socialization of Wealth in the twentieth. But whatever we call it, the movement is the same: the dipping of more and grimier hands into the wealth-bag of the nation, until today only the ultrastubborn fail to see that democracy, in determining income, is the next inevitable step to Democracy in political power.

27. See George Padmore, "The Pan-African Movement," in *W. E. B. Du Bois Speaks: Speeches and Addresses 1920–1963*, ed. Foner (New York, 1970), pp. 161–78.

28. Carroll Smith-Rosenberg's essay "The Female World of Love and Ritual," first published in 1975, has not only provided crucial images of American gynocentric community for historically minded readers but has also provided the proof that women were in their ordinary relations affectively vital to other women, despite having found neither articulation nor legitimation in public discourse or social institutions. See Smith-Rosenberg, "The Female World of Love and Ritual: Relations Between Women in Nineteenth-Century America," *Disorderly Conduct: Visions of Gender in Victorian America* (New York, 1985), pp. 53–76.

29. Fredric Jameson, "Reification and Utopia in Mass Culture," *Social Text* 1 (Winter 1979): p. 144.

JACQUELINE BOBO

Sifting Through the Controversy: *Reading* The Color Purple

T*he Color Purple,* the novel and the film, have both been the subject of intense opposition since the arrival of Alice Walker's book in 1982 and the release of Steven Spielberg's film in December 1985. On the surface, the dissension has centered on the image of black people in media. Both works present a negative portrait, proclaim some critics, of black men in particular and the black family in general.

These kinds of protests are not new, for black people have fought against negative depictions in film in many instances; notable among them were protests against *The Birth of a Nation* (1915), *The Green Pastures* (1936), *Gone With the Wind* (1939), and *Porgy and Bess* (1959). The primary difference in the criticism of the contemporary film is that the outrage over the works is not unanimous. Black women and black men, for the most part, are split, and at times, at odds over the effect of the works on the condition of black people in this country.

The nature of the debate over *The Color Purple* and the way it affected how the public received the film and produced a reading of it are the subjects of this investigation. There is, of course, a significant difference between the novel and the film, one being the work of a black woman, the other a mainstream media product constructed by a white male. There is also a critical difference in the way a novel and film are experienced. The reading experience

Callaloo: A Journal of African American and African Arts and Letters, Volume 12, Issue 2, Number 39, (1989 Spring): pp. 332–342. © The Johns Hopkins University Press.

is more personal and private, whereas watching a film, until it is released on videotape, involves sitting in a theater with many other people and being affected by their reactions. Although these are important differences between the Alice Walker book and the Spielberg film, the two works have become almost interchangeable in many people's minds.

The novel won the American Book Award and the Pulitzer Prize for Fiction in 1983 and was on the *New York Times* hardcover best-seller list for a number of weeks, but its impact was not as widespread as the film's. Although there were criticisms of the novel when it was published and there have long been attacks against Alice Walker, the protests accelerated in the wake of the film's release. The film reached an audience in several stages and each time induced a strong reaction. It was released during the holiday season in 1985, withdrawn from circulation in the fall of 1986, re-released theatrically at the beginning of 1987, and released on videotape July 1987. By October 1986 the film version of *The Color Purple* had made almost $100 million, and the rental of the videotape has been in the top twenty since its arrival in the video stores.[1] It is therefore safe to assume that more people have seen the film than have read the book. It is also a sure bet that many people's perception of the novel is based upon what they have seen or heard about the film.

The film *The Color Purple* has been constructed as controversial by the media coverage of the protests against it, as have the novel, and, by extension, Alice Walker. In a sort of revolving door operation each subject involved in the controversy has taken on a controversial aspect: the novel, the author, the film, the director. At times even the defenders of the works have come under fire. Armond White of the New York *City-Sun;* Vernon Jarrett of the Chicago *Sun-Times;* and Kwasi Geiggar, head of a Los Angeles group, the Coalition Against Black Exploitation, appeared as part of a panel on *Tony Brown's Journal* to debate the effect of the film. When White declared that there was something worthwhile that could come from the film, Jarrett replied that if White liked the film then he may as well be white.[2] In another instance, a clip of Whoopi Goldberg was shown on *The Phil Donahue Show* while Tony Brown was a panelist. Goldberg said that those who criticize *The Color Purple* for showing negative images of black men should also criticize Prince for the disturbing images he showed of black women being dumped in garbage cans in *Purple Rain*. Brown replied in response to her statement that there were those who practiced the art of saying what white people wanted them to say.[3]

When *The Color Purple* is referred to as controversial the inference is that the content of the work is incendiary rather than that the reaction to it has been negative. *The Color Purple,* novel and film, became inflammatory subject matter because there were those who did not like them rather than because the content of the works was offensive to everyone in the audience.

The distinction is a subtle and fine one, yet is important. If a cultural product is presented as controversial, this view affects the way in which it is perceived and its worth evaluated, initially, by an audience. The predominant reading, or meaning construction, of *The Color Purple* is that the works negatively depict black people, especially black men. Although the works are open to a variety of readings, this particular reading became "relatively fixed" at the moment they were constructed as controversial. This interpretation is especially true for those who have not seen the film and/or have not read the book.

Film scholar Annette Kuhn has developed a method of analyzing how a predominant reading of a film affects its reception. She analyzed a 1923 British film entitled *Maisie's Marriage* and the way in which censorship of the film constructed it as controversial. Because the film was viewed as controversial, it was assumed that the content of the film caused the censorship as well as the controversy. The content of the film had little to do with its reception by the public. What did affect its reception was its association with the name Marie Stopes, her favorable views on sexuality and birth control, and the negative sentiment about those topics in Britain at that time. Kuhn writes that the name of Marie Stopes and her book, *Married Love*, were well-known in 1920s Britain even by those who had not read the book: "If many people did not know precisely what Marie Stopes's ideas were, they certainly knew what they were about: sex and birth control."[4]

Kuhn contends that the film *Maisie's Marriage* acquired certain meanings because of discourses originating outside of the film text itself. These were debates about sexuality, sexual pleasure, and contraception, elements which, she feels, suffused the text at an unconscious as well as a conscious level, even though the film was not about these topics. The point that Kuhn makes about how a particular reading of *Maisie's Marriage* was produced is relevant for this assessment of the film *The Color Purple* in that the 1920s film and the 1980s film were both caught up in "power relations" between several discourses, at a particular historical moment, "over the conditions under which the film was to enter the public domain." Kuhn submits that *Maisie's Marriage* "constituted a strategic intervention in a broader debate as much because of the discourses surrounding the film as the content of the film itself."[5]

The discourses surrounding *The Color Purple* are those of mainstream media and black men. The black woman's discourse, as spoken by the black woman, has been less publicized than have the other two until recently. Black women's responses, with the exception of Dorothy Gilliam in *The Washington Post*, have mainly been in Left and alternative publications, rather than in mainstream media. These are not avenues of information in which the majority of black people have ready access. Black women's reactions, for the most part, have also been in rebuttal to the criticisms and in defense of Alice Walker and the novel, rather than prompted by their response to the film.

The broader debate over *The Color Purple* is about the authority of black women writers to set the agenda for imagemaking in fiction and film. It is this aspect of the controversy that constitutes *The Color Purple's* "strategic intervention." Although mainstream critiques and black male criticism of the film and novel have muddied the waters, a review of the criticism makes this clear.

The first reviews (late 1985) in mainstream newspapers and magazines did not address the protests from black men about the film. Television critics such as Gene Shalit, Gene Siskel, and Roger Ebert applauded the existence of the film; but most print reviews criticized Spielberg for mishandling the novel.[6] The critiques ranged from mild plot summaries and background articles on the making of the film to wild, sarcastic diatribes lampooning Spielberg for venturing outside of his normal environment in an attempt to make an "important" film. Spielberg's previous record of producing inane blockbuster movies was held up to substantiate his inability to recreate the novel *The Color Purple* into a worthwhile film.

Several critics referred to the "cloying and saccharine" musical score by Quincy Jones and the "fantasyland" atmosphere that Spielberg created. Many also ridiculed the buffoonish actions of some of the characters: one critic even suggesting that the characters Harpo and Mr. _____ appeared as if they had wandered in from the television situation comedy "The Jeffersons."[7] Vincent Canby wrote in *The New York Times* that there were "titters" throughout the audience at the critics' preview screening that he attended.[8] Another reviewer summed up Spielberg's effort as being "the first Disney film about incest."[9]

As the protests against the film received more media play, the tone of the critiques changed. Later critiques became much more vitriolic and attacked not only the film but also Alice Walker. Pauline Kael of *The New Yorker* did not like the book or the film. She felt that Alice Walker got away with "rampant female chauvinism."[10] John Simon in the *National Review* wrote that the film was "an infantile abomination from a perpetually young filmmaker" and that the book was no literary masterpiece. Simon wrote that the novel had been hyped out of all proportion to its worth and that it was "unable to transcend the two humanly legitimate but artistically burdensome chips on its shoulder, feminism and Black militancy."[11] The author of the piece in *New York* magazine headlined his article "Purple People-Eater" and called the film "a hate letter to Black men," then labeled the novel a "quick, heart-pounding read" and "candy passing itself off as soul food."[12]

The power relations that were and still are in struggle over *The Color Purple* are the dominant forces in society and black people. The media coverage of the protests from black men obscured this in that the conflict was framed as an in-house fight between black women and black men. Although this was certainly one facet of it, the larger issue concerned black women viewers' favorable response to the film, and the implications of this for the future course of black people's political activism. The women were identifying with many of the characters and the events in the film, and were going out to read the novel and other books written by black women writers.

The works of black women writers are more readily available now, and there is also a body of scholarship about the writers that places the current writers within a tradition dating back to the nineteenth century. In works by these writers, recurrent themes surface: that the black woman, historically, and as a figure in mainstream creative works has been sorely abused. During enslavement black women were worked as hard as men, used as breeders, then constructed in mythology as wanton and sexually lascivious. After slavery black women were usefully constructed as mean and evil castrating wenches, emasculating their male partners and further impeding the progress of the race. Contemporary works by black women writers, of which *The Color Purple* is part, are a corrective to prior notions of black women. Black women viewers of the film, through a complex process of negotiation, have reconstructed something useful from the film. In doing so, they have connected up with a larger movement of black women as cultural workers. The predominant element of this movement is the creation and maintenance of images of black women that are based on black women's constructions, history, and real-life experiences.

The first reviews of the film, not yet considering black people's responses, were reminiscent of mainstream reviews of previous Hollywood films with all-black casts. The reviewers talked about the film as being "universal" and a "must see" film about family relationships, much in the way that *Roots* was promoted as "the triumph of an American family," rather than the history of a people who had survived enslavement. The tone is patronizing and condescending. As the subversive nature of the film surfaced, not so much because of the content of the film, but because of the value that a particular segment of the audience (black women) derived from it, the critiques changed. The attempt was to neutralize or blunt the force of meaning construction. In two earlier articles I examined black women's response to the film, and as part of a larger study, I conducted a group interview with selected black women viewers of the film. On the whole, I have found that black women have engaged positively with *The Color Purple* and have extracted something useful from the film.[13]

The black women whom I interviewed talked about the controversy over the film and the novel. One said that she deliberately checked out the book from the library because of the news about a woman who wanted to have the book banned from the Oakland public schools.[14] She said:

I like to think that I'm one of these activists and if it ever came up in my children's school that I would have a say in whether it stays or goes. That's exactly what I was tearing into that book for. But when I got into the book, I changed my attitude because I thought, this is really great, and a whole other side of it was exposed.

The woman said that after she read the book she went to see the film, and she loved it. Her response to the controversy at the Oakland schools became one of outrage:

I said to myself if I could find that woman who said she didn't want the book in the library, I would have said to her "Now wait a minute. That's not fair." That's not fair for the mother, just because she did not want her child to read the book . . . [If that's the way she felt] she should go through the library and take care of every one she labeled that she did not want her child to read, and take *all* of them out.

Another woman said: "Why don't they protest what's on television every week? Fred Sanford and all of them." She said that many people who did not like the film felt it was an airing of black people's dirty laundry. Another woman responded that there was nothing wrong with that: "We don't always have to pretend that everything is hunky-dory. It could be that if I tell somebody and they tell somebody else then maybe I can get some answers to some problems I have."

Another woman wondered "where was all this hue and cry when the Blaxploitation films came out?" She also questioned films such as *Sounder*, which did not generate any protests, and in which the black man is always depicted as a loser. She added:

Listening to us talk here I'm beginning to see that it's [the protest over *The Color Purple*] a sexist thing, and that upsets me because black people in general are oppressed. We're in this together. We worked in the same fields together, we walked in the same chain coffle together. It's just sad because we all know that we wouldn't be here without the black woman having strength.

Other women in the group discussed the charge that neither the book nor the film was realistic. One said that someone who had seen the film declared that no man would allow a woman to take a razor to his neck after he had treated her so badly. Another replied: "They will beat you up, black both your eyes, and then go get right in the bed and go to sleep." This remark prompted another woman to add: "And then will have the nerve to want you to cook them something to eat." One woman tried to explore the reasons why some black men abused black women.

> My mother asked my Dad how come he would jump on her. Sometime when she hadn't done anything he would just jump on her, for GP. She asked him some years after they split up, and he told her he didn't know any better. That when he sat around with the guys . . . the guys would talk about how you had to keep a woman in line, you had to whip her ass every so often. And so he told Momma that's what he thought he was supposed to do to make sure he could be the man of the house.

In reaction to black women's favorable responses to the film, black male criticism of the film began to attain much more media space. In major newspapers, television programs, and radio talk shows for the past several years, any information about the film involved the protest from black males. In January 1986 *The New York Times* reported that the film was the dominant topic of conversation on radio and talk shows, in newspaper columns, at community forums and churches around the country. According to the article, the furor was about the film's depiction of black men and the division it had caused between black women and black men.[15]

One of the more vicious condemnations of the film and of Alice Walker was written by a black male columnist for *The Washington Post*, Courtland Milloy. Milloy wrote that some black women would enjoy seeing a movie about black men shown as "brutal bastards." Furthermore, Milloy contended, the book was demeaning. He stated: "I got tired, a long time ago, of white men publishing books by Black women about how screwed up Black men are." Milloy admitted in the article that he had not seen the film: "As far as I'm concerned I don't have to see this movie to write about it."[16]

Tony Brown, host of the weekly television program *Tony Brown's Journal* and a nationally syndicated columnist, wrote of the film that it was "the most racist depiction of Black men since *The Birth of a Nation* and the most anti-Black family film of the modern film era." Brown repeated these comments in several articles and on *The Phil Donahue Show* in April 1986. He said of Alice Walker's collaboration on the film: "She has done it at the expense of Black people and of Black men." Brown was challenged by a black woman in the Donahue audience, who stated that he had not seen the film. She questioned him about his responsibility as a journalist for making such incendiary comments about something of which he had no knowledge. Brown's reply to her was that he was black before he was a journalist, and that his responsibility was to black people.[17]

The Spring of 1986 produced a plethora of articles by black males critical of *The Color Purple*. William Willimon in *Christian Century* declared that he was "seeing red" over *The Color Purple* and the stereotypes of black males in the novel could "only have been created by a writer more interested in writing a polemic than a novel."[18] Gerald Early in *The Antioch Review* wrote that "*The Color Purple*, by Black feminist writer Alice Walker, is not a good novel"; therefore, Early concluded, it should have made an excellent Hollywood film. He felt it didn't. But Early's argument becomes suspect when he not only dispenses with Alice Walker's novel but dismisses the celebration of Black History Month as nothing more than an empty spectacle of a series of faces and dates commemorated in a "vacuum seal of pious duty."[19] Black independent filmmaker Spike Lee declared in *Film Comment* that the reason that Hollywood selected Alice Walker's novel to make into a film was that the black men are depicted as "one-dimensional animals." He stated further that Alice Walker had problems with black men and that "the quickest way for a Black playwright, novelist, or poet to get published has been to say that Black men are shit. If you say that, then you are definitely going to get media, your book published, your play done—Ntozake Shange, Alice Walker."[20]

Mel Watkins, in an article headlined "Sexism, Racism, and Black Women Writers" in the *New York Times Book Review* succinctly outlined the problem that black men had with the novel and the film. Watkins criticized Alice Walker and other black women writers who have written what he characterizes as negative stories about black men for trespassing outside the established rules of image-making in fiction. Watkins writes:

> Those Black women writers who have chosen Black men as a target have set themselves outside a tradition that is nearly as old as Black American literature itself. They have, in effect, put themselves at odds with what seems to be an unspoken but almost universally accepted covenant among Black writers.[21]

Watkins explains the covenant as one in which black writers did not expose "aspects of inner-community life that might reinforce damaging racial stereotypes already proffered by racist antagonists."

Mary Helen Washington has categorized the proliferation of artistic work by black women as "the renaissance of Black women writers" of the 1970s and 1980s. Within this new era the major thrust of the writers is the personal lives and collective histories of black women. The writers are reconstructing a heritage that has either been distorted or ignored. Washington writes that black women's experiences are very different from those that men have written about. Her statement about the content of black women's writing is a contradiction of Watkins's avuncular pronouncements. Referring to *Invisible Man* and *Native Son*, Washington writes: "There are no women in this tradition hibernating in dark holes contemplating their invisibility; there are no women dismembering the bodies or crushing the skulls of either women or men."[22]

Richard Wesley, screenwriter for the film based upon Richard Wright's novel *Native Son*, characterized the public assaults against *The Color Purple* as "image tribunals." Wesley wrote that these tribunals were mostly conducted by black males, usually in their thirties or older, who based their attacks on political concepts developed during the 1960s, an ideology that he contends has remained sacrosanct. The ideology proscribes that black men and women must maintain unity; but Wesley submits that that unity, as enacted by these men, only remains intact if the black man leads. According to proscription, the woman must be silent and let the man speak for the race. Wesley writes: "Few Black men in their right minds will come out and couch their objections to Walker's novel in those terms, but you can hear echoes of those sentiments in much of their criticism of her."[23]

The first objective of the criticisms against *The Color Purple* is to protect the turf of those who have set themselves up as "guardians of the Black image," as Wesley labels it. At a deeper level and much more significantly, the criticism is masking a movement by black women artists to probe into some significant issues in black people's lives and to chart a more tenable course for political action.

Many articles about black men's protest against *The Color Purple* link it to the outrage that was generated in 1976 with the Broadway production of Ntozake Shange's choreopoem *for colored girls who have considered suicide/when the rainbow is enuf* and Michele Wallace's *Black Macho and the Myth of the Superwoman* (1979). I think that the battlelines were drawn much earlier with the dismissal of Lorraine Hansberry in the 1960s. Others trace this trend as extending even farther back, to the 1920s and the 1930s, with Nella Larsen abandoning her writing career after she had been severely criticized by the writers of the 1920s Harlem Renaissance, and Richard Wright categorizing Zora Neale Hurston's novel *Their Eyes Were Watching God* (1937) as "counterrevolutionary and a continuation of the minstrel image."[24]

In 1984, during the twenty-fifth anniversary commemoration of *A Raisin in the Sun* (1959), several black writers lamented not only the death of Lorraine Hansberry in 1965, but the fact that her reputation as a worthwhile black artist had suffered because the architects of the "Black Aesthetic" found her writing deficient.[25] Aishah Rahman, in "To Be Black, Female and a Playwright," wrote that she was a witness to the negation of Lorraine Hansberry during the sixties black nationalist reign. The reasons given for dishonoring Hansberry, Rahman reveals, were that

1) the critics hailed *Raisin* as being not just a "Negro play" but one with "universal" dimensions—which was interpreted to mean that it made white folks feel comfortable at Black expense; 2) it was a "bourgeois" drama because the characters had "bourgeois" aspirations—that is they wanted some dignity, some money and a decent place to live; 3) it was a commercial success, which somehow made it less than a righteous work; and 4) it was "no-surprise-that-a-woman-would-be-the-first-Black-on-Broadway-because-they-could-get-through-the-barriers-more-easily-than-Black-men." I suppose the fact that Langston Hughes had a play produced on Broadway in 1935 called *Mulatto* either wasn't well known to my colleagues or did not serve their purposes.[26]

Rahman could have added that *A Raisin in the Sun* was the fifth play written by a black person and yet the only one written by a black woman to appear on the Broadway stage in the 1950s. In fact, Lorraine Hansberry's play was the only play written by a black woman to appear on Broadway up to that time.

Rahman calls the Black Arts Movement writers to task for criticizing the strong black mother, Lena Younger, that Hansberry created, while the major recurrent theme of the Black Arts writers was how the black woman was the major cause of their enslavement. The women these writers created were, writes Rahman, "perverted characters of someone's nightmare." As a writer, she said, "I was determined to pick up the standard of Lorraine Hansberry's legacy . . . by portraying Black women in real terms." The risk involved, she continues, is that she would be accused of "sabotaging the Black male image (as if to make women whole were, necessarily, to make men crippled)."

Salim Muwakkil connects the criticism of *The Color Purple* with a continuing attempt by black men to upgrade the black male image and the status of black males in society at the expense of black women. She cites, among other events, the move by Operation PUSH in Chicago to get the CBS affiliate station to hire two male minority anchors. The reason given by the PUSH leadership for demanding black male anchors was that "The Black male has always been castrated by white America and Black women have always been used to keep Black men in their place." Muwakkil sees these incidents, along with the complaints against the film and novel, as a struggle against black feminism. She feels that black people are at a "turbulent historical juncture" and the black women writers are starting to question "patriarchal assumptions that underlie this society." Black men are resisting this: "Black men, although they haven't shared much else in this society, have at least shared some perquisites of patriarchal culture and thus those privileges have assumed an exaggerated importance." Muwakkil sees the current dispute as an attempt by "ideological critics" to impose their judgments on the creative process. She feels this is a mistake: "The Black cultural nationalists of the '60s and '70s demonstrated anew the deadening effect such ideological requirements have on creative expression. Their various proscriptions and prescriptions aborted a historical moment pregnant with promise."[27]

All art, wrote Lorraine Hansberry, is social: "that which agitates and that which prepares the mind for slumber. The writer is deceived who thinks that he has some other choice. The question is not whether one will make a social statement in one's work—but *what* the statement will say."[28]

In what would later become known as an historic confrontation, Lorraine Hansberry was present at a meeting called by then Attorney General Robert Kennedy on May 24, 1963, to discuss the civil rights struggles in the South. In attendance at the Kennedy apartment overlooking Central Park South were James Baldwin, Lena Horne, Harry Belafonte, Dr. Kenneth Clark, among others, and Jerome Smith, a CORE Freedom Fighter recently returned from the South where he had been brutally beaten and jailed. The meeting became more and more heated, and Kennedy expressed impatience with a statement by Smith that he would not fight against Cuba. Lorraine Hansberry answered Kennedy's impatience, saying "You've got a great many very accomplished people in this room, Mr. Attorney General. But the only one who should be listened to is that man over there" (Jerome Smith). Hansberry later exploded when someone brought up the recent civil rights battles in the South and the impact this would have on Southern black men. She said that the country ought to also be concerned with the "specimens of white manhood" recently immortalized in photos with their knees on the breasts of black women who had been dragged to the ground.[29]

Alice Walker also writes about the black women who were civil rights activists in the South. In the poem "Revolutionary Petunias" she creates a black woman named Sammy Lou, who, though considered "incorrect" by the "venerated saints of the revolution," wins the final struggle with her oppressor. Sammy Lou performs the "incorrect" actions of going to church, praying, and naming her children after presidents and their wives, yet she is able to kill the white man who has murdered her husband. Walker writes of her that any black revolution, rather than calling her "incorrect," "will have to honor her single act of rebellion."[30]

Walker writes of the "contrary instincts" exhibited by black women throughout history. The artists, beginning with Phillis Wheatley in 1773, were torn by conflicting urges to create in a world in which they were not valued. Wheatley was unheralded in her time and later ridiculed as a fool. Other black women writers suffered that same fate of dismissal or rejection for the persistent "contrariness of will" that was the essence of their writing. Barbara Christian writes that this trait of contrariness and of counterpoint is the core of the present-day literature of black women. Christian sees it as a "philosophical orientation" of rebellion and radical revisioning that challenges traditional definitions and acts for the common good.[31]

Black women viewers of *The Color Purple* demonstrated this contrary instinct in giving a different reading to the film. Although a predominant negative reading of the film was given dominant exposure, black women were able to extract meanings of their own. The disputes over *The Color Purple* actually stimulated meaning production that connected with a larger movement of black women that is empowering black women and forming a potent force for change.

NOTES

1. Nina Darnton, *"Color Purple* to Re-Open Nationwide," *The New York Times* 9 January 1987: C6.

2. *Tony Brown's Journal* PBS, 6 April 1986.

3. *The Phil Donahue Show* 25 April 1986.

4. Annette Kuhn," 'The Married Love' Affair," *Screen* 27.2 (March–April 1986): p. 18.

5. Annette Kuhn, p. 5.

6. David Nicholson, "From Coast to Coast *Purple* Aroused Passions," *Black Film Review* 2.2 (Spring 1986): p. 18; Ishmael Reed, "Steven Spielberg Plays Howard Beach," *Black American Literature Forum* 21:1–2 (Spring–Summer 1987): p. 8. According to Reed, Siskel and Ebert addressed the controversy in the following week's show.

7. Kenneth Turan, "Movies," *California Magazine* 11 February 1986: p. 42.

8. Vincent Canby, "From a Palette of Cliches Comes 'The Color Purple,'" *The New York Times* 5 January 1986: p. 17.

9. David Ansen, "We Shall Overcome," *Newsweek* 30 December 1985: p. 59.

10. Pauline Kael, "Current Cinema: Sacred Monsters," *The New Yorker* 30 December 1985: p. 69.

11. John Simon, "Black and White in Purple," *National Review* 14 February 1986: p. 56.

12. David Denby, "Purple People-Eater," *New York* 13 January 1986: p. 56.

13. Jacqueline Bobo, *"The Color Purple:* Black Women as Cultural Readers," *Female Spectators: Looking at Film and Television,* ed. Deidre Pribram (London and New York: Verso, 1988): pp. 90–109; and *"The Color Purple:* Black Women's Responses," *Jump Cut* 33 (February 1988): pp. 43–51.

This article is based on my recently completed dissertation "Articulation and Hegemony: Black Women's Response to the Film *The Color Purple."* As part of the study I conducted an ethnography of reading with selected black women viewers of the film in December 1987 in California and October 1988 in Oregon. All references to women interviewed come from the 1987 study. For a discussion of the issues of readers' response to texts in media audience analysis see *Remote Control: Television, Audiences, and Cultural Power,* eds. Ellen Seiter, et al. (New York: Routledge, Chapman and Hall, Inc., in press). See also *Writing Culture: The Poetics and Politics of Ethnography,* James Clifford and George E. Marcus, eds. (Berkeley: University of California Press, 1986), and *Natural Audiences: Qualitative Research and Media Uses and Effects,* Thomas R. Lindlof (New Jersey: Ablex, 1987).

14. Alice Walker writes about this in "Finding Celie's Voice," *Ms.* December 1985: 71–72, p. 96. A mother of a student in an Oakland, California, public school objected to the novel *The Color Purple* and asked for the book to be removed from the school's library.

15. E. R. Shipp, "Blacks in Heated Debate Over 'The Color Purple,'" *The New York Times* 27 January 1986: A13.

16. Courtland Milloy, "A 'Purple' Rage Over a Rip-Off," *The Washington Post* 24 December 1985: B3.

17. *The Phil Donahue Show* 25 April 1986. Tony Brown was a part of a panel along with Michele Wallace, Donald Bogle, and Willis Edwards.

18. William H. Willimon, "Seeing Red Over *The Color Purple*," *Christian Century* 2 April 1986: p. 319.

19. Gerald Early, *"The Color Purple* As Everybody's Protest Art," *The Antioch Review* 44.3 (Summer 1986): p. 261.

20. Marlaine Glicksman, "Lee Way," *Film Comment* October 1986: p. 48.

21. Mel Watkins, "Sexism, Racism and Black Women Writers," *The New York Times Book Review* 15 June 1986: 36.

22. Mary Helen Washington, *Invented Lives: Narratives of Black Women 1860–1960* (New York: Anchor Press/Doubleday & Company, Inc., 1987): p. xxi.

23. Richard Wesley, "'The Color Purple Debate': Reading Between the Lines," *Ms.* September 1986: p. 90.

24. Barbara Christian, *Black Women Novelists: The Development of a Tradition, 1892–1976* (Westport, Connecticut: Greenwood Press, 1980): pp. 61–62.

25. Kalamu ya Salaam, "What Use is Reading?: Re-Reading Lorraine Hansberry," *The Black Collegian* March/April 1984: pp. 45–48; and, Aishah Rahman, "First Light of a New Day," *In These Times* 28 March–3 April 1984: pp. 8–9.

26. Aishah Rahman, "To Be Black, Female and a Playwright," *Freedomways* 19.4 (Fourth Quarter 1979): p. 257.

27. Salim Muwakkil, "Bad Image Blues," *In These Times* 9–15 April 1986: p. 23.

28. Lorraine Hansberry, "The Negro Writer and His Roots: Toward a New Romanticism," *The Black Scholar* March–April 1981: p. 5. This article is the first publication of a speech that Hansberry delivered March 1, 1959, before a conference of black writers.

29. Numerous sources detail the meeting with Robert Kennedy, including James A. Wechsler, "RFK & Baldwin," *The New York Post* 28 May 1963: p. 30, although Wechsler errs when he says that Baldwin directed Kennedy to listen to Smith. Arthur M. Schlesinger, Jr. and others who were there, Kenneth Clark and Hansberry herself, attribute the comment to Hansberry. See Schlesinger's *Robert Kennedy and His Times* (Boston: Houghton Mifflin, 1978): p. 345. For a further examination of the political and historical significance of Hansberry see Jacqueline Bobo, *Debunking the Myth of the Exotic Primitive: Three Plays by Lorraine Hansberry*, Master's Thesis, San Francisco State University, 1980.

30. Alice Walker, "From an Interview," *In Search of Our Mothers' Gardens* (New York: Harcourt, Brace, Jovanovich, 1983): p. 266.

31. Barbara Christian, "From the Inside Out: Afro-American Women's Literary Tradition and the State," *Center for Humanistic Studies Occasional Papers* #19 (University of Minnesota: 1987): p. 6.

PRISCILLA L. WALTON

"What She Got to Sing About?":
Comedy and The Color Purple

[Laughter] is a froth with a saline base. Like froth it sparkles. It is gaiety
itself. But the philosopher who gathers a handful to taste may find that the
substance is scanty and the aftertaste bitter.

(Bergson 190)

This observation, written in 1900 by Henri Bergson, in the conclusion
to his essay "Laughter," ironically anticipates the changes that occur in the
comic mode of the succeeding century when laughter's "froth" virtually
disappears and its "bitter aftertaste" comes to predominate. After 1900, literature—comedy in particular—becomes more acrimonious and discordant,
perhaps better to represent life in our century of "disorder and irrationalism"
(Sypher 201). The comic novel ceases to ring with the "silvery laughter" that
George Meredith applauds; rather it reverberates to the maniacal, paranoid
laughter in which Thomas Pynchon revels. In short, comedy enters the
realm of the absurd and begins to reflect the individual's disorientation in a
"senseless, chaotic" world.

Yet even within this context, it might seem anomalous to call Alice
Walker's 1982 work, *The Color Purple*, a comedy. The novel is arguably bleaker
than many of the others that are included in the mode, since it deals with
rape, incest, and social prejudice; yet the ideal "womanist" world in which it
culminates (Walker, Search xi) is joyous and celebratory—a condition of the

ARIEL: A Review of International English Literature, 21:2 (April 1990): pp. 59–74.

comic. Although its subject matter appears at times to counteract the levity expected of a comic novel and so to be at variance with the comic purpose, if we set aside our more traditional expectations of the mode and look rather at the intent of the comic, we see that *The Color Purple* rather closely adheres to its theoretical tenets.

While it is not my intention here to offer an absolute definition of comedy, some idea of what the comic signifies is necessary to come to an understanding of its relevance to *The Color Purple*. My discussion is selective: the characteristics I discuss relate more specifically to what theorists of the comic call "high comedy," or the "comedy of ideas," since Walker's novel is obviously not of the kind of comedy which elicits hearty guffaws from its readers. But this does not disqualify it from the mode, for theorists of the comic often note that laughter is a very deceptive criterion by which to assess it (Martin 74, Sypher 203). More often than not, high comedy concerns itself less with being 'funny' than with dramatizing possibilities and exploring potentials. If it does provoke laughter, it is because it mocks certain social conventions. Yet, it mocks because it devotes itself to social improvement and often provides a critique of societal limitations. James K. Feibleman suggests that comedy pursues the ideal:

> A constant reminder of the existence of the logical order as the perfect goal of actuality, comedy continually insists upon the limitations of all experience and of all actuality. The business of comedy is to dramatize and thus make more vivid and immediate the fact that contradictions in actuality must prove insupportable. It thus admonishes against the easy acceptance of interim limitations and calls for the persistent advance toward the logical order and the final elimination of limitations. (82)

Comedy seeks improvement in a "negative way," for it asserts that if it is only the limitations of actuality which prevent it from achieving perfection, then the limitations should be eliminated (96). Therefore, in a period of social change (like the twentieth century), comedy often assumes an increasing importance because it is more subversive in nature than tragedy (96) and seeks to improve society: "Better to stress the fact that however much value any actual situation may have, it is prevented from having more only by its limitations. Why, then, be satisfied?" (96). Because comedy continually exposes the limitations of the actual to highlight the ideal, many comic theorists emphasize its potentially "dangerous" and even "revolutionary" nature. Indeed, Wylie Sypher goes so far as to suggest that the comedian

> refuses to make . . . concessions to actuality and serves, instead, as chief tactician in a permanent resistance movement, or rebellion,

within the frontiers of human experience. By temperament, the comedian is often a fifth columnist in social life. (247)

All these criteria are relevant to *The Color Purple*, but of more specific interest at this point is the means by which comedy frequently displays its "revolutionary" tendency. If comedy is a subversive mode, it often succeeds in demonstrating the limitations of the social order through the incorporation of an excluded or marginalized individual. Northrop Frye perceives this as comedy's adaptation of the "*pharmakos*" or the victimized character who is "opposed to or excluded from the fictional society" and has "the sympathy of the audience" (*Anatomy* 48). The "*pharmakos*" generally appears in comedy in one of two ways and can be regarded as a "fool or worse by the fictional society, and yet impresses the real audience as having something more valuable than his [or her] society has" (48); or the "*pharmakos*" may choose to repudiate the society, and in doing so become "a kind of *pharmakos* in reverse" (48). The idea of the "*pharmakos*" also foregrounds what has been called comedy's "paradoxical nature," since in it frequently that which is "seemingly absurd [is] actually well-founded" (Martin 86) and therefore, in "the best sort of comedy," the "incongruous is finally seen to be congruent to a larger pattern than that which was originally perceived" (87).

While comedy seeks to improve society, often, particularly in its twentieth-century manifestations, it veers so close to tragedy that it is difficult to separate the comic from the tragic mode. But Frye suggests that this is because "tragedy is really implicit or uncompleted comedy [and] comedy contains a potential tragedy within itself" ("Argument" 455). If comedy completes itself, this completion is manifested in the new (or renewed) society which is evident in its conclusion. High comedy is not content to expose the limitations in a closed social order; once they have been exposed, it often offers what it perceives as the ideal, for in its aim for general improvement, it needs to provide an open society as an alternative to the closed or limited one it has dramatized. Comedy's theme, therefore, is often "the integration of society (*Anatomy* 43) and this social integration "may emphasize the birth of an ideal society" ("Argument" 454). As a result, "that which gets born at the end of comedy" may "not impress us as true, but as desirable," since unlikely "conversions, miraculous transformations, and providential assistance are inseparable from comedy" (*Anatomy* 170).

High comedy forces its dramatized order to "open in many directions" (Sypher 249). It becomes "an achievement of man as a social being" (Sypher 252) because it compels us to recognize our potential by mocking what is less than ideal in our practice. Hence, while it exposes the limitations of our society, it either eliminates these limitations and so renews its fictional order or it posits a new, ideal order in its conclusions. Like tragedy, therefore, comedy too offers a "road to wisdom" (Sypher 254), and the comic protagonist often learns through suffering (Sypher 254); but the comic differs from the tragic in that it never "despairs of man" (Sypher 254).

And Alice Walker's novel, *The Color Purple*, does not despair of "man" either, for it incorporates these elements of comedy: it makes the incongruous congruent to a larger pattern; it refuses to accept the limitations imposed on its fictional society; and it posits a new order which is presented in the novel as ideal. Even its tragic elements are not anomalous, since they are in accord with Frye's observation of "how frequently a comic dramatist tries to bring his action as close to a catastrophic overthrow of the hero as he can get it, and then remove the action as quickly as possible" (*Anatomy* 178).

However, if we are to apply these prescriptions to *The Color Purple*, we must first perceive it as a "high comedy," since it is only this mode which theoretically subscribes to the criteria discussed earlier. But "high comedy" invariably includes, and, in fact, culminates in the comedy of manners, and to characterize *The Color Purple* as such appears to be problematic, especially in light of M. H. Abrams's explanation that this mode

> deals with the relations and intrigues of men and women living in a polished and sophisticated society, relying for comic effect in great part on the wit and sparkle of the dialogue—often in the form of repartee, a witty conversational give-and-take which constitutes a kind of verbal fencing match—and to a lesser degree, on the ridiculous violations of social conventions and decorum by stupid characters such as would-be wits, jealous husbands, and foppish dandies. (26)

The male and female characters of *The Color Purple* do not live in a polished and sophisticated society, nor do they engage in what is traditionally considered sparkling and witty *repartee*. And the violations of social norms and decorum that occur are not perpetrated by foolish, stupid, or dandified characters but by female characters with whom we are expected to sympathize. However, the conventions of the comedy of manners are so clearly inverted in *The Color Purple* that we cannot but suspect it to be deliberate. Therefore, I would suggest that *The Color Purple* is a parodic inversion of the comedy of manners,[1] and so undercuts the form at the same time that it ironically adheres to its intentions—to improve and to open the closed social order it dramatizes.

Linda Hutcheon defines parody as "imitation with critical difference" (36). She also notes that parody too is potentially "revolutionary":

> The presupposition of both a law and its transgression bifurcates the impulses of parody: it can be normative and conservative, or

it can be provocative and revolutionary. . . . [P]arody can, like the
carnival, also challenge norms in order to renovate, to renew. (76)

In its parodic inversion of the comedy of manners, Walker's novel recalls
the works of Jane Austen, who, as Sypher observes, "devastates our compromises and complacencies—especially male complacency" and "placidly
undermines the bastions of middle-class propriety" (247). Austen too, of
course, frequently parodies various literary modes, particularly "the popular
romance fiction of her day" (Hutcheon 44), and through it "satirizes the traditional view of woman's role as the lover of men" (Hutcheon 44). But while
she may call into question the social mores of her time, Austen presents, in
the conclusions of her novels, a society in which women are integrated into
the traditional order. Walker, on the other hand, recalls Austen's work with
a "critical difference," since in her novel no compromises are brooked. She
goes further than her predecessor and rejects the society which imposes the
limitations and at the same time points out the exclusivity of literature, since
traditionally few novels that have achieved significant "recognition" have
dealt with anything other than a white social order or anything other than
a patriarchal society. (To this end she also reworks to some extent Samuel
Richardson's *Pamela* and the traditional endings of sexist fairy tales, specifically "The Frog Prince.")

By transposing the comedy of manners, Walker foregrounds the limitations she finds in it and so undercuts those social norms which it has incorporated and to which it ultimately contributes. Indeed, J. A. Cuddon suggests
that the comedy of manners has "for its main subjects and themes the behaviour and deportment of men and women living under specific social codes"
(139). This definition takes on new significance in relation to a novel like *The
Color Purple* because it subverts the form by parodically inverting its conventional notions of expected social codes.

Walker writes from the point of view of an outsider who is rebuffed by
a closed social order; yet in her novel she transcends these social restrictions
and envisions a world in which they cease to exist. *The Color Purple* is an intellectual comedy in that it is a comedy of ideas: it dramatizes possibilities and
completes itself in a vision of an ideal world[2]—a world which is matriarchal,
a parody of the boy-gets-girl endings of most comedies and fairy tales. This
world is also an ideal one which is in direct opposition to the rigidly closed
society that is in evidence in the opening pages of *The Color Purple*. However,
the tragic elements so apparent here are necessary to Walker's idea, since she
must work through the limitations of the closed order to give credence to the
utopian possibilities of her open, womanist world.

Walker dramatizes the crippling strictures of this old order through her
heroine, who is a social pariah. Celie is not just a woman, she is a black wom-

an; but she is not just a black woman, she is—as she later learns—a lesbian, and is, therefore, thrice removed from the white male heterosexual norm. By writing from the point of view of this seemingly socially aberrant individual, Walker exposes the limitations that society imposes on anything outside the norm and the narrow, restrictive lifestyle that it upholds. The society in evidence at the beginning of the novel is a totally closed society, which would not open to include Celie even if she wished it, since she cannot change the colour of her skin or her sex. Yet this social outcast is shown to be far wiser than the white patriarchy which excludes her. She is able to manifest at the conclusion of the work a society that "opens in many directions" (Sypher 249). And in doing so, she points up the limitations of life lived under the patriarchal norm by transcending them.

But before the ideal situation is reached, virtually every bastion of society is assaulted and little is left unscathed. Walker exposes the limitations in most social values and institutions and attacks the autonomy of the white male heterosexual norm which has generated them. It is difficult to pinpoint the prescriptions of this norm, primarily because they operate as the basis of our society and so seem self-evident to us. As Feibleman writes:

> It is a notorious historical observation that customs and institutions rarely enjoy more than a comparatively brief life; and yet while they are the accepted fashion they come to be regarded as brute givens, as irreducible facts, which may be depended upon with perfect security. (81)

However, by extrapolating from the text, we can reconstruct those social mores that Walker questions.

The prescriptions are formulated in the nuclear family, which perpetuates the notion of male and female roles. The male role dictates that man perform "manly" work, such as field work and carpentry (*Purple* 22, 27), and that he act as the head of his household and the maker of its laws (36, 37). The female role demands that woman be domestic; she must clean her house, cook, tend to the children (20), and obey her husband (37). It is not thought proper for men and women to trade these positions, and, if they do, they are subject to criticism and mockery (36). Marriage, which begins on this restrictive basis, merely perpetuates the stereotyped roles that its members are expected to play and again does not allow for deviation from them. Both the family and marriage are shown to operate on the assumption of feminine inferiority. Religion, in support of this order, preaches platitudes and casts narrow moral judgements upon those who are different or who refuse to conform to the conventions of family life (46). The laws effected by the patriarchy in the name of "equality" and "justice for all" merely function as a support to the existing order by keeping those outside that order "in their place" through the use of force (90, 91). While the theory behind the institution of the patriarchal order may have been altruistic and idealistic, Walker's novel shows how far from the ideal it has strayed in its practice. She therefore dramatizes these social values and institutions as they function in actuality and then redramatizes them in terms of the possible and the desirable.

The novel begins by portraying the family as a social unit which subjects girl children to a life of rape and terror: "First he put his thing up against my hip and sort of wiggle it around. Then he grab hold my titties. Then he push his thing inside my pussy. When that hurt, I cry. He start to choke me, saying You better shut up and git used to it" (1–2). The first three letters suggest that Celie's "father" kills her mother through abuse, at which point he ominously begins to eye her favourite sister, Nettie. Clearly, "a girl child ain't safe in a family of men" (42) and no woman in the household is inviolable. Nor is marriage a safe haven for Celie; it merely becomes an extension of her unhappy home life. Ironically, she is offered to Mr. _____ like a slave on an auction block, and Mr. _____ is more interested in her dowry than in her : "Mr. _____ say, That cow still coming? He say, Her cow" (12). In turn, Celie's wedding day is equally desolate, "I spend my wedding day running from the oldest boy. He twelve" (13). Marital sex is brutal and animalistic, and Celie later equates it with defecation, since it is hardly an act based on mutual fulfilment: "He git up on you, heist your nightgown round your waist, plunge in. Most times I pretend I ain't there. He never know the difference. Never ast me how I feel, nothing. Just do his business, get off, go to sleep" (81).

Celie's life is more a death-in-life, a life without hope, joy, or any indication of improvement. Nettie comments on this before she leaves: "I sure hate to leave you here with these rotten children, she say. Not to mention with Mr. _____. It's like seeing you buried, she say. It's worse than that, I think. If I was buried, I wouldn't to work" (18). But Celie does not despair, and her faith sustains her: "I just say, Never mine, never mine, long as I can spell G-o-d I got somebody along" (18).

While Celie may find a vent for her anguish in writing to God, religion itself is undercut when Shug Avery comes to town. Shug, who refuses to accept the limitations that society imposes on a woman's life, becomes the target for attack:

> Even the preacher got his mouth on Shug Avery, now she down. He take her condition for his text. . . . He talk about a strumpet in short skirts, smoking cigarettes, drinking gin, Singing for money and taking other women mens. Talk bout slut, hussy, heifer and streetcleaner. (46)

Not surprisingly, however, Celie does not hold with the virtues preached from the pulpit and repudiates conventional social behaviour as prescribed by Mr. _____'s father. Independently, she rejects the "virtues" which society applauds, and takes the ill Shug in to nurse. Astutely noticing his refusal to acknowledge her as a person, Celie discounts Mr. _____'s father's words: "Celie, he say, you have my sympathy. Not many women let they husband whore lay up in they house. But he not saying to me, he saying it to Mr. _____" (57). Celie chooses instead to champion Shug and responds: "Next time he come I put a little Shug Avery pee in his glass. See how he like that" (57).

Celie identifies with the rebellious Shug from the seventh page of the novel, when she finds her picture and begins to idolize the blues singer. Shug provides an ideal for Celie, since, unlike the other women in Celie's life, she is not broken through years of abuse. Pretty and different, she offers an alternative lifestyle:

> Shug Avery was a woman. The most beautiful woman I ever saw. . . . I see her there in furs. Her face rouge. Her hair like some thin tail. She grinning with her foot up on somebody motocar. Her eyes serious tho. Sad some. . . . An now when I dream, I dream of Shug Avery. She be dress to kill, whirling and laughing. (7)

Celie is also attracted to her stepdaughter-in-law, Sofia, an Amazon who refuses to be dominated by her husband, Harpo. But an independent woman has a more difficult time than one who meekly accepts her meagre lot in life. Ironically, Harpo wants Sofia to act like the submissive Celie : "I want her to do what I say, like you do for Pa. . . . But not Sofia. She do what she want, don't pay me no mind at all. I try to beat her, she black my eyes. Oh, boo-hoo, he cry" (66). Even though he loves Sofia, Harpo's marriage is troubled because society has taught him that this is not the way a woman should behave. Celie tries to reason with him, but to no avail; social conventions are too deeply ingrained in his mind:

> Sofia love you. You love Sofia . . . Mr. _____ marry me to take care of his children. I marry him cause my daddy made me. I don't love Mr. _____ and he don't love me. But you his wife, he say, just like Sofia mine. The wife spose to mind. (66)

Sofia becomes a victim of social injustice when she refuses to respect authority in the person of the white mayor's wife, who wants Sofia to work as her maid. When Sofia responds with a "hell no" (90), a brawl ensues and the police are called. The dangers of fighting back are clear since Sofia's punishment is hardly "just" or merited by her crime:

When I see Sofia I don't know why she still alive. They crack her skull, they crack her ribs. They tear her nose loose on one side. They blind her in one eye. She swole from head to foot. Her tongue the size of my arm, it stick out tween her teef like a piece of rubber. She can't talk. And she just about the color of eggplant. (92)

Society's justice is again satirized when the astute women realize that the only way to get Sofia released from the prison that is killing her is to plead that "justice ought to be done" (99) and to assert that Sofia will only be sufficiently punished when she becomes "some white lady maid" (99). After raping Squeak, the sheriff promptly takes action to ensure that Sofia will be "properly punished," and she is released into the mayor's custody, We realize how correct the women's assessment of society's "compassion" is when the mayor's (white) wife wishes to be "kind" to her maid and drives her to visit the family she has not seen in five years, only to make her leave in fifteen minutes (110–111). She later berates Sofia for her ingratitude.

The novel is often criticized for its melodramatic disposition, but I would suggest that this is a result of Walker's parodic inversion of Samuel Richardson's *Pamela*. Certainly the epistolary style of *The Color Purple* reminds us of Richardson's work, which, itself, is often melodramatic.[3] *The Color Purple* deliberately recalls *Pamela*, but ironically transposes it, for Pamela becomes reconciled to the world of men, and if she is accorded any stature within it, that stature is bestowed when Mr. B. learns to appreciate her, makes her his wife, and thus allows her entry into his world. Like Pamela, Celie too suffers at the hands of men, with the "critical difference" that she is never incorporated into their society. Rather, she overturns this order and instigates a new one, into which she allows Mr. _____ to enter when he rehabilitates himself.

Despite the almost overwhelming oppressiveness of Celie's life, she endures and finally begins to accept herself: "I'm pore, I'm black, I may be ugly and can't cook, a voice say to everything listening. But I'm here" (214). Yet, this self-acceptance is dearly bought, and Celie suffers extreme anguish when she learns that Mr. _____ has been hiding the letters which her sister, Nettie, has written. She is so angry that she nearly kills her husband and is saved only by Shug's replacing the destructive razor in her hand with a constructive needle—a symbolic act. However, Nettie's letters provide a further source of anguish for Celie, when, through them, she learns of her true parentage. At this point, her anger turns to despair, and she rejects God:

Yeah, I say, and he give me a lynched daddy, a crazy mama, a lowdown dog of a step pa and a sister I probably won't ever see again. Anyhow, I say, the God I been praying and writing to is a man. And act just like all the other mens I know. Trifling, forgitful and lowdown. (199)

But a woman—Shug—teaches Celie to love and to trust again, and when she offers to take Celie to Memphis, Celie's world is rejuvenated. In the pivotal dinner scene, when Celie and Squeak announce that they have decided to forge new identities by leaving their husbands, they refuse to conform to the old patriarchal order. Celie stabs Mr. _____ when he tries to slap her (271) and Squeak demands that she be called by her proper name : "Listen Squeak, say Harpo. You can't go to Memphis. That's all there is to it. Mary Agnes, say Squeak. Squeak, Mary Agnes, what difference do it make? It makes a lot, say Squeak. When I was Mary Agnes I could sing in public" (110).[4] The final pages of the novel are spent in dramatizing the positive aspects of society, by incorporating and revitalizing the social values and institutions in light of the new order.

The family itself becomes a positive force when Sofia changes it into an entity that succours and helps its members. She extends the nuclear family when she welcomes Squeak's children into her home and heals the breach that had existed between the two women, both rivals for Harpo's affections: "Go on sing, say Sofia I'll look after this one till you come back" (211) . Family is, therefore, no longer based on blood but on mutual love and respect. Shug and Celie form a new family unit when Celie learns the truth of her parentage, and Shug's tenderness helps her to overcome her despair: "Shug say, Us each other's peoples now, and kiss me" (189). Further, Shug's relationship with Celie takes on the sanctity that Celie's marriage with Mr. _____ lacked and offers a positive view of "non-marriage" as a union which proffers acceptance and concern: "Besides, she say. You not my maid. I didn't bring you to Memphis to be that. I brought you here to love you and help you get on your feet" (218).

Even religion is revitalized when it extends to encompass the segregated, and God loses "Its" colour and gender: "God ain't a he or a she, but a It. . . . It ain't a picture show. It ain't something you can look at apart from anything else, including yourself" (202). When religion loses the limitations imposed on it by a white, male hierarchy, faith "opens in many directions" (Sypher 249) and Celie's perception of God becomes all inclusive and whole. She comes to accept Shug's belief in a God who is "everything" (202) and begins to understand "It" need not be restricted to a church:

God love everything you love—and a mess of stuff you don't.
But more than anything else, God love admiration.
You say God vain? I ast.
Naw, she say. Not vain, just wanting to share a good thing. I

think it pisses God off if you walk by the color purple in a field
somewhere and don't notice it, (203)

Society itself can become more enlightened when its members are able
to repudiate the dictates of societal norms. Indeed, there is an attempt on the
part of the daughters to overcome the sins of the fathers when Eleanor Jane
tries to make reparation for her parents' treatment of Sofia by working for her:
"Do her peoples know? I ast. They know, say Sofia. They carrying on just like
you know they would. Whoever heard of a white woman working for niggers,
they rave. She tell them, Whoever heard of somebody like Sofia working for
trash" (288). The new society is not a closed order; it is open to all; even Mr.
_____ can be included when he realizes the errors of his ways, rejects his old,
narrow outlook, and learns the meaning of love:

> . . . he say something that really surprise me cause it so thoughtful
> and common sense. When it come to what folks do together with
> they bodies, he say, anybody's guess is as good as mine. But when
> you talk bout love I don't have to guess. I have love and I have been
> love. And I thank God he let me gain understanding enough to
> know love can't be halted just cause some peoples moan and groan.
> It don't surprise me you love Shug Avery, he say, I have love Shug
> Avery all my life. (277)

The novel's major narrative symbol is associated with the act of sewing:
Celie literally sews her life back together when she begins to design pants,
and Mr. _____'s salvation is symbolized when he begins to make shirts to
match them. Indeed, Mr. _____ asks Celie to marry him again, "this time in
the spirit as well as in the flesh" (290), but she refuses him because, as she
states, "I still don't like frogs" (290). Celie's reference to frogs recalls the fairy
tale, "The Frog Prince," which the novel parodically inverts. In this story, Mr.
_____ may kiss the "princess," but he undergoes no miraculous transformation
into a handsome prince; he remains a "frog." Celie, on the other hand, is still
able to "live happily ever after" without him, which, as mentioned earlier, undercuts the traditional boy-gets-girl endings of most fairy tales and comedies.
However, Celie does forgive Mr. _____ when she allows him to join in her
creative process, and her forgiveness constitutes the basis for the new society,
for men and even white women like Eleanor Jane, although viewed scepti-
cally, are allowed a chance to atone.

Since the novel attacks those bastions of society—family, religion, and
marriage—but also offers a rejuvenation of them in its final pages, it evi-
dently suggests that society itself is not what Walker questions and rejects
but rather the limitations that are imposed upon it and make it closed and

restrictive. The womanist utopia of the conclusion signifies a renewal of the initial social order because it is more accessible and more humane. Walker's utopia is "humanist" as well as womanist in the sense that it offers a revivification of humanity as a whole. This concept is epitomized in Celie's sewing.[5] Her first pair of pants are made out of army fabric—hard, stiff to the touch—which she later rejects in favour of soft, pliable material: "Shug finger the pieces of cloth I got hanging on everything. It all soft, flowing, rich and catch the light. This a far cry from the stiff army shit us started with, she say" (219). The clothes that Celie designs out of the new fabric enhance the people who wear them; she creates pants that are comfortable and designed with their wearer in mind:

> these pants are soft, hardly wrinkle at all, and the little figures in the cloth always look perky and bright. And they full round the ankle so if she want to sing in 'em and wear 'em sort of like a long dress, she can. (219)

Mr. _____'s shirts are also devised to be extensions of their wearer; they support life rather than stifle it: "Got to have pockets, he say. Got to have loose sleeves. And definitely you not spose to wear it with no tie. Folks wearing ties look like they being lynch" (290)

The clothes that Celie and Mr. _____ design celebrate rather than restrict people; they become a symbol of the humanist/womanist utopia manifested at the end of the novel. Indeed, this utopia becomes an Edenic paradise, as Thadious M. Davis suggests, for the arrival of Celie's son, *Adam* Omatangu, and the rest of her family from Africa

> signals the continuity of generations, the return (ironically perhaps) to the 'old, unalterable roots.' Their return is cause for a larger hope for the race, and for celebration within the family and community, because they have survived 'whole,' literally since they miraculously survive a shipwreck and symbolically since they have acquired definite life-affirming attitudes. (52)

This is precisely the note on which the novel ends, since the new order, the order that opens to the once segregated, is celebratory: "White people busy celebrating they independence from England July 4th, say Harpo, so most black folks don't have to work. Us can spend the day celebrating each other" (294). To paraphrase Martin, in Walker's comedy, the female/ black incongruous is seen to be more congruous than the white patriarchy, which made them incongruous in the first place by denying them entry into its closed society.

Therefore, while it may seem "incongruous" to classify *The Color Purple* as a comedy, it cannot truly be called anything else, for it seeks to improve society by eliminating the limitations prescribed by the societal norms. Meredith stresses that where "the veil is over women's faces, you cannot have society, without which the senses are barbarous and the Comic Spirit is driven to the gutters to slake its thirst" (31). In *The Color Purple*, the "veil," of which Meredith speaks, is lifted, the barriers between the sexes are razed, and a new world is erected on the ruins, in which the sexes meet on an equal footing and celebrate each other, life, and humankind.

Notes

1. I am indebted to Linda Hutcheon for showing me the significance of this aspect of the novel.

2. Romance too offers a utopia in its conclusion. However, romance offers idealized characters and incorporates other-worldly elements (Frye, *Anatomy* 186–195). To suggest that *The Color Purple* belongs to this genre, I think, would be to stretch a point. However, Frye does suggest that comedy will often overlap with romance in its conclusion (177) which seems to me to be the case here.

3. The similarity of the two male protagonists' names (Mr. _____ and Mr. B.) further supports the idea that the novel plays on Richardson's text.

4. Names are very important in this novel. Walker dramatizes the idea that when we name we possess, and as a result, the women reject the names accorded them by the patriarchy. On the other hand, Mr. _____ is also transformed into Albert when he sees the "errors of his ways" and convinces Celie of his sincere repentance. He, therefore, must be renamed to signify his renewal and his incorporation into the new order. It is also interesting to note that he loses the title—Mr.—which is used, to some extent, to subjugate Celie.

5. It is also symbolized in Celie's dialectal language which is proffered as natural and supportive of life. When she is given a chance to "improve" her speech, she says, "only a fool would want you to talk in a way that feel peculiar to your mind" (223).

Works Cited

Abrams, M. H. *A Glossary of Literary Terms.* 4th ed. New York: Holt, 1981.

Bergson, Henri. "Laughter." *Comedy.* Ed. Wylie Sypher. New York: Doubleday, 1956.

Cuddon, J. A. *A Dictionary of Literary Terms.* Harmondsworth: Penguin, 1982.

Davis, Thadious M. "Alice Walker's Celebration of Self in Southern Generations." *The Southern Quarterly: A Journal of the Arts in the South.* 21:4 (1983): pp. 39–53.

Feibleman, James K. "The Meaning of Comedy." *Aesthetics.* Toronto: Collins, 1949.

Frye, Northrop. *Anatomy of Criticism: Four Essays.* Princeton: Princeton University Press, 1973.

———. "The Argument of Comedy." *Theories of Comedy.* Ed. Paul Lauter. New York: Doubleday, 1964.

Hutcheon, Linda. *A Theory of Parody: The Teachings of Twentieth Century Art Forms.* New York: Methuen, 1985.

Martin, Robert Bernard. "Notes Toward a Comic Fiction." *The Theory of the Novel.* Ed. John Halperin. New York: Oxford University Press, 1974.

Meredith, George. "An Essay on Comedy." *Comedy.* Ed. Wylie Sypher. New York: Doubleday, 1956.

Sypher, Wylie. "The Meanings of Comedy." *Comedy.* Ed. Wylie Sypher. New York: Doubleday, 1956.

Walker, Alice. *In Search of Our Mothers' Gardens.* New York: Harcourt, 1983.

———. *The Color Purple.* New York: Pocket Books, 1982.

OM P. JUNEJA

The Purple Colour of Walker Women: Their Journey from Slavery to Liberation

Alice Walker, an activist during the Civil Rights Movement of the Blacks in the U. S., goes beyond the protest novels of Richard Wright, James Baldwin, Chester Himes and others to assert the ethnicity of her Black characters. Most of them are plain, ignorant Black women oppressed by a system beyond their comprehension. The oppression of these women is an outcome of American racism and sexism which are interconnected as modes of dominance. Walker asserts that the American society is a 'racist, sexist and colourist capitalist society'[1] which operates on the basis of unnatural hierarchical distinctions. The oppression of Black women by their husbands, brothers, lovers etc. is an outcome of this system.

Explaining the situation of the Black women in racist America Ellen Willis asserts that at a time when the American society is guided by the norms of 'whiteness' and 'maleness' white women have to fight for their feminism, Black men for their blackness but Black women have to fight their battle on two fronts because 'the Black woman suffers both racial and sexual invisibility.'[2]

Drawing them to the centre of her fictional world, Alice Walker adds a third dimension to the two-fold invisibility of her female protagonists, who very often are reduced to the level of animals and insects. Dehumanization of Black women protagonists, being the lot of the oppressed, is a result of their

The Literary Criterion, Volume 26, Number 3 (1990): pp. 66–76.

sense of powerlessness against the structure of dominant society, which they are unable to understand: 'In (their) day-to-day existence, they carry out a plot constructed by white society and choreographed by Black men.'[3]

Most of these women, like their men are trapped in the Georgia share cropping system which operated like an internal colony within the U. S. in 1920s and 1930s. Alice Walker draws these characters from the lives of her own ancestors. She says that she wrote *The Third Life of Grange Copeland* in the naturalistic tradition so that the history of the ante-bellum period of Blacks could be written in fictional terms. The novel therefore has a linear structure with events arranged in a chronological order. Alice Walker wanted this novel to be very realistic, almost 'visual' so that the reader is 'able to sit down, pick up that book and see a little of Georgia from the early twenties through the sixties.'[4] Walker takes us into this life through her women characters. The options for these Black women are very limited as they are trapped within the system. Like Margaret, Grange Copeland's wife in *The Third Life of Grange Copeland,* these women exemplify a state of 'suspension' in which life becomes a continuous agency. The novelist paints a graphic picture of the 'suspended' life of Margaret in the following passages:

> 'On Monday suffering from a hangover and after-effect of a violent quarrel with his wife the night before, Grange was morose, sullen, reserved, deeply in pain under the hot early morning sun. Margaret was tense and hard, exceedingly nervous. Brownfield moved about the house like a mouse. On Tuesday, Grange was merely quiet. His wife and son began to relax. On Wednesday. . . . Grange muttered and sighed . . . . he said things that made his wife cry. By Thursday, Grange's gloominess reached its peak . . . . By Friday, Grange was so stupefied with the work and the sun he wanted nothing but rest the next two days before it started all over again . . . .
>
> 'Late Saturday night Grange would come home lurching drunk, threatening to kill his wife and Brownfield . . . . Sunday morning, Grange would make his way . . . . to the Baptist church where his voice above all the others was raised in song and prayer.'[5]

This cycle of physical, emotional, mental and sexual oppression is broken only when Grange runs away from share-cropping Georgia to New York to define his manhood. Margaret, finding no creative outlet breaks this circle of her suspended life by committing suicide.

Mem, the wife of Brownfield, a sensitive, refined woman, is a dialectically polarized contrast to Margaret. Initially, their married life is almost idyllic. But the internal colonial share-cropping system is so oppressive that their life pattern soon becomes a repetition of the life-cycle of their forebears. Brownfield now beats her every Saturday 'trying to pin the blame for his failure on her by imprinting it on her face' (p. 55). His brutalisation is total.

Historically, the burden of Black man's rage against the oppression by the whiteman, has always been carried out by Black women who are used as their 'punching bag'. They are easier to knock out than the sharecropping system. Brownfield dramatises the tension inherent in this system. He is mean. Walker dramatises his meanness in order to contrast it with the tough resilence of Mem. Black women like Mem, generally, plain, ignorant, God fearing and church going, developed a resilience to the system. They, according to Walker, circumvented the system by their 'creative sparks' expressed in such crafts as quilting, gardening, cooking etc. Mem, initially expresses her creativity through these arts, but she cannot hold on to them for long on account of debumunization of Brownfield because of American sexism and racism.

Although Mem's 'creative sparks' arc extinguished for ever by Brownfield, her creative urge blossoms in her daughter Ruth who has been saved from the evil influence of Brownfield by Grange in his later incarnation.

The 'creative sparks' of the survival culture of the suspended Black women, again, is the theme of Walker's second novel, *Meridian*. The theme finds an appropriate expression in the character of Meridian. Meridian, to begin with, is a looney, crazy woman who has been abused physically and psychologically. But unlike the women characters in *The Third Life of Grange Copeland,* Meridian is provided with an opportunity to liberate herself by the Civil Rights Movement. Initially she involves herself in the movement fully. But as the Movement turns into a violent revolution, she questions the validity of the violent means to achieve revolutionary ends. She gains a sense of perspective and proportion through suffering, which she believes is essential to human development. The oppression which destroys all the creative sparks of Margaret and Mem, makes Meridian philosophical as she imbibes the collective wisdom of her people.

Alice Walker fights the myth of the Black motherhood as a stereotype of strength, self-abnegation and sacrifice. Margaret and Mem are abused mothers produced by the sharecropping system. Their idea of motherhood, though not stereotypical, is restrictive. Mem's attempt at providing a good and protective motherhood to Ruth fails, and the role is finally taken on by Grange Copeland. Meridian's idea of motherhood is not restrictive: 'she is torn between her own personal desire to become a mother and the fact that motherhood seems to cut her off from the possibilities of life and love'.[6] It is this contradiction in her desires which precipitates her quest to become a mother not in the biological sense of the term, but in the philosophical sense when she takes to non-violent resistance for the sake of children, The renunciation of her cell, her sleeping bag and her role to Truman, again, is symbolic of the role of the mother earth that she had played. Truman climbs shabbily into Meridian's bag and realizes the terror of the role of mother earth that he has now to play. She therefore passes on the struggle to defend life to Truman in order to understand the sacredness of life fully, symbolizing the awakening of the spirit, and also the beginning of another individual search. The novel is thus used as a contemplative and analytical tool.

The narrative technique that she uses to emphasise the contemplative nature of her novel is that of a collage so that it works on the mind in different patterns. She calls it 'a crazy quiet story'[7] as it jumps back and forth in time and works on many different levels including that of myth. This method is helpful in evolving metaphor and symbolism as an integral part of *Meridian.*

Alice Walker believes that as an American she has inherited three cultures: European, African and Amerindian. A faith in the presence of spirits is common to all the three cultures. She therefore dedicates her novel, The *Colour Purple:*

'To the spirit
Without whose assistance
Neither this book
Nor I
Would have been
Written'[8]

Walker's faith in the presence of spirits is mainly a consequence of Afro-American heritage of animism, which the Black Americans share with their African forebears. The Igbos of Nigeria, for example, believe in the existence of the spirit world. The concept of 'Chi' therefore is central to Igbo cosmology. Explaining the concept of 'Chi' in Igbo cosmology, Chinua Achebe, the doyen of African writers, states that the Igbos believe that the world in which they live has its double and 'counterpart in the realm of spirits. According to this belief a human being is only one half of a person as the other half being 'Chi' lives in the 'spiritland' where dead ancestors recreate a life comparable to their earthly existence. This 'spiritland, asserts Achebe, 'is not only parallel to the human spirit but is also similar and physically contiguous with it, for there is constant coming and going between them in the endless traffic of life, death and reincarnation.'[9]

The concept of 'Chi' is similar to Alice Walker's concept of animism which she asserts is a 'belief that makes it possible to view all creation as living, as inhabited by spirits'.[10] This world view essentially emphasises the oneness of the universe: animate or inanimate.

The spirit of animism is so pervasive in *The Colour Purple* that Celie's last letter is addressed to 'Dear God. Dear Stars, dear trees, dear sky, dear peoples. Dear Everything Dear God' (p. 242).

Celie addresses her letters to God sharing her confidences with Him, who serves as the epistolary confidant in the narrative discourse of *The Colour Purple*. She views God initially as a man with whom she can share her confidences and who can provide her the necessary protection from the world around her, Shug, the female liberator infuses self-confidence in her. This changes her perspective. Now she looks at God as a man who acts like other men 'trifling, forgetful and' lowdown' (p. 164). Shug's love helps Celie regain her inner strength and wisdom, which liberates her from the customary image of God as a white haired man with big feet and a beard. Her journey to liberation therefore changes her perception of God from the white Christian God to the black animistic all-pervasive God without a fixed image: the God of 'Dear stars, dear trees, dear sky, dear Everything.'[11]

Initially, in her traumatized, isolated state of mind God works as a 'shadow confidant' to whom she can neither mail her letters, nor can she completely convey her thoughts, leave alone the sharing of her feelings and emotions. As a 'shadow confidant' God, however, performs the dual functions of listening to her story and also of providing a repository for her confessions.[12] The first letter combines these two functions when she writes:

"Dear God,
    I am fourteen years old. I: have been always a good girl. May be, you can give me a sign letting me know what is happening to me.
    ..." (p. 1).

With these laconic opening remarks she tells the tale of sexual oppression of her Mama by Pa and her own sexual abuse by Pa later on. This unsigned letter therefore is symbolic of the sexual abuse of the Black woman by Black man; a lover or a husband, a father or a brother. The poignancy of the confidential mode of the epistolary discourse is intensified in the next prayerful letter:

"Dear God,
    My Mama dead. She die screaming and cussing .... I'm big. I can't move fast enough. By the time I git back from the well, the water be warm. By time I git the tray ready the food be cold. By time I git all the children ready for school it be dinner time. He don't say nothing ...." (p. 4)

Celie's use of the bare, laconic patois of the Southern Blacks is an expression of her individual consciousness and personality. Walker also uses Celie's idiolect as an act of defiance, a polemic against American racism and sexism. The novelist takes liberty with the sacrosanct English language to declare Celie's independence from the system. Nettie, on the contrary, uses

Standard English. Her language at the end of the novel becomes stiff and unexpressive, whereas Celie's English "despite its grammatical errors and simple vocabulary, is eloquent and beautiful."[13]

Celie like Mem and Margaret is a "suspended"[14] woman. Her unwed mother dies before she is married to Albert who is always referred to as Mr. _____ in her letters. Kate, who comes to visit Albert, her brother, advises Celie to fight to improve her wretched condition. Celie writes—

> "I don't say nothing. I think bout Nettie, dead. She fight, she run away. What good it do? I don't fight, I stay where I'm told. But I'm alive" (p. 21).

Though her vision is limited her motive to survive is positive. Shug Avery, a black singer, broadens her vision by teaching self-worth and love to Celie who develops a lesbian relationship with her. Shug's singing transforms Celie's personality. She recognizes her self-worth when Shug sings a song in her name: "First time somebody made something and name after me" (p. 65). She writes to God. Celie now recognizes Shug as her lover.

When Albert and Grady go out, Shug and Celie receive a letter from Nettie, accidentally. Nettie, in fact, had been writing to Celie ever since she left home for working with the missionaries in Africa. Albert never delivered these letters to Celie because they contained the true story of their life. Despite the fact that Nettie receives no reply, she keeps on writing to Celie:

> "I remember one time you said your life made you feel so ashamed you couldn't even talk about it to God, you had to write it, bad as you thought your writing was. Well, now I know what you meant. And whether God will read letters or no, I know you will go on writing them. Anyway, when I don't write to you I feel as bad as I do when I don't pray, locked up in myself and choking on my own heart. I am so lonely, Celie" (p. 110).

Thus, by handing over the narrative to Nettie, Walker changes the confidence system of the narrative discourse. Celie now has the letters of Nettie. Though she knows that her letters would never reach Nettie, she finds in her an active "confidant", and therefore bids farewell to the "shadow confidant"— that is, God. Her tone and language also change accordingly. Her last letter to God on page 151 is remarkably poignant:

> "Dear God,
>   That's it, say Shug. Pack your stuff. You coming back to Tennessee with me.

But I feels daze.

My daddy lynch. My mama crazy. All my little half brothers and sisters no kin to me. My children not my sister and brother. Pa not my Pa.

You must be sleep". (p. 151).

The letter opens with a sense of ending: "That's it, say Shug, Pack your stuff". The finality and urgency of the situation is further intensified in the epistolary discourse of transmission in the third paragraph which consists of only twenty-seven words bereft of auxiliaries. The sense of shocked discovery of her past liberates her from all the ties of kinship, literal or metaphoric. She therefore snaps her ties with God, the "shadow confidant," in favour of an active confidant, Nettie, to whom she writes: "I don't write to God no more, I write to you" (p. 164). This is the longest letter that Celie has written so far. It aptly sums up the change in her views about God. She no more recognizes the old white man as her God which she now identifies with trees, birds, air and other people. Meridian's faith in non-violence becomes a way of perception with Celie who writes, "I knew that if I cut a tree, my arm would bleed". Her vision of life is essentially animistic which encompasses life in its totality: "I think it pisses God off if you walk by the colour purple in a field somewhere and don't notice it" (p. 167).

This principle of the "Colour Purple" implies universal love encompassing entire life. Walker's saintly women characters realize it through suffering. Celie celebrates it when she challenges Albert's male chauvinistic objections: "you a lowdown dog is what's wrong, I say. It's time to leave you and enter into creation. And your dead body just the welcome net I need" (p. 170).

Celie achieves selfhood mainly with the help of Shug Avery, but Nettie's contribution cannot be ignored. Nettie's letters, in fact, not only tell the hidden story of her life, they broaden her vision by projecting the problems of the Black American on the wider horizon of European colonialism. The story of colonization of the bush village, Olinka, particularly reminds one of the Black African writers like Chinua Achebe (*Things Fall Apart* and *Arrow of God*), Ngugi wa Thiong'O (*A Grain of Wheat* and *Petals of Blood*) and many others. Walker's story of the colonization of Olinka is similar to such stories in the novels of T. M. Aluko, though with a difference. While the story of colonization told by the African writers presents an insider's point of view, Alice Walker tells 'the tale from the view point of a Black American, an. outsider who has lived in an "internal colony" within the U. S. and runs away to Africa to escape the oppression of the system.

Nettie's African experience again brings the question of roots of the Black American in to sharp focus. Celie's children, Adam and Olina, feel at home in Africa. They enjoy the African food, their customs and way of life.

Both of them become very fond of Tasbi, the African girl. The marriage of Tasbi and Adam at the end of the novel signifies the birth of a new Black world where the best of both the worlds will be preserved. Nettie's cyclical journey over a period of thirty years from a small southern town in the U. S. to New York to London to Olinka in Africa and back to her small town in the U. S.—all very ably described in her letters to Celie, is also the cyclical journey of the Black Americans in search of their roots which, according to the novelist, are not anywhere else but in the U.S.

Significantly, this journey is made by a woman who goes to Africa with her Christian God and comes back enriched with the experience of animism. In the meanwhile Celie too renounces the white God, a symbol of American racism and sexism, for African animism. Her identification with trees, birds, air and other human beings represents the natural state of living free from all kinds of oppression.

Celie's journey of self-discovery is symbolic of the "Womanist process"[15] embedded in the Afro-American folk-art tradition of their survival culture. This is a tradition in which the Black American women, despite heavy oppression, expressed their creativity in such crafts as gardening, cooking and quilting. The art of quilting, for example, allowed them to satisfy their creative urge in bits and pieces of waste material to create new designs. Quilting therefore represents the two-way process of art: economy and functionalism. Alice Walker captures the spirit of this womanist process by using the epistolary style in *The Colour Purple*. The distinct and original narrative tone of the novel approximates it to the oral code of the vernacular idiom of the South. The concentrated distillation of language, again, allows the novelist to strip off the layers of American civilization to hone down to the core of human existence and the working of the principle of "Colour Purple": the celebration of universal love and freedom through sisterhood. To sum up then the journey of Walker women in search of the principle of "Colour Purple" is to restate the role of the Black woman as a creator and also to define her relationship with the change in American society. This is, perhaps, best stated by Walker in a poem:

". . . . . . . because women are expected to keep silent about their close escape. I will not keep silent

> No, I am finished with living
> for what my mother believes
> for what my brother and father defend
> for what my lover elevates
> for what my sister, blushing, denies or rushes
> to embrace.

Besides
my struggle was always against
an inner darkness I carry with myself
the only known keys
to my death. . . . . . .

. . . . the healing
of all our wounds
is forgiveness
that permits a promise
of our return
at the end."

NOTES

1. Alice Walker in her interview with Claudia Tate in Claudia Tate (ed), *Black Woman Writers at Work* (New York: Continuum, 1983): pp. 175–187.

2. Ellen Willis, "Sisters under the Skin? Confronting Race and Sex", *Voice Literary Supplement*, No. 8, June 1982, pp. 1–19.

3. Betty. J. Parker-Smith, "Alice Walker's Women: In search of some Peace of Mind" in Mari Evans (ed.) *Black Women Writers (1950-1980): A Critical Evaluation* (New York: Anchor/Double, 1984): pp. 478–493.

4. Claudia Tate, op.cit.

5. Alice Walker, *The Third Life of Grange Copeland* (New York: Harcourt Brace, 1970): pp: 11–13.

6. Alice Walker, "In Search of Our Mother's Gardens" *MS*, 2 (May 1974): pp. 64–65.

7. Barbara Christian, *Black Women Novelists: The Development of Tradition, 1892–1976* (London: Greenwood, 1980): p. 220.

8. Claudia Tate, op.cit., p. 176.

9. Alice Walker, *The Colour Purple* (New York: Harcourt Brace Jovanovich, 1982).

10. Chinua Achebe, "Chi in Igbo Cosmology" in *Morning yet on Creation Day* (London: Heinemann, 1977): p. 95.

11. Alice Walker in an interview with John O'Brien (ed,). *Interviews with Black Writers.* (New York: Liveright, 1973): p. 193.

12. Janet Gurkin Altman, *Epistolary: Approaches to a Form* (Columbus: Ohio State University Press, 1982): p, 58.

13. Katie Jones, "Dialect. Idiolect, Sociolect: Transformations of English in the Works of Raja Rao, Samuel Selvon, and Alice Walker. *Chimo*. No. 11, Fall 1985, pp. 4–13.

14. Barbara Christian, "The Black Woman Artist as Wayward" in Mari Evans (ed.) *Black Women Writers* (1930–1980). (New York: Anchor/Double, 1954): p. 469.

15. Alice Walker, *Good Night Willy Lee, I'll see you in the Morning* (New York: Harcourt Brace Jovanovich, 1984): p. 53.

CHARLES L. PROUDFIT

Celie's Search for Identity: A Psychoanalytic Developmental Reading of Alice Walker's The Color Purple

> It is my belief and my faith that whenever you are trying to convey a sense
> of a common reality to people, they will want to read and hear about it.
> —Alice Walker, "The Eighties and Me"

Since the publication of Alice Walker's *The Color Purple*, both novel and author continue to elicit a wide range of praise and censure from an increasing number of black and white, female and male reviewers, literary critics, and general readers. At one extreme are those who find the work "an American novel of permanent importance" (Prescott 67); who place the author "in the company of Faulkner" (Smith 183); and who praise Walker for her creation of the unique voice of her protagonist, Celie, a "poor, ugly, uneducated [black girl] . . . [from] rural Georgia," for "the universality of the themes of redemptive love, strength in adversity, independence, and self-assertion through the values of community," and for "creating a unique set of people who speak to the *human* condition" (McFadden 139–143). At the other extreme are those who feel that the novel should be "ignored" rather than "canonized" (Harris, "On *The Color Purple*" 155); who place Walker "closer to Harriet Beecher Stowe than to [Zora Neale] Hurston" (Pinckney 18); and who censure Walker for the creation of an unrealistic plot (Towers 36), for the "depiction of violent black men who physically and psychologically abuse their wives and children. . . [and for the] depiction of lesbianism" (Royster 347), and for peopling her

Contemporary Literature Volume 32, Number 1 (Spring 1991): pp. 12–37. ©1991 by the Board of Regents of the University of Wisconsin System.

novel with characters who "themselves do not seem to respond to [some form of] internal logic" (Harris, "Victimization" 9). Walker herself relates that her mother finds the book's language "offensive" and humorously describes a parent's attempt to have the novel banned in a California public school system ("Coming in from the Cold" 55–58). Between these extreme critical positions, one finds a growing body of measured literary criticism that addresses both the novel's formal qualities and thematic concerns[1] and that validates the novel's having been awarded in 1983 both the American Book Award for Fiction and the Pulitzer Prize.

Although from the beginning critics have recognized the importance of the theme of "female bonding" in Celie's search for and development of a mature female identity,[2] no one, to my knowledge, has viewed either this theme or the protagonist's character development from the perspective of contemporary psychoanalytic developmental psychology. Such a psychoanalytic developmental reading will help illuminate Walker's literary portrayal of the importance of the mother for the female infant, child, and adult as she struggles to separate, to individuate, to develop her own identity, and to make a final choice of love object; will suggest the need to reconsider certain negative criticisms of the novel, such as unequal narrative voices, unrealistic character development, faulty plot, unbelievable events, and a lesbian relationship "that represents the height of silly romanticism" (Harris, "On *The Color Purple*" 157); and will help account for the contrasting literary portraits of Celie and Nettie.

This reading is based upon a mother-daughter bond that, according to several current psychoanalytic theorists on female development, has its origins in deep, primitive ties to the mother of infancy and is a bond that must be worked through *again and again during a woman's lifetime.*[3] Walker's descriptions of Celie's bonding, first with the biological mother of infancy and later with suitable mother surrogates, is psychologically realistic and ranges from the ministrations of Celie's younger sister Nettie, to Kate and Sofia, and to Shug's facilitating Celie's sensual awakening to adult female sexuality and a healthy emotional life. This "female bonding," which occurs over an extended period of time, enables Celie—a depressed survivor-victim of parent loss, emotional and physical neglect, rape, incest, trauma, and spousal abuse—to resume her arrested development and continue developmental processes that were thwarted in infancy and early adolescence. These processes are described with clinical accuracy; and, as they are revisited and reworked in Celie's interactions with appropriate mother surrogates, Celie is enabled to get in touch with her feelings, work through old traumas, and achieve an emotional maturity and a firm sense of identity that is psychologically convincing.

Since some readers may not be familiar with psychoanalytic developmental psychology, often referred to as object relations theory, I should first like to make several observations about this approach to the study of child development and then acquaint the reader with several concepts and theories of the English analyst and pediatrician D. W. Winnicott that inform my developmental reading of the text.[4] Stated simply, psychoanalytic developmental psychology is the study of the infant's and the child's development that focuses upon the unconscious, conscious, and maturational processes that *occur within the mother-infant/child matrix.* The infant's and child's object relations are both internal (intrapsychic) and external (the child experiences itself as separate from other objects [like mother or father] "objectively perceived" [Winnicott, *Maturational Processes* 57]). Most object relations theorists postulate that at birth the human infant is psychologically merged with its mother.[5] Winnicott asserts that *"There is no such thing as a baby";* rather, "one sees a 'nursing couple" *(Through Paediatrics* 99). Margaret Mahler observes that "from the beginning the child molds and unfolds in the matrix of the mother-infant dual unit" *(5).* Although Mahler, Winnicott, and other object relations theorists differ in their understanding of the developmental process that, if successfully "completed," allows for the emergence of a healthy, creative self, they do agree that this process occurs within the mother-infant/child matrix (Greenberg and Mitchell). Furthermore, Winnicott, Mahler, and others agree with Daniel Stern: "Development is not a succession of events left behind in history. It is a continuing process, constantly updated" (260).[6] Walker's fictional treatment of Celie's continuing development into middle age appears to be in agreement with this psychoanalytic developmental view.

Although a psychoanalytic literary critic might draw upon several schools of object relations in offering a developmental reading of Walker's *The Color Purple,* I believe that Winnicott's concepts and theories offer the most helpful insights into the psychological dynamics that underlie Walker's literary portrayal of the significance of "female bonding" for the resumption of Celie's arrested developmental processes in the early part of the novel. Furthermore, Winnicott's view of the origin of what he calls the "True Self" and the "False Self" not only illuminates the contrasting literary portraits of Celie and her younger sister Nettie but also enables the reader to observe how Walker creatively uses diction, sentence structure, tone, and style in the sisters' letters to each other in order to create "authentic" and "inauthentic" voices. Finally, Winnicott's assertion that the developmental issues of infancy "are never fully established, and continue to be strengthened by the growth that continues in later childhood, and indeed in adult life, even in old age" (*Maturational Processes* 74) lends credence to Celie's lengthy developmental process—a process that has been severely criticized (Harris, "Victimization" 16). Since Walker's fictive description of Celie's developmental history includes a brief sketch of the first several years of her life (*Color Purple* 160–161), I will begin with Winnicott's concept of "primary maternal preoccupation" (*Maturational Processes* 85).

Winnicott observes that many expectant mothers experience a special psychological state during the latter part of their pregnancies and for several weeks after childbirth, in which they turn their attention inward and focus on the needs of the unborn and newly born. He calls this organized state "primary maternal preoccupation" and believes that the most successful mothers experience it. He believes that the mother and her newborn should be viewed as "a unit" (*Maturational Processes* 39) and asserts that the "good-enough mother" (57, 145; *Playing* 10),[7] who is empathetically attuned to her infant's needs, provides a "holding environment" (*Maturational Processes* 44–50, 86), in which the infant moves "from being merged with the mother to being separate from her, or to relating to her as separate and 'not-me'" (45). During this time the "good-enough mother" serves both as an auxiliary ego for the immature ego of the infant (44, 56–63) and as a "mirror" in which the infant sees itself reflected: "[When] the mother is looking at the baby ... *what she looks like is related to what she sees there*" (*Playing* 112). According to Winnicott, the "good-enough mother" provides the infant over time with enough such positive reflections of self that the infant begins to develop a "True Self" (118). If, however, a "mother [who is not good enough] reflects her own mood or, worse still, the rigidity of her own defenses" (112), then the infant perceives rather than apperceives (113), and we have the beginning of a compliant "False Self" (*Maturational Processes* 145). The origins of the "True Self" and the "False Self" begin *before* the infant has "separated off the 'not me' from the 'me'" (158), that is, roughly prior to the sixth month.

Although Winnicott eschews a strict stage theory of infant development, he does note that the infant passes through several phases on its journey toward the development of a self. In the first phase of *absolute dependence,* the mother provides a facilitating environment (womb/first few weeks of life) for the totally helpless infant (*Maturational Processes* 87–88). In the next phase of *relative dependence,* the infant comes to separate the "not me" from the "me"; and from about six months to twenty-four months the infant becomes *"aware of dependence,"* comes to *"know in his mind* that mother is necessary,"* and "gradually the need for the actual mother (in health) becomes fierce and truly terrible" (88). By two years of age, Winnicott believes that the infant has begun to develop inner capacities that will enable him or her to deal more effectively with loss (88). Prior to three years of age, however, loss of the mother or mothering agent can have profound adverse psychological effects upon a child. Finally, Winnicott asserts that throughout these phases of infant development "the whole procedure of infant-care has as its main characteristic a steady presentation of the world to the infant. ... It can only be done by continuous management by a human being who is consistently herself. ... This of course applies to father too" (87–88). These developmental concepts and theories, especially the "good-enough mother," "the holding environment," the "mirror role of the mother," and the origin of the "True Self" and the "False Self," underlie Walker's dramatic theme of "female bonding" and help illuminate the author's literary portrayal of Celie's lengthy search for and achievement of a mature female identity and healthy object relations.

Walker, like Charlotte Brontë in *Jane Eyre* (one of Walker's favorite novels in childhood [Steinem 92]) begins *The Color Purple in medias res:* Celie, like Jane, is poised on the edge of adolescence after a childhood of loss, deprivation, and abuse. With Celie's first anguished letter to God, Walker enables the reader to enter into the private thoughts and emotional state of her traumatized, guilt- and shame-ridden, and depressed fourteen-year-old protagonist, who has been repeatedly raped and impregnated by the man (Alphonso) whom she believes to be her biological father: "Dear God, I am fourteen years old. ~~I am~~ I have always been a good girl. Maybe you can give me a sign letting me know what is happening to me" (11). Celie draws a line through "I am" and writes "I have always been a good girl," because the child victim of rape and incest often blames herself for her trauma; or, worse still, believes that this bad thing has happened to her because *she* is bad and therefore deserves it. Celie writes to God because she is ashamed of what is happening to her (122) and because of the threat from Alphonso that immediately precedes Celie's first letter: *"You better not never tell nobody but God. It'd kill your mammy"* (11). Threats and forced secrecy are usual parts of incest (Herman 88; Russell 132–133). The style of this letter, and of those that immediately follow, is characterized by short, choppy sentences, halting rhythms, repetitive grammatical structures of subject, verb, object, concrete physical descriptions in an ongoing present, and matter-of-fact tone. It is a style that mirrors Celie's traumatized cognitive processes and depressed emotional state. We learn that Celie's depression is partly caused by her repressed rage when later in the novel Sofia asks her what she does when she gets mad: "I think. I can't even remember the last time I felt mad, I say. I used to git mad at my mammy cause she put a lot of work on me. Then I see how sick she is. Couldn't stay mad at her. Couldn't be mad at my daddy cause he my daddy. Bible say, Honor father and mother no matter what. Then after while every time I got mad, or start to feel mad, I got sick. Felt like throwing up. Terrible feeling. Then I start to feel nothing at all" (47). Even the color purple, a mixture of the primary colors red (rage) and blue (depression), suggests Celie's mood in the initial letters. The color is also symbolic of the bruises resulting from the beatings inflicted upon Celie first by Alphonso (whom she later learns is her stepfather) and then her husband Albert.

In Celie's second letter, written about a year later, Celie's mother has died, screaming and cursing her pregnant daughter. After the birth of Celie's second child, Alphonso gives her infant son away, as he had her infant daughter, though Celie believes that he has killed them. She stops menstru-

ating after the second birth. During the next five years, Celie lives at home
with Alphonso, his new young wife, and a growing number of their children;
she serves as a maid, and as protector of her younger sister Nettie against
Alphonso's sexual advances. At twenty, Celie is married off to Albert, a wid-
ower with children, who also abuses her. Nettie joins them but is soon told
by Albert to leave.

It is not until sometime later, when Albert brings home his old flame
Shug Avery, that Celie is enabled, with Shug's help, to find Nettie's letters
to her. These letters, written after Nettie goes to live with the missionaries
Corrine and Samuel but hidden by Albert, reveal to Celie the truth of her
origin. She discovers that Alphonso is not her biological father and that she
lived for the first two years of her life as the only child in a loving family. The
father adored his pregnant wife and, we would expect, his daughter Celie. But
one night, when she was barely two years old, her successful father's store and
blacksmIth shop were burned and destroyed; he and his two brothers were
dragged from their homes and hanged by jealous white merchants; and, when
his mutilated and burned body was brought home to his wife by neighbors,
she gave birth to Nettie and suffered an emotional breakdown:

> Although the widow's body recovered, her mind was never the same.
> She continued to fix her husband's plate at mealtimes just as she'd
> always done and was always full of talk about the plans she and her
> husband had made. The neighbors, though not always intending
> to, shunned her more and more, partly because the plans she talked
> about were grander than anything they could even conceive of for
> colored people, and partly because her attachment to the past was
> so pitiful. She was a good-looking woman, though, and still owned
> land, but there was no one to work it for her, and she didn't know
> how herself; besides she kept waiting for her husband to finish the
> meal she'd cooked for him and go to the fields himself. Soon there
> was nothing to eat that the neighbors did not bring, and she and
> her small children grubbed around in the yard as best they could.
>
> While the second child was still a baby, a stranger appeared in
> the community, and lavished all his attention on the widow and her
> children; in a short while, they were married. Almost at once she
> was pregnant a third time, though her mental health was no better.
> Every year thereafter, she was pregnant, every year she became
> weaker and more mentally unstable, until, many years after she
> married the stranger, she died.
>
> Two years before she died she had a baby girl that she was too
> sick to keep. Then a baby boy [in fact Celie's kidnapped babies
> (12–13)]. These children were named Olivia and Adam. (161)

Thus, in a single evening, the two-year-old Celie experiences several catastrophic losses: (1) the death of a loving father; (2) the emotional loss of a loving mother (at first through a psychotic episode and later through sickness and depression); (3) the loss of a safe and nurturing family environment; and (4) the loss of her place as an only child. During the next several months, Celie and her newborn baby sister Nettie experience hunger, neglect, and other deprivations. When Alphonso appears on the scene within the year and "lavished all his attention on the widow and her children," Celie's and Nettie's physical needs were probably met, but their mentally unstable, ill, and often pregnant mother would not have been able to provide either of her daughters with the "good-enough mothering" that they needed. Given the description of Alphonso in Celie's early letters, he would not have been temperamentally fit to serve as a mother substitute. We can reasonably postulate that Celie became mother surrogate to Nettie, as well as to her ill and half-crazed mother's unwanted babies.[8] When Celie's mother goes "to visit her sister doctor over Macon" (11), Alphonso rapes Celie and begins to use her as a sexual replacement for his exhausted wife—a not uncommon situation in actual cases of father-daughter incest (Herman 47–49).

This dramatic literary portrait of Celie as a traumatized and depressed survivor-victim of parent loss, physical and emotional neglect, rape, incest, and spousal abuse, which one black female critic finds unbelievable (Harris, "On *The Color Purple*" 155–156), is in fact a clinically accurate description of what Leonard Shengold calls "soul murder":

> Soul, or psychic, murder involves trauma imposed from the world outside the mind that is so overwhelming that the mental apparatus is flooded with feeling. The same overstimulated state can result as a reaction to great deprivation. The terrifying too-muchness requires massive and mind-distorting defensive operations for the child to continue to think and feel and live. The child's sense of identity (that is, the emotional maintenance of the mental images of his or her self) is threatened. Our identity depends initially on good parental care and good parental caring—on the transmitted feeling that it is good that we are there. . . . What happens to the child subjected to soul murder is so terrible, so overwhelming, and usually so recurrent that the child must not feel it and cannot register it, and resorts to a massive isolation of feeling, which is maintained by brainwashing (a mixture of confusion, denial, and identifying with the aggressor). A hypnotic living deadness, a state of existing "as if" one were there, is often the result of chronic early overstimulation or deprivation. As [Sandor] Ferenczi (1933) put it, "The [abused] child changes into a mechanical obedient automaton." . . . But the automaton has murder within. (24-25)

As a survivor of deprivation in childhood and of overstimulation in adolescence and young adulthood, Celie exhibits several characteristics of those
who have experienced "soul murder." When her husband Albert, whom she
addresses as "Mr. _____ "until the very end of the novel, orders Celie to get his
belt and then beats her, she isolates her feelings: "It all I can do not to cry. I
make myself wood. I say to myself, Celie, you a tree" (30). Unable to deal with
her feelings of jealousy and rage (46), Celie identifies with her male aggres-
sors: when Harpo asks her how to make his wife Sofia mind, Celie writes, "I
don't mention how happy he is now. How three years pass and he still whistle
and sing. I think bout how every time I jump when Mr. _____ call me, she
[Sofia] look surprise. And like she pity me. Beat her, I say" (43). And Celie,
like other victims of "soul murder" who have been reduced to "a mechanical
obedient automaton," harbors a murderous rage that almost surfaces when
Albert's father denigrates Shug (58–59) and when she learns that Albert has
for many years been intercepting and hiding Nettie's letters (114–115).

How does Celie survive her early losses and subsequent "soul murder"
and begin to move successfully through the developmental stages arrested in
infancy and adolescence toward a mature female identity? How is she enabled
to take pleasure—her own pleasure—in creative work and unselfish love as an
adult? In short, how is Celie able first to verbalize and then to fulfill with her
authentic living the promise inherent in those Stevie Wonder verses quoted
by Walker at the beginning of her novel: *"Show me how to do like you / Show
me how to do it"*?

Alice Walker writes: "Let's hope people can hear Celie's voice. There
are so many people like Celie who make it who come out of nothing. People
who triumph" (Anillo and Abramson 67). According to psychoanalytic developmental psychology, however, a successful survivor does not emerge "out of
nothing"; Celie, as a successful survivor, is able to learn "how to do it" because
(1) her family of origin gave her "good parental care" during the first two years
of her life;(2) she is able to make use of several nurturing surrogate mother
figures, foremost among whom is "the Queen Honeybee" herself, Shug Avery;
and (3) as a survivor of "soul murder" she uses "adaptive powers and talents"
(Shengold 7).[9] In the remainder of this paper, I shall first speculate upon the
psychological state of the pretraumatized two-year- old Celie viewed from
the perspective of psychoanalytic developmental psychology; then attempt
to show how Celie "bonds" with developmentally appropriate mother surrogates (Winnicott's "good-enough mother") as she resumes working through
several developmental processes that were traumatically halted at age two and
that need to be readdressed in her skewed and delayed adolescence in order
for her to achieve psychological maturity and a firm sense of identity; and,
finally, compare Celie and Nettie as examples of what Winnicott calls the
"True Self" and the "False Self."

Since Samuel's story of Celie's family of origin before its destruction includes a father who was a successful farmer and landowner, who prospered at whatever he turned his hand to, and who adored his wife (160), we can infer that Celie's first two years of life were spent in a supportive, caring family environment in which her basic physiological and psychological needs were met. We can assume that Celie bonded successfully with her mother and received "good-enough mothering." We find this mutually loving, triangular yet preoedipal family re-experienced by Celie in several places in the text. When Albert's father pays his son and Celie, now in her twenties, a call and denounces Shug Avery as a "whore," Albert and Celie, each of whom loves Shug, exchange a glance, and Celie writes: "This the closest us ever felt. He [Albert] say, Hand Pa his hat, Celie" *(59)*. A little while later, Albert's brother Tobias drops by with a box of chocolate for the "Queen Honeybee." After Shug enters and sits by Celie without looking at Albert, Celie has a moment of intense self-awareness: "Then I see myself sitting there quilting tween Shug Avery and Mr. _____. Us three set together gainst Tobias and his fly speck box of chocolate. For the first time in my life, I feel just right" (61). Finally, in Celie's last letter, written in her early fifties, she describes herself and Albert and Shug "sitting out on the porch after dinner. Talking. Not talking. Rocking and fanning flies. . . . sitting on the porch with Albert and Shug feel real pleasant" (249). These adult experiences of Celie's are pleasurable because they are unconsciously experienced as that loving relationship she had had with her preoedipal father and mother during the latter part of her first two years of life. They help fulfill the need that has remained for such family object relations since the early separations.

Celie's father's adoration of his pregnant wife and mother of his daughter also strongly suggests that femaleness and femininity were highly valued by both mother and father, and that Celie's core gender identity is femaleness. According to Robert Stoller, our "core gender identity is the sense we have of our sex—of maleness in males and of femaleness in females. . . . It is a part of, but not identical with, what I have called gender identity—a broader concept, standing for the mix of masculinity and femininity found in every person. . . . Core gender identity develops first and is the central nexus around which masculinity and femininity gradually accrete" ("Primary Femininity" 61). Stoller's research leads him to believe that "core gender identity" is solidified for the most part by the end of the second year; gender identity, however, is determined by a wide variety of biological, psychological, social, and cultural influences and is usually not finalized until middle or late adolescence.[10] Thus, by two, Celie's "core gender identity," her sense of femaleness, is fairly well established, and the groundwork has been laid for the further development of her "gender identity."

Perhaps most important for Celie's ability to bond successfully with females in adolescence and young adulthood, and thus to resume her development of an identity, of a "True Self" in Winnicott's terminology, is her partial but incomplete resolution of a transitional developmental phase that occurs roughly between six and twenty-four months. Winnicott calls this phase "relative dependence" and describes the infant's need for its mother at this time as "fierce and truly terrible." Since the infant has not yet developed the permanent capacity to image mother either consciously or unconsciously when she is absent, the infant is subject to being overwhelmed with "separation anxiety." Mahler offers the term "rapprochement crisis" for this phase and describes it as a time of ambivalence, when the infant's needs for separateness and autonomy and identity formation are in conflict with its need for mother (76–120). If the mother is understanding and empathetic at this difficult time, the infant will, in the third year, go on to develop a stable sense of self and others. If, however, there are serious maternal failures, severe adult psychopathology may result, and the developmental tasks of adolescence, especially the finalizing of gender identity and a firm sense of self, will be made even more difficult. Since Celie loses her "good-enough mother" at the height of her "rapprochement crisis," when she has yet to develop stable conscious and unconscious images of mother and her identity formation is in the early stages of development, it is hardly surprising that Celie should later respond to the ministrations of women and resume the developmental tasks of separation, autonomy, and identity formation.

Although the white, patriarchal God Celie writes to in the first part of the novel never sends her a sign (175–176), life does—primarily in the form of caring and nurturing black women. These "good-enough mothers," with the notable exception of Shug Avery, take the initiative; they intuit the depressed and traumatized Celie's deeply buried needs and break through her defensive passivity. When Nettie runs away from home to escape Alphonso's unwanted sexual advances and joins Celie and Albert, she teaches Celie "spelling and everything else she think I need to know. . . . to teach me what go on in the world" (25).

Nettie not only tries to give Celie the tools that will free her, she also, even more importantly, conveys to Celie her belief that Celie is of value. Kate, one of Albert's sisters, convinces him of Celie's need for clothes and takes her to a store to select cloth so that a dress can be made. When Celie is overcome with emotion and cannot speak, Kate reassures her and says: "You deserve more than this. Maybe so. I think" (28). And when Sofia, Harpo's wife and Albert's daughter-in-law, suggests that Celie and she make quilt pieces, Celie writes: "I run git my pattern book. I sleeps like a baby now" (47).

It is the seemingly inappropriate nightclub singer Shug Avery, however, who provides Celie with an extended period of "female bonding"; who, with unconditional love, provides a "holding environment" in which Celie's nascent self is reflected back to itself; and, who, as surrogate and "good-enough mother," and lover, helps Celie to complete the development of those capacities that enable her to deal more effectively with loss, to finalize her gender identity and choice of mature love object, and to develop a stable sense of self. One might argue that the development of a nurturing and positive relationship between these two women is improbable. Celie, until she hears Shug's name spoken, appears as a passive victim. After she is married to Albert, women who become mother surrogates have to reach out to her. How then can Shug's name and her picture, provided to her by Alphonso's new wife (16), mobilize the depressed and passive Celie actively to seek a "good-enough mother" in Shug? And when the two women meet for the first time, the deathly ill Shug's first words are "You sure *is* ugly" (50).

What may appear inappropriate and improbable is seen not to be so when we acknowledge Celie's developmental history, her unconscious need to complete those developmental tasks that have been skewed and/or arrested — and most important initially, her adolescent longing for a transitional, idealized role model, figures that adolescents often draw from the entertainment and sports worlds: "Shug Avery was a woman. The most beautiful woman I ever saw. She more pretty then my mama. She bout ten thousand times more prettier then me. I see her there in furs. Her face rouge. Her hair like somethin tail. She grinning with her foot up on somebody motorcar. Her eyes serious tho. Sad some. I ast her to give me the picture. An all night long I stare at it. An now when I dream, I dream of Shug Avery" (16).

After Celie's immediate positive response to the glamorous figure in the photograph, she focuses on the singer's "serious" and "sad eyes." In so doing, she moves from her adolescent need to cathect a transitional, idealized role model to her unconscious infantile need to master the trauma of losing the emotional availability of her "good-enough mother." Her initial negative encounters with the ill Shug parallel Celie's frustrated infantile efforts to break through her mother's psychosis and later her depression and deteriorating mental and physical condition. Celie perseveres, however, for she knows from the expression of the eyes in the photograph that *this* woman has the ability to mirror Celie back to herself. *"What* [mother] *looks like is related to what she sees there,"* asserts Winnicott (*Playing* 112), and Celie's experience confirms this. When she sees Shug's "serious" and "sad" eyes, she sees into her own murdered soul. When Alphonso is trying to convince Albert that Celie would make him a good wife despite her ugliness, Celie takes out Shug's picture, looks in her eyes, and "Her eyes say Yeah, it *bees* that way sometime" (18). Celie's ability to use Shug's eyes as a mirror is predicated upon earlier, positive, and unconscious mirror reflections from a "good-enough mother" of happier days. Indeed, Celie's ability to use Shug Avery herself as a mother surrogate for female bonding is predicated upon "good-enough mothering" during the first two years of Celie's life.

Once Celie has cathected Shug's photograph, her image permeates Celie's conscious and unconscious mind. Shug serves both as a "goodenough [preoedipal] mother" and as a libidinal object. On her wedding night, Celie thinks of Shug and, knowing that Albert and Shug were lovers, puts her arm around him (21). When Kate takes her to the store to buy cloth for her dress, Celie wonders what color Shug would wear (28). After hearing that Shug and her "orkestra" are coming to town, Celie carries an announcement with Shug's picture on it in her pocket all day and wants desperately to go that night: "Not to dance. Not to drink. Not to play card. Not even to hear Shug Avery sing. I just be thankful to lay eyes on her" (33). And when Albert brings the sick Shug home to recuperate, Celie, though flooded with emotions and desiring to heal her, cannot move until she "see her eyes" *(50)*. When Shug finally looks up at her, Celie notices those parts of Shug's face that a nursing infant would see: "her face black. . . . She got a long pointed nose and big fleshy mouth. Lips look like black plum. Eyes big, glossy" (50).

Celie not only devours Shug with her eyes but wishes to incorporate her with her mouth. As she nurses Shug back to health, Celie at first hungrily looks at her naked body: "First time I got the full sight of Shug Avery long black body with it black plum nippies, look like her mouth, I thought I had turned into a man" (53). After Celie gives Shug coffee and a cigarette, she has a compulsion to take "hold of her hand, tasting her fingers in my mouth" (55). Shug, in her capacity as a "good-enough mother," is unconsciously experienced by Celie as the maternal breast—a libidinal object. Celie's intense hunger is soon satisfied by the physical presence of this woman whose nickname, in combination with "nippies," forms a Southern expression for a pacifier. Later, Celie washes and combs Shug's hair, saving the strands that "come out in my comb. . . . I work on her like she a doll or like she Olivia—or like she mama. I comb and pat, comb and pat. First she say, hurry up and git finish. Then she melt down a little and lean back gainst my knees. That feel just right, she say. That feel like mama used to do. Or maybe not mama. Maybe grandma" (57).

Although Celie has found a "good-enough mother" in Shug, it is only when Shug can provide an extended "holding environment" that Celie can build upon the efforts of previous mother surrogates and, in bonding with Shug, complete her previously stymied psychological development. One night Shug takes the initiative and asks to sleep with Celie. When Shug asks Celie how it was making love "with your children daddy," Celie begins to tell another person for the first time about her rape and incest. Uncertain of Shug's response, Celie soon pauses: "I lay there quiet, listening to Shug breathe." After several more painful revelations, she pauses again: "Shug so quiet I think she sleep. After he through, I say, he make me finish trimming his hair. I sneak a look at Shug. Oh, Miss Celie, she say. And put her arms round me. They black and smooth and kind of glowy from the lamplight. I start to cry too. I cry and cry and cry. Seem like it all come back to me, laying there in Shug arms. How it hurt and how much I was surprise" (108–109). This bedroom scene is the beginning of Celie's working through her rape trauma with abreaction and reconstruction of the traumatic events. Shug, as a "good-enough mother," provides a "holding environment" that enables Celie to verbalize and to get in touch with long-repressed memories and feelings and work them through. Her severe dissociative state and cognitive deficiencies improve after this abreaction, as evidenced by the increasingly grammatical, stylistic, and tonal complexity of her letters.

It is also in this bedroom scene that the two women become lovers. Once again, Shug takes the initiative. After unburdening herself with words and tears, and unable consciously to recall the love of her preoedipal parents, Celie angrily says, "Nobody ever love me." Shug immediately responds: "I love you, Miss Celie. And then she haul off and kiss me on the mouth." After Celie responds with a kiss, the two kiss repeatedly—then touch—and then Celie says: "Then I feels something real soft and wet on my breast, feel like one of my little lost babies mouth." And then: "Way after while, I act like a little lost baby too" (109).

Even though Celie's sensuous "female bonding" with Shug leads to a deeply experienced and lengthy lesbian relationship between the two women, Shug continues to serve Celie as a "good-enough mother" who ministers to the unconscious developmental needs of her child. Besides "mirroring" and providing a "holding environment," Shug also remains "consistently herself" (Winnicott, *Maturational Processes* 87) and allows for moments of quiescent transitional relatedness which, according to Winnicott, are essential for the development of a stable and personal self: "It is only when [the infant experiences himself] alone (that is to say, in the presence of someone) that the infant can discover his own personal life" (34). Celie describes the first of many such moments following their first night together: "Me and Shug sound asleep. Her back to me, my arms round her waist. What it like? Little like sleeping with mama, only I can't hardly remember ever sleeping with her. Little like sleeping with Nettie, only sleeping with Nettie never feel this good. It warm and cushiony, and I feel Shug's big tits sorta flop over my arms like suds. It feel like heaven is what it feel like, not like sleeping with Mr. _____ at all" (110).

Shug occasionally acts as an "auxiliary ego" for Celie and helps her modulate states of excitement. When Shug tells Celie that Albert has been hiding Nettie's letters to her over the years, leading her to believe that her sister was dead, Celie is flooded with murderous rage and, without Shug's intervention, would have cut Albert's throat with his razor (114–115). Later, when Celie's rage toward Albert makes her sexually impotent with Shug, Shug identifies Celie's emotional state and tells her that strong emotions, such as "being mad, grief, wanting to kill somebody" (136), make one impotent. Shug then suggests that together they make Celie a pair of pants, thus giving Celie a lesson in sublimation: "A needle and not a razor in my hand, I think" (137).[11]

Shug also helps Celie to verbalize her feelings about Albert openly and to separate from him (180–183); long before they become lovers she gives Celie a lesson in and appreciation of her female reproductive organs (79–80); and her open bisexual behavior (which offends some critics)[12] and her special blend of masculine and feminine gender identity facilitates Celie's completion of her own adult sexual orientation (choice of a love object) and gender identity. When Shug takes Celie to her house in Memphis, described by Celie as "big and pink and look sort of like a barn," in order "to love you and help you get on your feet" (188, 190), she provides Celie with a literal and psychological womblike "holding environment" in which Celie flourishes. While there, Celie discovers that she has a creative and unique talent as a designer of "perfect pants," for women and men, and, with Shug's financial backing, she establishes her own clothes business, "Folks-pants, Unlimited," and thereby achieves economic independence: "Dear Nettie, I am so happy. I got love, I got work, I got money, friends, and time" (193).

But before Celie can complete her final developmental task, the achievement of an autonomous and stable sense of self, she learns that Sofia's mother has died and returns home for the funeral. As she approaches Harpo's and Sofia's house, Celie acknowledges to herself: "I feels different. Look different. Got on some dark blue pants and a white silk shirt that look righteous. Little red flat-heel slippers, and a flower in my hair. I pass Mr. _____ house and him sitting up on the porch and he didn't even know who I was" (195). When Albert walks up to Celie after the funeral, she looks "in his eyes and I see he feeling scared of me. Well, good, I think. Let him feel what I felt" (199). These internal and external changes are soon followed by an unexpected inheritance.

Sometime after returning to Memphis and Shug, Celie learns from Alphonso's wife Daisy that Alphonso is dead and that Nettie and Celie have inherited their dead parents' land and the house and dry goods store that Alphonso rebuilt. When Celie wonders what Nettie and she would sell in such a store, Shug quickly replies, "How bout pants?" (216). Celie and Shug return home to look at the property and the buildings, and Celie spends the summer getting the house ready for Nettie, her husband, Celie's grown children, Shug, and herself. When she returns home to Shug, Celie's lover and "good-enough mother" inadvertently provides her with a painful opportunity to complete her development of an autonomous and stable sense of self.

"My heart broke," Celie writes to Nettie, after hearing from Shug that she "got the hots for a boy of nineteen" (218–219). Although Shug protests that she still loves Celie and will return to her once she has had her "last fling," Celie regresses briefly, returns to *writing* about her feelings—but then is able to verbalize her love for Shug "whatever happens, whatever you do" (221). Celie finds it necessary, however, to leave Shug's house, and she returns to her own, where she undergoes a period of healthy mourning. At first Celie has little desire to live and writes Nettie that "the only thing keep me alive is watching Henrietta [Sofia's ill daughter] fight for her life" (222). She breaks into tears after telling Albert how Shug taught her how to sublimate her murderous rage for him by helping her to make her first pair of pants (223). And one of the darkest days of her life occurs when she receives both a telegram informing her that Nettie's homeward bound ship has been sunk by German mines and all of her letters written to Nettie—unopened: "I sit here in this big house by myself trying to sew, but what good is sewing gon do? What good is anything? Being alive begin to seem like a awful strain" (225). Alone and despairing, believing herself bereft of sister, adult children, and her "good-enough mother," Celie confronts her existential aloneness and struggles to complete both her mourning process and her final developmental task.

As time passes, Celie occasionally questions Shug's love: "I stand looking at my naked self in the looking glass. What would she love? I ast myself. . . . My body just any woman's body going through the changes of age. . . . My heart must be young and fresh though, it feel like it blooming blood. . . . But look at you. When Shug left, happiness desert" (229). Although she periodically receives a post card from Shug, there is no mention of her return. Celie and Albert often spend time talking about their love for Shug and sharing their happy and sad memories—an activity that furthers the mourning process. After six months have passed, Celie sums up the first part of that process:

> Well, your sister too crazy to kill herself. Most times I feels like shit but I felt like shit before in my life an what happen? I had me a fine sister name Nettie. I had me another fine woman friend name Shug. I had me some fine children growing up in Africa, singing and writing verses. The first two months was hell, though, I tell the world. But now Shug's six months is come and gone and she ain't come back. And I try to teach my heart not to want nothing it can't have.
>
> Besides, she give me so many good years. Plus, she learning new things in her new life. Now she and Germaine staying with one of her children. (235)

This extract from a letter to Nettie not only conveys the authentic voice of successful mourning but shows us that Celie is beginning to move beyond her need for a "good-enough mother" and, as a developing, autonomous, and stable self, Celie is able to express appreciation for Shug's generosity and even derive pleasure from the thought that Shug is "learning new things in her new life."

The mourning process is slow, however, and Celie is subject to a variety of contrasting thoughts and feelings about Shug: "I wish I could be traveling with her, but thank God she able to do it. Sometimes I feel mad at her. Feel like I could scratch her hair right off her head. But then I think, Shug got a right to live too. She got a right to look over the world in whatever company she choose. Just cause I love her don't take away none of her rights" (236). At times Celie regresses and unconsciously experiences Shug as the sad mother of her childhood: "What I love best bout Shug is what she been through, I say. When you look in Shug's eyes you know she been where she been, seen what she seen, did what she did. And now she know" (236). There comes a time, however, when Celie's mourning process has done its work, and she is able to consciously acknowledge and unconsciously experience Shug's separateness, uniqueness, and autonomy, as well as her own: "And then, just when I know I can live content without Shug, just when Mr. _____ done ast me to marry him again, this time in the spirit as well as in the flesh, and just after I say Naw, I still don't like frogs, but let's us be friends, Shug write me she coming home. Now. Is this life or not? *I be so calm.* If she come, I be happy. If she don't, I be content. And then I figure this the lesson I was supposed to learn" (247–248). Celie has indeed learned *"how to do like you."* Through years of "female bonding" and "good-enough mothering," Celie has, in middle age, created a mature, stable, and autonomous identity for herself; she is what Winnicott would call a "True Self."

Nettie's literary portrait, however, contrasts sharply with Celie's; literary critics usually discuss this contrast in terms of the "narrative voices" that emerge from the letters. Whereas Celie's "voice" is praised by many,[13] including one of Walker's harshest critics (Harris, "On *The Color Purple*" 156), Nettie's "voice," and her letters, have, like the novel itself, received a wide variety of negative and positive criticism. On the negative side are those who find Nettie's voice to be nondistinctive (Towers 36) and inauthentic (Robinson 2); her letters to be "often mere monologues on African history" (Watkins 7), didactic (Smith 182), "unconvincing" (Davis 53), "preachy" (McFadden 140), and "extraneous to the central concerns of the novel" (Harris, "On *The Color Purple*" 157); and her language "dull, devitalized, too correct. . . . written in 'white' missionary language" (Tucker 92). On the positive side are those who praise Nettie's and Celie's "voices" in terms of the authentic folk voice that emanates from the novel (Watkins 7; Chambers 54) and who find that Nettie's letters provide "important thematic parallels. . . [and] essential plot information" (McFadden 140), foster change in Celie (Fifer 158; Babb 114), and "add substantially to the depth and variety of the entire novel" (Tucker 91), while Nettie's language, "conventional, educated diction," bodies forth "the new self Nettie has created with her new language" (Fifer 155, 158). Thus at one extreme Towers and Robinson assert that Nettie is "essentially uncharacterized" (Towers 36) and has "no personality" (Robinson 2), and at the other extreme Fifer argues that Nettie, through mastering a new language, standard English, has created a new self for herself (158).

Whether one views Nettie's "narrative voice" or literary portrait as superficial or complex, her intellectual and educated mind contrasts vividly with the emotional intensity of her victimized older sister. In fact, Nettie gives the appearance of having overcome the traumatic incidents of their childhood and adolescence more successfully than Celie and presents herself as a healthier character throughout her letters. But is this so? I suggest that the reverse is the case: that is, that Celie, often against overwhelming odds, works toward and achieves a stable and authentic sense of self, a "True Self," and that Nettie, who is cared for and protected by Celie until she joins the black missionaries Corrine and Samuel, the adoptive parents of Celie's two children, develops in infancy the beginning of a "False Self" that is strengthened and formed by her immediate family environment and the educational system. Approaching Nettie's literary portrait in terms of Winnicott's "False Self" helps account for the divergence of critical opinion concerning the authenticity of Nettie's "voice." Should Nettie appear to be what she is not, then those critics who find her "voice" authentic have been misled by her "False Self," and those critics who find her "voice" superficial have penetrated Nettie's "False Self." Before proceeding with this developmental reading, I should like to review Winnicott's thoughts about the origin and development of the "False Self."

Winnicott believes that the "False Self" originates during the first stage of object relationships (*Maturational Processes* 145); that is, prior to the sixth month of life, before the infant has "separated off the 'not me' from the 'me'" (58). The not "good-enough mother" mirrors her own self to the infant rather than mirroring the infant back to itself, thereby making the infant perceive rather than apperceive, and it complies with mother and her needs. The infant, according to Winnicott, begins to develop "an aspect of the personality that is false (false in that what is showing is a derivative not of the individual [True Self] but of the mothering aspect of the infant-mother coupling)" (58). The adult who has a "False Self" system uses it "to hide and protect the True Self, whatever that may be" (142); the "False Self" "does [this] by compliance with environmental demands" (147). Winnicott also posits a continuum for "False Personalities": "At one extreme: the False Self sets up as real and it is this that observers tend to think is the real person.... The True Self is hidden" (142–143), while "In health: the False Self is represented by the whole organization of the polite and mannered social attitude, a 'not wearing the heart on the sleeve,' as might be said" (143). Finally, Winnicott observes that "when a False Self becomes organized in an individual who has a high intellectual potential there is a very strong tendency for the mind to become the location of the False Self" (144).[14]

When Nettie's infancy is compared with Celie's, it is obvious that each is born into a "different family" and that each has a strikingly different developmental history. Whereas Celie spends the first two years of her life in an intact, loving, traditional family with "good- enough mothering," Nettie spends the first several months of her life experiencing severe physical and emotional deprivation and the first several years complying with the emotional needs of a depressed and mentally unstable mother. Although Celie was in all probability able to offer some mothering to Nettie in the early as well as the later years, she could not have been a "good-enough mother" in Winnicott's sense. Thus it is reasonable to speculate that Nettie, in order to survive, quickly learned to comply with her environment; out of necessity she developed a "False Self" at the expense of her "True Self." The text appears to corroborate this speculation. During Nettie's adolescent years, first at home with Alphonso and later with Celie and Albert, Celie encourages Nettie "to keep at her books" (14) in order to escape her older sister's fate—and Nettie complies. When Albert decides that Nettie has to leave, Celie tells her to look up the wife of the "Reverend Mr. _____ " (26)—and Nettie complies. And when Samuel and Corrine ask Nettie if she would like to join them in their African missionary enterprise, Nettie accepts, "But only if they would teach me everything they knew to make me useful as a missionary. . . . and my real education began at that time" (124).

Several critics have observed how effectively Nettie responds to and complies with her immediate environment. Valerie Babb notes that Nettie's first letter to Celie (119) "reads in a manner consistent with Celie's oral style" and that after "her missionary employers, Corrine and Samuel, have had a hand in her education. . . Nettie's letters are rendered completely in the standard" (113). Elizabeth Fifer describes Nettie as "controlled, religious, and idealistic" (163) and draws our attention to Celie's initial "bewilderment at the new self Nettie has created with her new language: 'What with being shock, crying and blowing my nose, and trying to puzzle out words us don't know, it took a long time to read just the first two or three letters" *(158)*. Lindsey Tucker finds Nettie's letters to be "written in 'white' missionary language. Metaphorically speaking, Nettie wears her language much like she wears Corrine's clothing—without total authenticity or comfort" (92). Tucker then asserts: "In spite of a new home, a new career, and a new self, at the end of the novel, Celie has held onto one precious possession, her language. Although urged to become 'educated,' to learn to talk as the books do, she refuses to change her speech patterns by submitting to white language" (92). Restated in psychological terms, we might say that Celie will not and, in fact, cannot compromise the integrity of her "True Self," whereas Nettie's compliance with "white' missionary language" is in keeping with the protective nature of the "False Self." Nettie's "real education," it appears, is the final development of a "False Self" system that has found a home in Nettie's superior intellect.

In the next-to-last scene of *The Color Purple*, Celie's "True Self" and Nettie's "False Self," as well as their family and loved ones, are reunited. Although Trudier Harris calls this a "fairy-tale" ending ("On *The Color Purple*" 160), I believe that the reunification scene offers a psychological validity that transcends the contrivance of plot, and that this psychological validity consists in offering closure to the developmental processes that began with the sisters' births. Celie, feeling "real pleasant" as she sits "on the porch after dinner" between Albert and Shug (249), has developed a mature, autonomous, and "True" self, has been reunited with her lover Shug, and has also on an unconscious level been reunited with her preoedipal father (Albert) and mother (Shug). Just as it is appropriate that the altered Albert, who sent Nettie away thirty years before, should be the first to recognize her among a group of people who have gotten out of a car with their luggage at the end of the drive, so too is it psychologically appropriate that Celie's and Nettie's meeting should be described from the perspective of very little children:

> When Nettie's foot come down on the porch I almost die. . . . Then us both start to moan and cry. Us totter toward one nother like us use to do when us was babies. Then us feel so weak when us touch, us knock each other down. But what us care? Us sit and lay there on the porch inside each other's arms.
>
> After while, she say *Celie.*
>
> I say *Nettie.*
>
> Little bit more time pass. Us look round at a lot of peoples knees. Nettie never let go my waist. This my husband Samuel, she say, pointing up. These our children Olivia and Adam and this Adam's wife Tashi, she say.
>
> I point up at my peoples. This Shug and Albert, I say. (250)

Not only does this emotional meeting of two middle-aged sisters enable them to regress and re-experience unconsciously earlier infantile needs for each other, but their "True" and "False" selves are validated with this encounter. Nettie brings nothing to this reunion that is truly hers—including herself. Thirty years earlier, when she had sought refuge with Samuel and Corrine, they treated her like family, "Like family might have been, I mean" (121). In becoming a missionary and going to Africa, she assumes "'white' missionary language" and a professional role. And when she arrives at Celie's and her house, she is accompanied by a dead woman's husband and a living woman's grown children. In order to complete this developmental portrait of Nettie as a "False Self," Walker has her win a hollow "oedipal victory": "You may have guessed that I loved [Samuel] all along; but I did not know it. Oh, I loved him as a brother and respected him as a friend, but Celie, I love him bodily, *as a man!"* (211). Corrine's suspicion that Olivia and Adam are, in fact, Samuel's and Nettie's children is incorrect (158–159, 168–169); what she does sense, however, is Nettie's love for the oedipal father. Nettie, unlike Celie, was not traumatized at the height of the rapprochement period, when a child *needs* its mother. Therefore, she passes through that "triangular period" that Freud termed the "Oedipus complex" (roughly from two and a half to six years) as a "False Self." Celie, on the other hand, appears to have been largely unaffected by her passage through the oedipal years. Her traumatic losses at two and subsequent "soul murder" appear to have precluded the unfolding of this stage.

In contrast to Nettie, everything that Celie brings to this reunion is truly hers. As Nettie approaches, Celie, who "stand swaying, tween Albert and Shug" (250), is supported by her symbolic preoedipal family of origin as well as her lover Shug and now friend Albert. "Nettie stand swaying tween Samuel and . . . Adam" (250). Celie's "True Self," forged out of years of abuse and suffering and "female bonding," is face-to-face with Nettie's "False Self," created through compliance with the outside world in order to survive a chaotic infancy and childhood. Nettie, who appears to have everything, including husband, grown children, Celie, and her inheritance, lacks one essential thing—an authentic life. Celie, who has survived loss, "soul murder," incest, and physical and emotional abuse, has, in the process, acquired a home, a career, friends, and a lover and has developed an authentic self that enables her to live an authentic life. Celie, unlike Nettie, is able to participate in mature object relationships: as a "True Self," Celie can both successfully mourn the inevitable losses of life and go on to form new relationships and live authentically and deeply in the present moment (Winnicott, *Maturational Processes* 221, 148–149).

Although this psychoanalytic developmental reading of Walker's *The Color Purple* is limited in scope and makes no pretension to address the many aesthetic, moral, and sociological problems and issues raised by this complex and controversial work of fiction, I have illuminated several of the unconscious developmental processes that underlie Walker's presentation of "female bonding" and that facilitate Celie's search for and attainment of a mature, autonomous, and authentic sense of identity that enables her to live an authentic life. Drawing upon Winnicott's concepts of the "good-enough mother," the "mirror role of the mother," "the holding environment," and the origin of the "True Self" and the "False Self," I have traced the development of Celie's "True Self" and Nettie's "False Self" and, in the process, have addressed specific negative criticisms of the novel, such as unequal narrative voices, unrealistic character development, faulty plot, unbelievable events, and the "fairy-tale" quality of the lesbian relationship between Celie and Shug as well as Celie's and Nettie's reunion—arguing that a psychological reading of the text shows many of these negative criticisms to be spurious. Walker has given us in *The Color Purple* a brilliant psychological developmental novel (dedicated *"To the Spirit:* / Without whose assistance / Neither this book / Nor I / Would have been / Written"; Walker has "listened with the third ear" — her own unconscious). Celie's fictive narrative voice, that "speaks" to us though mute and that is never "heard" by those to whom she writes, transcends the limitations of her isolation and of the novel; as victim and survivor, Celie attests to the importance of "good-enough mothering" in the early years and to the healing power of human relationships.

NOTES

1. See especially Fifer, Babb, Chambers, Cheung, and Tucker.
2. See Prescott 68; Smith 182; McFadden 141–142; Steinem 90; Lenhart 3; Fifer 162–163; Shelton 386–387; McKenzie 54–57; Pinckney 17; Chambers 56–57; Tucker 85–90; Cheung 168; and Lewis 79–80.
3. See Deutsch 20; Ritvo; Blos; Bergman; and Dalsimer, "Introduction" 1–12.
4. For a succinct and useful summary of D. W. Winnicott's theories of psychoanalytic developmental psychology, see Khan. For a more complete study, see Davis and Walibridge.
I wish to thank James E. Marquardt, psychoanalyst and colleague, for reading an earlier version of this paper and for offering clarification of several psychoanalytic developmental concepts.
5. For Winnicott, the "mother" is the infant's "primary caretaker," and the "infant" refers to that phase of life "prior to word presentation and the use of word symbols. The corollary is that [infancy] refers to a phase in which the infant depends on maternal care that is based on maternal empathy rather than on [the] understanding of what is or could be verbally expressed" (*Maturational Processes* 40).
The terms "good-enough mother" and "primary caretaker" are, for Winnicott and other object relations theorists, not gender specific, even though in our culture the infant's primary caretaker is usually the biological mother. These terms are used to discuss the clinically observed importance of an adult person for the early psychological development of the infant. The focus of this paper is upon the importance of early object relations in the text for later change and development in adulthood, and not upon the current feminist political issues surrounding motherhood. I trust my readers will not accuse me of insensitivity to these issues.
6. See also Winnicott, *Maturational Processes* 73–74; and Mahler 3.
7. Elsewhere Winnicott writes: "If the inherited potential is to have a chance to become actual in the sense of manifesting itself in the individual's person, then the environmental provision must be adequate. It is convenient to use a phrase like 'goodenough mothering' to convey *an unidealized view* of the maternal function" (qtd. in Davis and Wallbridge 35; emphasis added).
8. Hilda S. Roliman-Branch writes: "Auxiliary mothering by older siblings supplements the mother's care and even replaces it entirely. The infant's need for attachment to a human object can be satisfied by another child" (412).
9. Shengold discusses the effects of "soul murder" upon artistic creativity in the works of three literary survivors: Dickens, Chekhov, and Kipling (181–208; 209–232; 233–283). Several critics have observed that Celie survives through the act of writing (Davis 50–52; Fifer 155–156; Chambers 59; Tucker 82–83; and Cheung 162).

10. For further psychoanalytic thinking about "core gender identity" and "gender identity," see Chodorow; Stoller, "Current Concepts" 793–796; Tyson, "Developmental Line" 61–63 and 72–84, and "Current Concepts" 796–799; and Tyson and Tyson.

11. "Paul Lewis observes that Shug twice uses humor to deflect Celie's murderous rage (*Color Purple* 134–135), and that Celie likewise uses humor to make the angry and embittered Sofia laugh for the first time "in three years" (*Color Purple* 99). He identifies it as "gallows humor" and asserts that such humor both "create[s] distance from our pain, . liberat[ing] us at least temporarily from otherwise inescapable torment" and helps further the humanity of "Miss Celie and Sofia, [and] even Albert and his foolish son Harpo" (80). I wish to thank my colleague Professor Siegfried Mandel for bringing Lewis's book to my attention.

12. See Harris, "Victimization" 9–10; and Royster 368.

13. See Watkins 7; Smith 183; McFadden 142; Fifer 155; and Chambers 54.

14. For a brilliant contemporary psychoanalytic study of the "False Self," see Miller.

Works Cited

Anillo, Ray, and Pamela Abramson. "Characters in Search of a Book." *Newsweek* 21 June 1982: p. 67.

Babb, Valerie. "*The Color Purple:* Writing to Undo What Writing Has Done." *Phylon: The Atlanta University Review of Race and Culture* 47 (1986): pp. 107–116.

Bergman, A. "On the Development of Female Identity: Issues of Mother-Daughter Interaction during the Separation-Individuation Process." Symposium on "The Many Faces of Eve." University of California at Los Angeles, Feb. 1984.

Blos, Peter. "Modifications in the Traditional Psychoanalytic Theory of Female Adolescent Development." *Adolescent Psychiatry* 8 (1980): pp. 8–24.

Chambers, Kimberly. "Right on Time: History and Religion in Alice Walker's *The Color Purple*." *CLA Journal* 31(1987): pp. 44–62.

Cheung, King-Kok. "'Don't Tell': Imposed Silences in *The Color Purple* and *The Woman Warrior*." *PMLA* 103 (1988): pp. 162–173.

Chodorow, Nancy. *The Reproduction of Mothering: Psychoanalysis and the Sociology of Gender.* Berkeley: University of California Press, 1978.

Dalsimer, Katherine. *Female Adolescence: Psychoanalytic Reflections on Literature.* New Haven: Yale University Press, 1986.

Davis, Madeleine, and David Wallbridge. *Boundary and Space: An Introduction to the Work of D. W. Winnicott.* New York: Brunner/Mazel, 1981.

Davis, Thadious M. "Alice Walker's Celebration of Self in Southern Generations." *Southern Quarterly Review* 21.4 (1983): pp. 39–53.

Deutsch, H. *The Psychology of Women.* Vol. 1. New York: Grune, 1944. 2 vols.

Fifer, Elizabeth. "The Dialect and Letters of *The Color Purple.*" *Contemporary American Women Writers.* Ed. Catherine Rainwater and William J. Scheick. Lexington: University of Kentucky Press, 1985: pp. 155–171.

Greenberg, Jay R., and Stephen A. Mitchell. *Object Relations in Psychoanalytic Theory.* Cambridge: Harvard University Press, 1983.

Harris, Trudier. "From Victimization to Free Enterprise: Alice Walker's *The Color Purple.*" *Studies in American Fiction* 14 (1986): pp. 1–17.

———. "On *The Color Purple*, Stereotypes, and Silence." *Black American Literature Forum* 18 (1984): pp. 155–161.

Herman, Judith Lewis. *Father-Daughter Incest.* Cambridge: Harvard University Press, 1981.

M. Masud R. Khan. Introduction. Winnicott, *Through Paediatrics* xi-1.

Lenhart, Georgeann. "Inspired Purple?" *Notes on Contemporary Literature* 14.3 (1984): pp. 2–3.

Lewis, Paul. *Comic Effects: Interdisciplinary Approaches to Humor in Literature.* New York: State University of New York Press, 1989.

Mahler, Margaret, Fred Pine, and Anni Bergman. *The Psychological Birth of the Human Infant: Symbiosis and Individuation.* New York: Basic, 1975.

McFadden, Margaret. Rev, of *The Color Purple*, by Alice Walker. *Magill's Literary Annual.* Ed. Frank N. Magill. Vol. 1. Englewood Cliffs, NJ: Salem, 1983: pp. 139–143. 2 vols.

McKenzie, Abilene Christian. "*The Color Purple's* Celie: A Journey of Selfhood." *Conference of College Teachers of English Studies* 51(1986): pp. 50–58.

Miller, Alice. *Prisoners of Childhood.* Trans. Ruth Ward. New York: Basic, 1981. Rpt. as *The Drama of the Gifted Child.* Trans. Ruth Ward. New York: Basic, 1986.

Pinckney, Darryl. "Black Victims, Black Villains." Rev, of *The Color Purple*, by Alice Walker; *The Color Purple*, a film by Steven Spielberg; *Reckless Eyeballing*, by Ishmael Reed. *New York Review* 29 Jan. 1987: pp. 17–20.

Prescott, Peter S. "A Long Road to Liberation." Rev, of *The Color Purple*, by Alice Walker. *Newsweek* 21 June 1982: pp. 67–68.

Ritvo, S. "Adolescent to Woman." *Journal of the American Psychoanalytic Association* 24 (1976): pp. 127–37.

Robinson, Daniel. "Problems in Form: Alice Walker's *The Color Purple.*" *Notes on Contemporary Literature* 16 (1986): p. 2.

Rollman-Branch, Hilda S. "The First Born Child, Male Vicissitudes of Preoedipal Problems." *International Journal of Psycho-Analysis* 47 (1966): pp. 404–415.

Royster, Philip M. "In Search of Our Fathers' Arms: Alice Walker's Persona of the Alienated Darling." *Black American Literature Forum* 20 (1986): pp. 347–370.

Russell, Diana E. *The Secret Trauma: Incest in the Lives of Girls and Women.* New York: Basic, 1986.

Shelton, Frank W. "Alienation and Integration in Alice Walker's *The Color Purple.*" *CLA Journal* 28 (1985): pp. 382–392.

Shengold, Leonard. *Soul Murder: The Effects of Childhood Abuse and Deprivation.* New Haven: Yale University Press, 1989.

Smith, Dinitia. "Celie, You a Tree." Rev, of *The Color Purple*, by Alice Walker. *Nation* 4 Sept. 1982: pp. 181–183.

Steinem, Gloria. "Do You Know This Woman? She Knows You: A Profile of Alice Walker." *Ms.* June 1982: pp. 36–37+.

Stern, Daniel N. *The Interpersonal World of the Infant: A View from Psychoanalysis and Developmental Psychology.* New York: Basic, 1985.

Stoller, Robert J. In "Current Concepts of the Development of Sexuality." Scientific Proceedings: Panel Report by Sara A. Vogel. *Journal of the American Psychoanalytic Association* 37 (1989): pp. 787–802.

———. "Primary Femininity." *Female Psychology: Contemporary Views.* Ed. Harold P. Blum. Spec. issue of *Journal of the American Psychoanalytic Association* 24 (1976): pp. 59–78.

Towers, Robert. "Good Men Are Hard to Find." Rev, of *The Color Purple*, by Alice Walker. *New York Review of Books* 12 Aug. 1982: pp. 35–36.

Tucker, Lindsey. "Alice Walker's *The Color Purple*: Emergent Woman, Emergent Text." *Black American Literature Forum* 22 (1988): pp. 81–95.

Tyson, Phyllis. In "Current Concepts of the Development of Sexuality." Scientific
    Proceedings: Panel Report by Sara A. Vogel. *Journal of the American Psychoanalytic
    Association* 37 (1989): pp. 787–802.
———. "A Developmental Line of Gender Identity, Gender Role, and Choice of Love
    Object." *Journal of the American Psychoanalytic Association* 30(1982): pp. 61–86.
Tyson, Phyllis, and Robert Tyson. *Psychoanalytic Theories of Development: An Integration.* New
    Haven: Yale University Press, 1990.
Walker, Alice. *The Color Purple.* New York: Washington Square, 1983.
———. "Coming in from the Cold: Welcoming the Old, Funny-Talking Ancient Ones into
    the Warm Room of Present Consciousness, Or, Natty Dread Rides Again!" National
    Writers Union. New York, Spring 1984; Black Women's Forum. Los Angeles, 17 Nov.
    1984. Rpt. in *Living by the Word.* New York: Harcourt, 1988: pp. 54–68.
———. "The Eighties and Me." *Publishers Weekly* 5 Jan. 1990: p. 21.
Watkins, Mel. "Some Letters Went to God." Rev, of *The Color Purple,* by Alice Walker. *New
    York Times Book Review* 25 July 1982: p. 7.
Winnicott, D. W. *The Maturational Processes and the Facilitating Environment.* New York:
    International Universities, 1965.
———. *Playing and Reality.* London: Tavistock, 1971.
———. *Through Paediatrics to Psycho-Analysis.* New York: Basic, 1975.

DIANE GABRIELSEN SCHOLL

With Ears to Hear and Eyes to See:
Alice Walker's Parable The Color Purple

To call *The Color Purple* a radical novel is not to make a surprising charge, considering the alarming number of critics who have protested the novel's raw language, its frank depiction of sexual expression, particularly lesbianism, and its bitter castigation of male and female sex roles. Its somewhat avant-garde epistolary narration also might earn the novel my designation of "radical," since the major portion of the letters are penned by a semi-literate black woman.

However, my claim for the radically Christian nature of the novel might meet with surprised opposition, given the vague spiritualist cast of the author's own theology and the pantheism expressed by Shug Avery in the novel's apparent theological center: "I believe God is everything. . . . Everything that is or ever was or ever will be. And when you can feel that, and be happy to feel that, you've found It" (178).[1] Indeed, Celie's letters to God give way in *The Color Purple* to her communication with her lost sister, a trade with which she seems quite happy, and her increasing self-reliance leaves her little need or inclination to continue her relationship with the Christian God of her earlier and more vulnerable days.

While the generalized awareness of God's presence in "a blade of corn" and in "the color purple" is not definitively Christian, the novel's Christianity instead rests in its qualities of extended parable, its movement through a

---

Christianity and Literature, Volume 40, Number 3 (Spring 1991): pp. 255–266.

realistically improbable sequence of narrative reversals toward a conclusion that defies realistic expectations. In fact, the world of the novel is figuratively turned upside down in the course of Celie's changing fortunes; and such radical alterations, the stuff and substance of the Gospels' paradoxical stories, inform the story of Celie with an energy that is distinctly biblical.

Readers consistently have argued that such improbable turns and reversals of fortune render the novel both unrealistic and unconvincing. Thus, Trudier Harris challenges the fundamental character changes Celie undergoes throughout the novel's unpredictable course and, in particular, takes on Alice Walker's choice of a resolution for the novel: "While the reader is inclined to feel good that Celie does survive, and to appreciate the good qualities she has, she or he is still equally skeptical about accepting the logic of a novel that posits so many changes as a credible progression for a character." Such radical changes ask "more of the reader than can reasonably be expected" (16).

Harris picks a central bone of contention with Walker, charging that in the novel "the issues are worked out at the price of realism" (6). In fact, almost immediately following its publication *The Color Purple* was attacked for its lack of verisimilitude. "Black people don't talk like that," charged a leading black women's magazine that turned down an opportunity to print excerpts from the novel (qtd. Walker, *Living* 63). Walker's essay "Coming in from the Cold" rejects this allegation, maintaining that she used the voice and language of her step-grandmother for Celie. But Walker indicates here a concern that goes well beyond the faithful recording of dialect:

> Celie's speech pattern and Celie's words reveal not only an intelligence that transforms illiterate speech into something that is, at times, very beautiful, as well as effective in conveying her sense of the world, but also what has been done to her by a racist and sexist system, and her intelligent blossoming as a human being despite her oppression demonstrates why her oppressors persist even today in trying to keep her down. For if and when Celie rises to her rightful, earned place in society across the planet, the world will be a different place, I can tell you (*Living* 64)

Walker suggests the figurative possibilities for Celie's character and for the novel as a whole, and she leads us toward a recognition of *The Color Purple*'s necessary resolution, a major transformation of Celie's place in the world and, more significantly, a transformation of the world itself. The means to this interesting but problematic resolution is parable, which defies realism's effort to convey the 'ordinary" and plausible course of events in its depiction of a topsy-turvy world where the unlikely and unpredictable are indeed most likely to happen.

The novel is most obviously the story of Celie's changing fortunes, and its central pattern displays a kinship to Victorian novels as Celie gradually overcomes the oppressive conditions of her despised situation, achieving in the end the prosperity and family security she has longed for. A black Jane Eyre? Celie seems to be one, though in moving toward its concluding re-union scene *The Color Purple* takes its readers through an even more dizzy-ing series of ironic reversals than does the nineteenth-century novel. Celie, sexually abused by her father and married against her will to the infamous Mr., learns to love the provocative blues singer Shug Avery and then herself, acquires self-esteem and financial independence as a maker of pants, becom-ing increasingly more expressive in their fabric and design, and learns to her surprise and satisfaction that her real father, lynched before she could remem-ber him, has left her a house and a dry goods store. Near the end of the novel she lacks nothing but her sister Nettie, whose letters from the mission field in Africa were long denied her by the malicious Mr. but are regained through the ministrations of wily Shug. When the steamship on which Nettie and her family have been returning to America is torpedoed during World War II, Celie's well of fortune seems to have dried up. But Nettie and her new hus-band Samuel, together with Celie's grown children whom she has not seen since her supposed "daddy" spirited them away in their infancy, are restored to Celie at the novel's close to complete her happiness.

Too good to be true? The story's outward attempt at successful res-olution is belied by the energetic tension throughout, for Celie's story is marked by narrative reversals, ironic in their defiance of expectations and often comical in their improbable and unpredictable nature. Repelled by Mr.'s insensitive sexual advances, she likens men to frogs and finds herself powerfully attracted to his mistress instead: "First time I got the full sight of Shug Avery long black body with it black plum nipples, look like her mouth, I thought I had turned into a man" (53). Shug makes no effort to hide her contempt for adoring Celie at first, but gradually she is won over by Celie's enduring kindness and becomes her lover and strongest ally, leav-ing Mr. baffled and much put out. This reversal of alliances is thoroughly in character for the novel. Celie loses her children, the unwelcome results of her "daddy's" incestuous violence, only to learn that they are alive and have been adopted by the missionaries Samuel and Corrine. Similarly, after Nettie is lost to Celie, she reappears when her withheld letters are found in Mr.'s trunk by ally Shug, letters chronicling her years spent in missionary service in the very household where the children Adam and Olivia are being reared. Nettie's letters further reveal that she and Celie share another father, the industrious storekeeper who was lynched for his success, thereby removing from the children the taint of incestuous origins and from Celie the burden of an abusive "daddy."

Such ironic reversals are the stuff of which *The Color Purple* is made. Lovesick Harpo moons after Sofia but finds he is no match for her physical strength and prepossessing size. He likes washing dishes, while she likes to chop wood. Embarrassed by his failure to control his wife as his father dominates the submissive Celie, he embarks on a marathon eating binge designed to make him Sofia's match but winds up tearful and sick, consoled in Celie's arms. When he and Sofia part, he takes up with Squeak, a diminutive shadow of her predecessor, who begins as Sofia's feisty combatant but who at the end of the story has become her loyal friend, entrusting Sofia with the care of her child while she pursues her singing career. Harpo and Sofia provide for their children and for Squeak's (she by this time has resumed her rightful name o Mary Agnes) in a large and spontaneous extended family, a considerable reversal of their first expectations of married life.

Sofia's personal fortunes shift considerably during the course of the novel, too. Jailed for attacking the mayor and his wife, behavior they find most unbecoming in a black woman, she is mercilessly beaten and sentenced to solitary confinement Due to the improbable intervention of Harpo's mistress, Squeak, she is freed to work as a maid for the mayor's wife, the job she originally refused with contempt in the scene which resulted in her jailing. Having gone to some effort to teach the mayor's wife to drive a car, Sofia is at last rewarded with Miz Millie's offer to drive her home to see her children for Christmas. But even before they set out the trip seems doomed, according to Sofia's account which Celie records in her letter:

> Well, say Sofia, I was so use to sitting up there next to her teaching her how to drive, that I just naturally clammed into the front seat.
> She stood outside on her side the car clearing her throat.
> Finally she say, Sofia, with a little laugh, This *is* the South.
> Yes ma'am, I say.
> She clear her throat, laugh some more. Look where you sitting, she say.
> I'm sitting where I always sit, I say.
> That's the problem, she say. Have you ever seen a white person and a colored sitting side by side in a car, when one of 'em wasn't showing the other one how to drive it or clean it?
> I got out the car, opened the back door and clammed in. She sat down up front. Off us traveled down the road, Miz Millie hair blowing all out the window. (102)

Relegated to passenger status in the back seat, Sofia has a short-lived Christmas. Miz Millie proves unequal to the task of backing up and clearing Jack and Odessa's yard, where Sofia's children have been staying in their mother's absence. Her frantic gear-stripping leaves the car unable to make the journey home, and Jack must drive both the mayor's wife and Sofia back in his pickup.

The crux of the story is the ironic role-shifting between Sofia and the mayor's wife. Sofia, outwardly the recipient of the mayor's charity, is obviously the most capable member of his household, secretly admired and feared by the family. Her competence is proven when she must assume the upper hand as driving instructor to Miz Millie, who nonetheless insists on changing roles back to the familiar pattern when she installs Sofia in the back seat. Ironically, the roles are reversed again by her failure to turn around in Jack and Odessa's yard, which leaves Sofia the obedient and helpful servant to the outward eye, as she sacrifices her afternoon with her children, but which makes her the silent victor as she chalks up still another instance of white incompetence and mismanagement "White folks is a miracle of affliction" (103).

It is the conspicuous nature of these ironic reversals throughout *The Color Purple* that gives the novel its qualities of parable. Such narrative turns, contrary to expectation and to precedent, suggest of course the arbitrary nature of assigned roles for men and women and for black and white people, as the characters burst the bonds of acceptable behavior. But such reversals have a deeper, unsettling effect as well: they push us beyond the comfortable assumptions of our culture-bound lives and serve to upset our certainties about the larger reality in which we live. Sofia winds up in the driver's seat, figuratively speaking, both in this episode and much later when the mayor's problem-besieged family continues to seek her advice. Celie's husband leaves behind his abusive behavior to take up women's work, emerging improbably as her confidante and not her tormentor.

Such narrative turns cause us to remember the parables, in which it is not the priest or the Levite who offer aid to the traveler set upon by robbers but the unlikely Samaritan who binds up his wounds and pays for his lodging; the prodigal son gets a warm welcome when he returns, overshadowing his dutiful brother. John Crossan in *The Dark Interval: Towards a Theology of Story* addresses the contradiction at the heart of parables, which "are meant to change, not to reassure us" (56). He characterizes parable as the opposite of myth, which has as its aim restoration of order and reconciliation. "Parable brings not peace but the sword, and parable casts fire upon the earth which receives it" (55). Is this not what The *Color* Purple, weaving craftily from one narrative reversal to another, does to us? Crossan maintains both a destructive and a creative role for parable:

> The surface function of parable is to create contradiction within a given situation of complacent security but, even more unnervingly, to

challenge the fundamental principle of reconciliation by making us
aware of the fact that we *made* up the reconciliation. Reconciliation
is no more fundamental a principle than irreconcillation. You have
built a lovely home, myth assures us; but, whispers parable, you are
right above an earthquake fault. (57)

So Celie's narrative characteristically pulls the rug out from under us, sweep-
ing away our certainties with an unsettling procession of contradictions.

But Celie's letters to God which reveal the radically changing nature of
events in her life are only part of The *Color* Purple. Nettie's letters to Celie
comprise another part, and although Nettie fails to acquire a voice the way
Celie does, never emerging as a spellbinding narrator, there is method to
her narrative inclusions. She writes from the other side of the world about a
cultural experience that is in some respects the reverse of that in which Celie
lives: most human beings are black, and white people are in the minority.
The Africans with whom Nettie lives tell a different version of the creation
story from Genesis, one which emphasizes white people as an aberration, an
interruption or reversal of the usual case, and which puts the blame on black
people for casting out their unacceptable white children, Adam and Eve. In
this embedded parable from the other side of the world, the theme of betrayal
and guilt within the human family is underscored, an ironic commentary on
the treatment Celie, Sofia, and other black characters have received at the
hands of white people throughout their lives.

Nettie's letters provide other embedded parables within the novel,
among them the story enacted for the missionaries as part of the welcoming ceremony that marks their arrival in the African village. A wealthy chief
plants cassava fields, yams, cotton, and millet to sell to white traders. He
grows increasingly greedy and soon takes over the land on which the roofleaf
grows to cultivate more crops for sale. When a storm destroys the roofs of
the village during the rainy season, villagers fall ill and die. Only after several
years have enough roofleaves grown back to adequately protect the villagers,
who continue to suffer adverse fortune due to their self-serving and now ban-
ished chief. Here again are the themes of betrayal, resulting destitution, and
culpability, described as the intrinsic story of the African village and not the
story imposed by the white oppressors alone. It is a story that suggests Mr.'s
brutal treatment of Celie on the other side of the world and also her "daddy's"
betrayal of her trust, and it serves to put such actions in a new light, causing
readers to look beyond the oppression of blacks by the white establishment as
the prevailing condition for brutality and betrayal.

Such embedded parables set in a counter-continent serve their place
within the overall parable. *The Color Purple* ends with a scene of reconciliation, a reunion that begins when Celie makes her peace with a contrite Mr.,

who has taken up sewing and housekeeping and collects seashells. More significantly for Celie, he is willing to talk about their past and attempts to understand and apologize for his excessive domination. They resume their relationship on a radically altered basis—as members of an extended family that embraces Shug, Harpo and Sofia and their combined brood, and finally Nettie, Samuel, Olivia, Adam, and the African Tasbi as well. The resolution of the novel offers us an apocalyptic vision of the "peaceable kingdom" established by human beings in search of love and justice.

But in order to establish the "peaceable kingdom" it has been necessary to turn the world figuratively upside down, to reverse roles and to subvert the structure of a society dominated by white people with the occasional complicity of black victims of oppression, such as Mr. and Celie's "daddy" Alphonso. While it might seem that all contradictions are resolved in the concluding reunion scene, in fact the existence of an exploitative and racist society, in which oppressors and victims both reveal their propensity for self-seeking and domination, sets the reconciliation firmly on an "earthquake fault." Tashi and Adam have undergone the African rite of scarification, a figurative fall from the innocence of childhood, and they know that visibly marked as they are they face an uncertain future in the American South. The problems of the world outside the reunited "family" suggest the "made-up" nature of the resolution. *The Color Purple,* then, confronts us with an ending that is not an ending, the ultimate paradox in a series of narrative paradoxes.

Much critical attention has been given to the novel's derivation from black folklore which, as Keith E. Byerman maintains, provides contemporary African-American writers "access to their racial history, not only as a content of struggles for freedom, literacy, and dignity, but also as a form of dialectical experience, practice, and belief" (2).[2] For Byerman, "folklore serves in this literature as the antithesis of closed, oppressive systems" (3); it "can be made to contradict the representations of the past and of reality offered by apologists for oppression" (4). Contemporary African-American writers tend to produce "open-ended stories which do not force a resolution on conflicts which are, both in literary and historical terms, inherently unresolvable" (9).

Byerman judges Walker's novel to be lacking when it is measured by these standards:

> Walker seeks to resolve the dialectic by making all males female (or at least androgynous), all destroyers creators, and all difference sameness. In this process, she must move outside the very conflicts that generated the sewing, the blues singing, and the voice of Celie herself. Such an effort makes sense for one who wishes to articulate a political position; resolution creates sacred, utopian space which justifies the ideology on which it is based. But this creation is in

fact another system that requires the same denial of history and difference as the order it has supplanted. To live "happily ever after," as the folk characters do in *The Color Purple*, is, ironically, to live outside the folk world" (169)

Byerman views Walker's choice of an 'allegorical" form as an effort to "transcend history," and he charges that in so doing Walker "has neutralized the historical conditions of the very folk life she values" (170).

Such an evaluation of the novel's resolution, however, seems to overlook the obvious figurative implication of the ending. Certainly *The Color Purple* fails to close with convincing realism, and indeed such a conclusion would be totally out of keeping with the highly improbable developments in the novel. Walker chooses instead to resolve the novel in a vision of peace and plenty, a vision that would be deluding as a realistic possibility (given the reader's awareness of the oppressive conditions that continue to threaten the characters) but serves to point us toward the end of history. The novel's ending is then both a false bottom and a figurative depiction of ultimate redemption.

Furthermore, the ahistorical feature of Walker's resolution which Byerman regards as its deficiency is consistent with the requirements of its nature as parable. It is in the nature of biblical parable to transcend the precise historical moment without avoiding the historical implications of story and its multiple ways of being heard and understood.[3] The biblical parables emerge from their historical context to strike the listener or reader in other contexts, and in this sense the stories are always new, never to be resolved fully but instead open and subject to shifting significance. Jesus attests to the "openness" of parable in Matthew 13:52 when he teaches his disciples: "Therefore every scribe who has been trained for the kingdom of heaven is like a householder who brings out of his treasure what is new and what is old."

Walker's sense of story, deriving from black folklore its heightened awareness of paradox and of a subversive dialectic, draws from the Bible's storytelling also, and particularly from the radical stories of the Gospels, punctuated by ironic reversals and rife with a subversive principle of contradiction and mystery as they are. Folklore shares some of the qualities of parable both in narrative structure and in the pervasive element of secrecy, the sense of hidden mystery accessible only to the initiated.

Henry Louis Gates, Jr., describes the indebtedness of African-American authors, including writers of early slave narratives and contemporary figures such as Walker, to the African traditional figure of the "signifying monkey" who interprets the Word of God and serves to baffle, mystify, and contradict in stories from African folklore. According to Gates, "signifying" in African-American culture retains a relationship to its origins in folklore, since it implies speaking with an element of "doubleness," often with an ironic or satirical intent and meaning.[4] While such "signifying" might indeed be a feature of the dialogue reported by Celie in *The Color Purple,* the most obvious way in which the novel maintains the character of a mysterious or "hidden" text is in Celie's original effort to write letters to God, letters that reveal but simultaneously conceal from the world the abuse inflicted on her by her "daddy." The letters therefore have a contradiction at their core and convey a kind of "doubleness," "signifying" themselves.

Certainly Jesus' role is characteristically that of "signifier," demonstrated in Matthew when the disciples ask him to explain his habit of speaking in parables. "To you it has been given to know the secrets of the kingdom of heaven, but to them it has not been given" (13:11), he answers them. "For to him who has will more be given, and he will have abundance; but from him who has not, even what he has will be taken away" (13:12). "This is why," he explains, "I speak to them in parables, because seeing they do not see, and hearing they do not hear, nor do they understand" (13:13). Frank Kermode characterizes the world depicted by Jesus in the book of Matthew as "a world of paradox," in which

> Jesus' followers are of more value than sparrows, yet God, who is with the sparrows when they fail (10:30), will nevertheless not prevent men from falling; for, according to the most bleakly majestic paradox of all, "He that findeth his life shall lose it: and he that loseth his life for my sake shall find it" (1439). Under this new authority the world is turned upside down; it becomes unacceptable to "the wise and prudent" and acceptable only to the simple or silly, to "babes" (11:25). Indeed, to accept it requires Ignorance of all that the new authority does not vouchsafe (11:27); yet by another disorienting paradox this apparently impossible charge becomes an easy yoke and a light burden (11:28–30). (393)

The "riddling" nature of Jesus' teachings conspires with the unpredictability of the parables to create a "world of paradox" essentially similar to Celie's world of seeming radical disorder, an improbable world of shifting meanings in which practically no one at the end occupies the same place in which he or she began.

Crossan calls parable "the dark night of story" (60), but he confers upon it the power that enables the reader's transcendence. Parables, he maintains, "shatter the deep structure of our accepted world and thereby render clear and evident to us the relativity of story itself. They remove our defenses and make us vulnerable to God. It is only in such experiences that God can touch us, and only in such moments does the kingdom of God arrive" (122). In *The Color Purple* the concluding reunion is then like the story's false bottom,

giving way after the preparatory narrative reversals to the novel's true tran-
scendent ground as it points beyond history without evading the historical
circumstances of racial violence and oppression.

Walker's writing indicates the author's commitment to a new social order.
"I believe in change: change personal, and change in society," she says in an interview. "I have experienced a revolution (unfinished, without question, but one
whose new order is everywhere on view) in the South. And I grew up—until
I refused to go—in the Methodist church, which taught me that Paul *will*
sometimes change on the way to Damascus, and that Moses—that beloved old
man—went through so many changes he made God mad" (*Search* 252).

Yet she has resisted a narrow didacticism in *The Color Purple*, an over-
stated and obvious endorsement of social change, and certainly some of her
critics who maintain that she subjugates the art of storytelling to her ideology
in this novel have overlooked the tension, the dialectic, the intentional paradox both of her narrative turns and of her improbable resolution. Her biblical
heritage is one shaping influence on her art in this powerful novel, and it is
this same heritage that prepared her to read the fiction of another Georgia
author, Flannery O'Connor. In Walker's essay "Beyond the Peacock," a tribute
to O'Connor, she characterizes the author she admires:

> She believed in all the mysteries of her faith. And yet, she was
> incapable of writing dogmatic or formulaic stories. No religious
> tracts, nothing haloed softly in celestial light, not even any
> happy endings, It has puzzled some of her readers and annoyed
> the Catholic Church that in her stories not only does good not
> triumph, it is not usually present. Seldom are there choices, and
> God never intervenes to help anyone win. To O'Connor, in fact,
> Jesus was God, and he won only by losing. (*Search* 15)

O'Connor, like Walker, understood the essential role of parable as an agent
of change, of transfiguring redemption. The reader need only think of the
ironic reversals in a story such as "Parker's Back" or the shifting fortunes
in "The Displaced Person." It is the capacity of parable to unsettle our
complacency, to prevent our ossification, to open up new possibilities that
usher in the kingdom of God. Walker's methodical destruction of our social
certainties is her means to the revelation, her provocative challenge issued
in the spirit and the narrative technique of the Gospels. In extending this
challenge she effects a transcendence of history by appearing to resolve the
conflicts at the heart of *The Color Purple*, but only so that her parable can
unsettle us more profoundly, striking at the roots of our historical circum-
stance as we, like the householder in Matthew 13, uncover in the treasure
"what is new and what is old."

NOTES

1. Walker describes her own religious views in a 1973 interview "Although I am constantly involved, internally, with religious questions—and I seem to have spent all of my life rebelling against the church and other people's interpretations of what religion is—the truth is probably that I don't believe there is a God, although I would like to believe it. Certainly I don't believe there is a God beyond nature. The world is God. Man is God. So is a leaf or a snake." But she goes on to qualify her opinion: "Like many, I waver in my convictions about God, from time to time. In my poetry I seem to be for; in my fiction, against" (*Search* 265). Drawing on the volume *In Love and Trouble: Stories of Black Women,* Walker discusses several contradictory ways in which Christianity appears in her work: "In other stories, I am interested in Christianity as an imperialist tool used against Africa ('Diary of an African Nun') and in voodoo used as a weapon against oppression ('The Revenge of Hannah Kernhuff')" (*Search* 266).

One persuasive reading of *The Color Purple* emphasizes the novel's derivation from African-American folk magic, suggesting that in Walker's taking the role of "medium" she is identifying with black women of her lineage as the source of her creative power. Pryse thus discusses "conjuring" in its relationship to the oral storyteller's art "Like [Zora Neale] Hurston, Walker also finds 'magic' in combining folk and female material, transforming the power of the root-doctor's conjure" (15).

Despite Walker's stated resistance to Christianity and the popular perception that she chooses other "religious" systems of belief and inspiration, one story stands out from the collection *In Love and Trouble* for its radically Christian nature. The old black woman in "The Welcome Table" commits the social indiscretion of going to the white people's church on a Sunday morning. When she fails to take the polite hints extended to her, she is ejected from the congregation and ultimately walks down the road with a benevolent Jesus to her peaceful death. In its many ironic reversals of social roles, expectations, and events, this story uses the formal structure of parable also and suggests its derivation from the biblical heritage of Walker's church-going childhood. The title is from a spiritual.

2. Byerman's introduction discusses black writers emerging in the late 1960s who shaped what he terms a new black aesthetic in their use of African-American folklore. He refers to African-American culture as a "dialectic," recognized by W. E. B. DuBois as "double-consciousness." Out of this "dialectic" emerged "a folk life emphasizing both faith and rebellion, integrity and trickster behavior, accompanied by mother-wit and stubborn hope. Characterized by a desire for freedom, it also recognizes that the struggle is long and the enemy formidable. It is, in other words, a double-faced culture, looking to the outside to measure the opposition and to the inside to gain sustenance for both the specific historical struggle and the universal pains and pleasures of human life" (2).

3. See Bruns's discussion of the significance of historical context in biblical hermeneutics.

4. Gates points to Walker's radical effort to "step outside the white hermeneutical circle" (258) represented by a white God toward a black female tradition. He discusses several ways in which *The Color Purple* "signifies," notably in Walker's "ironic use of a speakerly language which no person can ever speak, because it exists only in a written text." The central irony is that "people who speak dialect *think* that they are saying standard English words; when they write the words that they speak as 'dis' or 'dat,' therefore, they spell 'this' and 'that'" (255).

Works Cited

Bruns, Gerald L. "Midrash and Allegory: The Beginnings of Scriptural Interpretation." *The Literary Guide to the Bible*. Ed. Robert Alter and Frank Kermode. (Cambridge: Belknap-Harvard University Press, 1987): pp. 625–646.

Byerman, Keith E. *Fingering the Jagged Grain: Tradition and Form in Recent Black Fiction*. Athens: University of Georgia Press, 1985.

Crossan, John. *The Dark Interval: Towards a Theology of Story*. Niles: Argus, 1975.

Gates, Henry Louis, Jr. *The Signifying Monkey: A Theory of Ape-American Literary Criticism*. New York: Oxford University Press, 1988.

Harris, Trudier. "From Victimization to Free Enterprise: Alice Walker's *The Color Purple*." *Studies in American Fiction* 14 (1986): pp. 1–17.

Kermode, Frank. *The Genesis of Secrecy: On the Interpretation of Narrative*. Cambridge: Harvard University Press, 1979.

———. "Matthew." *The Literary Guide to the Bible*. Ed. Robert Alter and Frank Kermode. (Cambridge: Belknap-Harvard University Press, 1987): pp. 387–401.

Pryse, Marjorie. "Zora Neale Hurston, Alice Walker, and the 'Ancient Power' of Black Women." *Conjuring: Black Women, Fiction, and Literary Tradition*. (Bloomington: Indiana University Press, 1985): pp. 1–24.

Walker, Alice. *The Color Purple*. New York: Washington Square, 1983.

———. *In Love and Trouble: Stories of Black Women*. New York: Harcourt, 1973.

———. *In Search of Our Mothers' Gardens*. New York: Harcourt, 1983.

———. *Living by the Word Selected Writings, 1973–1987*. New York: Harcourt, 1988.

LINDA SELZER

Race and Domesticity in The Color Purple

An important juncture in Alice Walker's *The Color Purple* is reached when Celie first recovers the missing letters from her long-lost sister Nettie. This discovery not only signals the introduction of a new narrator to this epistolary novel but also begins the transformation of Celie from writer to reader. Indeed, the passage in which Celie struggles to puzzle out the markings on her first envelope from Nettie provides a concrete illustration of both Celie's particular horizon of interpretation and Walker's chosen approach to the epistolary form:

> Saturday morning Shug put Nettie letter in my lap. Little fat queen of England stamps on it, plus stamps that got peanuts, coconuts, rubber trees and say Africa. I don't know where England at. Don't know where Africa at either. So I still don't know where Nettie at. (102)

Revealing Celie's ignorance of even the most rudimentary outlines of the larger world, this passage clearly defines the "domestic" site she occupies as the novel's main narrator.[1] In particular, the difficulty Celie has interpreting this envelope underscores her tendency to understand events in terms of personal consequences rather than political categories. What matters about

---

African American Review, Volume 29, Number 1 (Spring 1995): pp. 67–82. © 1995 Linda Selzer.

not knowing "where Africa at"—according to Celie—is not knowing "where Nettie at." By clarifying Celie's characteristic angle of vision, this passage highlights the intensely personal perspective that Walker brings to her tale of sexual oppression—a perspective that accounts in large part for the emotional power of the text.

But Walker's privileging of the domestic perspective of her narrators has also been judged to have other effects on the text. Indeed, critics from various aesthetic and political camps have commented on what they perceive as a tension between public and private discourse in the novel.[2] Thus, in analyzing Celie's representation of national identity, Lauren Berlant identifies a separation of "aesthetic" and "political" discourses in the novel and concludes that Celie's narrative ultimately emphasizes "individual essence in false opposition to institutional history" (868). Revealing a very different political agenda in his attacks on the novel's womanist stance, George Stade also points to a tension between personal and public elements in the text when he criticizes the novel's "narcissism" and its "championing of domesticity over the public world of masculine power plays" (266). Finally, in praising Walker's handling of sexual oppression, Elliott Butler-Evans argues that Celie's personal letters serve precisely as a "textual strategy by which the larger African-American history, focused on racial conflict and struggle, can be marginalized by its absence from the narration" (166).

By counterposing personal and public discourse in the novel, these critics could be said to have problematized the narrative's domestic perspective by suggesting that Walker's chosen treatment of the constricted viewpoint of an uneducated country woman—a woman who admits that she doesn't even know "where Africa at"—may also constrict "the novel's ability to analyze issues of "race" and class.[3] Thus Butler-Evans finds that Celie's "private life preempts the exploration of the public lives of blacks" (166), while Berlant argues that Celie's family-oriented point of view and modes of expression can displace race and class analyses to the point that the "nonbiological abstraction of class relations virtually disappears" (833). And in a strongly worded rejection of the novel as "revolutionary literature," bell hooks charges that the focus upon Celie's sexual oppression ultimately deemphasizes the "collective plight of black people" and "invalidates . . . the racial agenda" of the slave narrative tradition that it draws upon ("Writing" 465).[4] In short, to many readers of *The Color Purple*, the text's ability to expose sexual oppression seems to come *at the expense of* its ability to analyze issues of race and class.[5]

But it seems to me that an examination of the representation of race in the novel leads to another conclusion: Walker's mastery of the epistolary form is revealed precisely by her ability to maintain the integrity of Celie's and Nettie's domestic perspectives even as she simultaneously undertakes an extended critique of race relations, and especially of racial integration. In particular, Walker's domestic novel engages issues of race and class through two important narrative strategies: the development of an embedded narrative line that offers a post-colonial perspective on the action, and the use of "family relations"—or kinship—as a carefully elaborated textual trope for race relations. These strategies enable Walker to foreground the personal histories of her narrators while placing those histories firmly within a wider context of race and class.

Both the novel's so-called "restriction of focus to Celie's consciousness" (Butler-Evans 166–167) and one way in which Walker's narratology complicates that perspective are illustrated by the passage quoted above. Celie's difficulty interpreting the envelope sent by Nettie at first only seems to support the claim that her domestic perspective "erases" race and class concerns from the narrative. But if this short passage delineates Celie's particular angle of vision, it also introduces textual features that invite readers to resituate her narration within a larger discourse of race and class. For where Celie sees only a "fat little queen of England," readers who recognize Queen Victoria immediately historicize the passage. And if the juxtaposition of the two stamps on the envelope—England's showcasing royalty, Africa's complete with rubber trees—suggests to Celie nothing but her own ignorance, to other readers the two images serve as a clear reminder of imperialism. Thus Africa, mentioned by name for the first time in this passage, enters the novel already situated within the context of colonialism. Importantly, Walker remains true to Celie's character even as she recontextualizes the young woman's perspective, because the features of the envelope Celie focuses upon are entirely natural ones for her to notice, even though they are politically charged in ways that other features would not be (for example, Celie night have been struck by more purely personal—and more conventional—details, such as the familiar shape of her sister's handwriting). Embedded throughout *The Color Purple*, narrative features with clear political and historical associations like these complicate the novel's point of view by inviting a post-colonial perspective on the action and by creating a layered narrative line that is used for different technical effects and thematic purposes.[6] That Celie herself is not always aware of the Full political implications of her narration (although she becomes increasingly so as the novel progresses) no more erases the critique of race and class From the text than Huck's naïveté in *Huckleberry Finn* constricts that work's social criticism to the boy's opinions. This individual letter from Nettie thus provides readers with a textual analogue for the novel's larger epistolary form, illustrating one way in which the novel's domestic perspective is clearly "stamped" with signs of race and class.

But it is not only through such narrative indirection and recontextualization that the novel engages issues of race and class. Walker's domestic narrative undertakes a sustained analysis of race through the careful development of family relationships—or kinship—as an extended textual trope for race relations. Any attempt to oppose political and personal discourses in the novel collapses when one recognizes that the narrative adopts the discourse of family relations both to establish a "domestic ideal" for racial integration and to problematize that ideal through the analysis of specific integrated family groupings in Africa and America.

I. "She says an African daisy and an English daisy are both flowers, but totally different kinds"

Important throughout the narrative, the kinship trope for race relations is articulated most explicitly late in the novel when a mature Celie and a reformed Albert enjoy some communal sewing and conversation. Celie herself raises the issue of racial conflict by drawing on the Olinka "Adam" story that has been handed down to her through Nettie's letters. Beginning with the explanation that ". . . white people is black peoples children" (231), the Olinka narrative provides an analysis of race relations expressed explicitly in terms of kinship.

According to the Olinka creation narrative, Adam was not the first man but the first white man born to an Olinka woman to be cast out for his nakedness—or for being "colorless" (231). The result of this rejection was the fallen world of racial conflict, since the outcast children were, in Celie's words, "so mad to git throwed out and told they was naked they made up they minds to crush us wherever they find us, same as they would a snake." Offered specifically as an alternative to the Judeo-Christian account of Adam, this parable also offers readers an alternative account of Original Sin—defined not in terms of appropriating knowledge or resisting authority but precisely in terms of breaking kinship bonds: "What they did, these Olinka peoples, was throw out they own children, just cause they was a little different" (232). Significantly, by retelling the Olinka narrative, Celie is able to express naturally some rather sophisticated ideas concerning the social construction of racial inferiority, since the myth defines that inferiority as a construct of power relations that will change over time. For the Olinka believe that someday the whites will "kill off so much of the earth and the colored that everybody gon hate them just like they hate us today. Then they will become the new serpent" (233).

The Olinka creation narrative also raises a question central to the novel's larger design: Is progress in race relations possible? Some Olinka, notes Celie, answer this question by predicting that the cycle of discrimination will repeat itself endlessly, that ". . . life will just go on and on like this forever," with first one race in the position of the oppressor and then the other. But others believe that progress in racial harmony is possible—that Original Sin may be ameliorated-through a new valorization of kinship bonds: ". . . the only way to stop making somebody the serpent is for everybody to accept everybody else as a child of God, or one mother's children, no matter what they look like or how they act" (233).[7] These latter Olinka, then, express a *domestic ideal* for race relations, one that counters the sin of discrimination—based on an ideology of essential difference—with an ethic of acceptance that is grounded upon recognition of relation, or kinship.

But the universalist ethos of the domestic ideal for race relations is put to the test by the larger narrative's development of historically situated, integrated kinship groupings in both Africa and America. Of particular importance are two family groupings: the white missionary Doris Baines and her black African grandchild in Africa, and Sofia and her white charge Miss Eleanor Jane in America. In both cases the specific integrated domestic groupings serve to expose and to critique the larger pattern of racial integration found in their respective countries.

Nettie meets Doris and her adopted grandson on a trip from Africa to seek help for the recently displaced Olinka in England, a trip Nettie calls "incredible" precisely because of the presence of an integrated family on board ship: It was "impossible to ignore the presence of an aging white woman accompanied by a small black child. The ship was in a tither. Each day she and the child walked about the deck alone, groups of white people falling into silence as they passed" (193). Compared to the overtly racist actions of the other whites who ostracize Doris and her grandson, The English missionary's relationship with the boy at first seems in keeping with the ethic of treating all people as "one mother's children." Indeed, Doris describes her years as the boy's "grandmamma" as "the happiest" years of her life (196). Furthermore, Doris's relationship to the African villagers also seems preferable to that of other white missionaries because, rather than wanting to convert "the heathen," she sees "nothing wrong with them" in the first place.

But the relationship between the white woman and her African grandson is actually far from ideal, and Nettie's letters subtly question the quality of their "kinship." If the boy seems "fond of his grandmother"—and, Nettie adds, "used to her"—he is also strangely reticent in her presence and reacts to Doris's conversation with "soberly observant speechlessness" (196). In contrast, the boy opens up around Adam and Olivia, suggesting that he may feel more at home with the transplanted black Americans than with his white grandmother.[8] Indeed, the boy's subdued behavior around his grandmother raises questions about the possibility of kinship across racial lines, while his ease with the black Americans suggests that feelings of kinship occur almost spontaneously within racial groups.

The nature of Doris's honorary "kinship" with the Akwee villagers is questioned more seriously still, beginning with her reasons for taking up missionary work in the first place. As a young woman Doris decided to become

a missionary not out of a desire to help others but in order to escape the rar-
efied atmosphere of upper-class England and the probability of her eventual
marriage to one of her many "milkfed" suitors, "each one more boring than
the last" (194). Although Doris describes her decision to go to Africa as an
attempt to escape the stultifying roles available to women in English society,
it is important to note that Nettie does not take Doris's hardships very seriously and draws upon fairytale rhetoric to parody the woman's upper-class
tribulations: "She was born to great wealth in England. Her father was Lord
Somebody or Other. They were forever giving or attending boring parties that
were not fun."[9] From Nettie's perspective as a black woman familiar with the
trials of the displaced Olinka, Doris's aristocratic troubles seem small indeed,
and Nettie further trivializes the white woman's decision to become a missionary by emphasizing that the idea struck Doris one evening when she "was
getting ready for yet another tedious date" (194).

The self-interest that prompts Doris to become a missionary also characterizes the relationship she establishes with the Akwee upon her arrival
in Africa. There she uses her wealth to set up an ostensibly reciprocal arrangement that in fact reflects her imperial power to buy whatever she wants:
"Within a year everything as far as me and the heathen were concerned ran
like clockwork. I told them right off that their souls were no concern of mine,
that I wanted to write books and not be disturbed. For this pleasure I was prepared to pay. Rather handsomely." Described as a mechanism that runs "like
clockwork," Doris's relationship to the Akwee clearly falls short of the maternal ideal for race relations expressed in the Olinka myths. In fact, Doris's
relationship to the villagers is decidedly *pa*ternal from the outset, since her
formal kinship with the Akwee begins when she is presented with "a couple
of wives" (195) in recognition for her contributions to the village.[10] The fact
that she continues to refer to the Olinka as "the heathen" in her discussions
with Nettie implies that, in spite of her fondness for her grandson, Doris never overcomes a belief in the essential "difference" of the Africans attributed
to her by the Missionary Society in England: "She thinks they are an entirely
different species from what she calls Europeans. . . . She says an African daisy
and an English daisy are both flowers, but totally different kinds" (115). By
promoting a theory of polygenesis opposed to the Olinkan account of racial
origins, Doris calls into question her own ability to treat the Akwee as kin.
The true nature of her "reciprocal" relationship with the Akwee is revealed
when she unselfconsciously tells Nettie that she believes she can save her villagers from the same displacement the Olinka suffered: "I am a very wealthy
woman," says Doris, "and I *own* the village of Akwee" (196).

Stripped of both the religious motivation of the other missionaries and
the overt racism of the other whites, Doris Baines through her relationship with
the Akwee lays bare the hierarchy of self-interest and paternalism that sets the

pattern for race relations in larger Africa. Indeed, from the moment that young Nettie first arrives in Africa she is surprised to find whites there "in droves," and her letters are filled with details suggestive of the hegemony of race and class. Nettie's description of Monrovia is a case in point. There she sees "bunches" of whites and a presidential palace that "looks like the American white house" (119). There Nettie also discovers that whites sit on the country's cabinet, that black cabinet members' wives dress like white women, and that the black president himself refers to his people as "natives"—as Nettie remarks, "It was the first time I'd heard a black man use that word" (120). Originally established by ex-slaves who returned to Africa but who kept "close ties to the country that bought them" (117), Monrovia clearly reveals a Western influence in more than its style of architecture, and its cocoa plantations provide the colonial model of integration that defines the white presence elsewhere in Africa—from the port town "run by a white man" who rents out "some of the stalls . . . to Africans" (127) all the way up to the governor's mansion where "the white man in charge" (144) makes the decision to build the road that ultimately destroys the Olinka village. Indeed, the later displacement of the Olinka villagers by he English roadbuilders—the main action in the African sections of *The Color Purple*—simply recapitulates the colonial process of integration already embedded in Nettie's narrative of her travels through the less remote areas of Africa.

From her eventual vantage point within the Olinka's domestic sphere, Nettie becomes a first-hand witness to this process of colonization-a process in which she and the other black missionaries unwittingly participate. For although Nettie's reasons for going to Africa differ from Doris Baines's in that they, like those of the other black missionaries, include a concern for the "people from whom [she] sprang" (Ill), she is trained by a missionary society that is "run by white people" who "didn't say a thing about caring about Africa, but only about duty" (115). Indeed, missionary work is tied to national interest from the time Nettie arrives in England to prepare for the trip to Africa:

> . . . the English have been sending missionaries to Africa and India and China and God knows where all, for over a hundred years. And the things they have brought back! We spent a morning in one of their museums and it was packed with jewels, furniture, fur, carpets, swords, clothing, even *tombs* from all the countries they have been. From Africa they have *thousands* of vases, jars, masks, bowls, baskets, statues—and they are all so beautiful it is hard to imagine that the people who made them don't still exist. And yet the English assure us they do not. (116–117)

Charting the course of empire through a catalogue of the material culture appropriated by missionaries from "all the countries they have been" (and, chillingly, from peoples who no longer exist), this passage brilliantly under-scores Walker's ability to maintain the integrity of the narrative's personal perspective—here that of a young girl's wonder at her first glimpse into the riches of her African heritage—even as she simultaneously invites readers to resituate that perspective in a wider context of race and class. In fact, throughout the African sections of the novel, Walker's embedded narrative enables readers to sympathize with the hopes and disappointments of the black missionaries while it simultaneously exposes the limitations of their point of view.

This narrative complexity becomes especially important in the passages concerning Samuel and Corrine's Victorian aunts, Theodosia and Althea, whom the narrative asks readers both to sympathize with and to judge harsh-ly. On the one hand, as representatives of a group of black women missionar-ies who achieved much against great odds, the narrative asks readers to see these women and their accomplishments as "astonishing":

> . . . no sooner had a young woman got through Spelman Seminary than she began to put her hand to whatever work she could do for her people, anywhere in the world. It was truly astonishing. These very polite and proper young women, some of them never having set foot outside their own small country towns, except to come to the Seminary, thought nothing of packing up for India, Africa, the Orient. Or for Philadelphia or New York. (199)

On the other hand, the narrative levies its harshest criticism of mission-ary work not against the white missionary Doris Baines but against Aunt Theodosia—and particularly against the foolish pride she takes in a medal given to her by King Leopold for "service as an exemplary missionary in the King's colony." The criticism is levied by a young "DuBoyce," who attends one of Aunt Theodosia's "at homes" and exposes her medal as the emblem of the Victorian woman's "unwitting complicity with this despot who worked to death and brutalized and eventually exterminated thousands and thousands of African peoples" (200). Like the other political allusions embedded in Walker's narrative, the appearance of Du Bois in Aunt Theodosia's domes-tic sphere recontextualizes Nettie's narrative, and his comments serve as an authoritative final judgment upon the entire missionary effort in Africa.

By structuring Nettie's letters around missionary work, then, Walker achieves much. First, that work provides Nettie and the other black mission-aries with a practical and credible pathway into the African domestic sphere. Second, the institutional, historical, and ideological connections between phi-lanthropy and colonialism enable Walker to use that domestic sphere and the example of Doris Baines's integrated family to expose the missionary pattern of integration in larger Africa. Finally, the embedded narrative line enables Walker to remain true to her characters even as she anatomizes the hierarchy of race and class that is first pictured in miniature on Nettie's envelope.

II. "He said he wouldn't do it to me if he was my uncle"

If the integrated family of Doris Baines and her adopted African grandson exposes the missionary pattern of integration in Africa as one based on a false kinship that in fact *denies* the legitimacy of kinship bonds across racial lines, the relationship between Miss Sophia and her white charge, Miss Eleanor Jane, serves an analogous function for the American South. Sophia, of course, joins the mayor's household as a maid under conditions more overtly racist than Doris Baines's adoption of her Akwee family: Because she answers "hell no" (76) to Miss Millie's request that she come to work for her as a maid, Sophia is brutally beaten by the mayor and six policeman and is then imprisoned. Forced to do the jail's laundry and driven to the brink of madness, Sophia finally becomes Miss Millie's maid in order to escape prison. Sophia's violent confrontation with the white officers obviously foregrounds issues of race and class, as even critics who find these issues marginalized elsewhere in *The Color Purple* have noted. But it is not only through Sophia's dramatic *public* battles with white men that her story dramatizes issues of race and class. Her domestic relationship with Miss Eleanor Jane and the other members of the mayor's family offers a more finely nuanced and extended critique of racial integration, albeit one that has often been overlooked.[11]

Like Doris Baines and her black grandson, Sophia and Miss Eleanor Jane appear to have some genuine family feelings for one another. Since Sophia "practically . . . raise[s]" (222) Miss Eleanor Jane and is the one sympathetic person in her house, it is not surprising that the young girl "dote[s] on Sophia" and is "always stick[ing] up for her" (88), or that, when Sophia leaves the mayor's household (after fifteen years of service), Miss Eleanor Jane continues to seek out her approval and her help with the "mess back at the house" (174). Sophia's feelings for Miss Eleanor are of course more ambivalent. When she first joins the mayor's household, Sophia is completely indifferent to her charge, "wonder[ing] why she was ever born" (88). After rejoining her own family, Sophia resents Miss Eleanor Jane's continuing intrusions into her family life and suggests that the only reason she helps the white girl is because she's "on parole. . . . Got to act nice" (174). But later Sophia admits that she does feel "something" for Miss Eleanor Jane "because of all the people in your daddy's house, you showed me some human kindness" (225).

Whatever affection exists between the two women, however, has been shaped by the perverted "kinship" relation within which it grew—a relationship the narrative uses to expose plantation definitions of kinship in general and to explode the myth of the black mammy in particular. Separated from her own family and forced to join the mayor's household against her will, living in a room under the house and assigned the housekeeping and childraising duties, Sophia carries out a role in the mayor's household which clearly recalls that of the stereotypical mammy on the Southern plantation. However, as someone who prefers to build a roof on the house while her husband tends the children, Sophia seems particularly unsuited for that role. And that is precisely the narrative's point: Sophia is entirely unsuited for the role of mammy, but whites—including and perhaps especially Miss Eleanor Jane—continually *expect* her to behave according to their cultural representations of the black mother. It is, in fact, these expectations that get Sophia into trouble in the first place, for when Miss Millie happens upon Sophia's family and sees her children so "clean" (76), she assumes that Sophia would make a perfect maid and that Sophia would like to come and work in her household. Similarly, Miss Eleanor Jane assumes that Sophia must return her family feelings in kind, without considering Sophia's true position in her household. The young white woman's stereotypical projections become clear when she can't understand why Sophia doesn't "just love" her new son, since, in her words, "all other colored women I know love children" (224–225).

An historical appropriation of domestic discourse for political ends, descriptions of the black mammy were used by apologists for slavery to argue that the plantation system benefited the people whom it enslaved by incorporating supposedly inferior blacks into productive white families.[12] And Sophia explicitly ties her employers to such plantation definitions of racial difference: "They have the nerve to try to make us think slavery fell through because of us. . . . Like us didn't have sense enough to handle it. All the time breaking hoe handles and letting the mules loose in the wheat" (89). But through Sophia's experience in the mayor's household, the narrative demonstrates that it is Miss Millie, the mayor's wife, who is actually incompetent—who must be taught to drive by Sophia, for example, and who even then can't manage a short trip by herself. Thus, when she suddenly decides to drive Sophia home for a visit, Miss Millie stalls the car and ruins the transmission, the mistress unable to master driving in reverse. Too afraid of black men to allow one of Sophia's relatives to drive her back home alone, Miss Millie reveals her childlike dependence upon Sophia, who must cut short her first visit with her children in five years to ride home with the distraught white woman. Sophia's position as domestic within the mayor's household thus enables Walker to subvert the discourse of plantation kinship by suggesting that it actually supports a group of people who are themselves incompetent or, in Sophia words, "backward, . . . clumsy, and unlucky" (89).

Predicated on this plantation model of integration, relations between whites and blacks throughout the American South reveal a false kinship not unlike that of Doris Baines and the Akwee. But in this instance the false kinship is doubly perverse because it conceals an elaborate network of actual kinship connections. Thus Miss Eleanor Jane's husband feels free to humor Sophia by referring to the importance of black mammies in the community—". . . everybody around here raise by colored. That's how come we turn out so well" (222)—while other white men refuse to recognize the children they father with black women. As Celie says of Mr. _____'s son Bub, he "look so much like the Sheriff, he and Mr. _____ almost on family terms"; that is, "just so long as Mr. _____ know he colored" (76–77). Like the apologists for slavery, then, the Southern whites in *The Color Purple* keep alive a counterfeit definition of family while denying the real ties that bind them to African Americans.

In fact, the underlying system of kinship that exists in the American South has more to do with white uncles than black mammies, as is clear from the scene in which Sophia's family and friends consider various stratagems for winning her release from prison. By asking, "Who the warden's black kinfolks?" (80), Mr. _____ reveals that kinship relations between whites and blacks are so extensive in the community that it may be assumed that *someone* will be related by blood to the warden. That someone, of course, is Squeak. Hopeful that she will be able to gain Sophia's release from the warden on the basis of their kinship, the others dress Squeak up "like she a white woman" with instructions to make the warden "see the Hodges in you" (82). In spite of the fact that the warden does recognize Squeak as kin "the minute [she] walk[s] through the door" (83)—or perhaps *because* he recognizes her—the warden rapes Squeak, denying their kinship in the very act of perverting it. As Squeak herself recounts, "He say if he was my uncle he wouldn't do it to me" (85). Both an intensely personal and highly political act, Squeak's rape exposes the denial of kinship at the heart of race relations in the South and underscores the individual and institutional power of whites to control the terms of kinship—and whatever power those definitions convey—for their own interests.[13]

It is specifically as an act of resistance to this power that Sophia comes to reject Miss Eleanor Jane's baby and thereby to challenge the Olinka kinship ideal for race relations. From the time her son is born, Miss Eleanor Jane continually tests out Sophia's maternal feelings for him, "shoving Reynolds Stanley Earl in her face" almost "every time Sofia turn[s] around" (223). When an exasperated Sophia finally admits that she doesn't love the baby, Miss Eleanor Jane accuses her of being "unnatural" and implies that Sophia should accept her son because he is "just a little baby!" (225)—an innocent who, presumably, should not be blamed for the racist sins of his fathers. From Sophia's vantage point as a persecuted black woman, however, Reynolds Stanley is not "just a sweet, smart, cute, *innocent* little baby boy." He is in fact the grandson and namesake of the man who beat her brutally in the street, a man whom he also resembles physically. A "white something without much hair" with "big stuck open eyes" (223), Reynolds Stanley also takes after his father, who is excused from the military to run the family cotton gin while Sophia's own boys are trained for service overseas. To Sophia, Reynolds Stanley is both the living embodiment of and literal heir to the system that oppresses her: "He can't even walk and already he in my house messing it up. Did I ast him to come? Do I care whether he sweet or not? Will it make any difference in the way he grow up to treat me what I think?" (224). Reminding Miss Eleanor Jane of the real social conditions that separate her from Reynolds Stanley in spite of his "innocence," Sophia articulates a strong position counter to the Olinka kinship ethic of treating everyone like one mother's children: ". . . all the colored folks talking bout loving everybody just ain't looked hard at what they thought they said" (226).

In subverting the plantation model of kinship in general and the role of mammy that it assigns to black women in particular, then, Sophia's position as an unwilling domestic in the mayor's household underscores the importance of the personal point of view to the novel's political critique of race relations. Indeed, the personal point of view of *The Color Purple* is central to its political message: It is precisely the African American woman's *subjectivity* that gives the lie to cultural attempts to reduce her—like Sophia—to the role of the contented worker in a privileged white society.[14]

III. "White people off celebrating their independence. . . . Us can spend the day celebrating each other"

The Color Purple closes with a celebration of kinship, its concluding action composed of a series of family reunions: Sophia patches things up with Harpo; Shug visits her estranged children (for the first time in thirty years); and the novel's two narrators, Celie and Nettie, are joyfully and tearfully reunited. Even Albert and Celie are reconciled, his change of heart signaled by his earning the right to have his first name written. Coming after Celie has achieved both economic independence and emotional security, the reunions at the end of *The Color Purple* testify to the importance of kinship to the happiness of every individual. Appropriately, then, when the two sisters fall into one another's arms at last, each identifies her kin: Nettie introduces her husband and the children, and Celie's first act is to "point up at [her] peoples . . . Shug and Albert" (243). But in addition to suggesting that the individual realizes her full potential only *within* the supporting bonds of a strong kinship group (no matter how unconventionally that group might be defined), the conclusion to *The Color Purple* also addresses the vexing question posed by the Olinka Adam narrative: Is progress in race relations possible? By bringing to closure two earlier narrative threads—one dealing with Sophia and Miss Eleanor Jane, and the other with Sophia's relationship to work—the novel suggests that progress in race relations is possible. But the narrative's ending also contains arresting images of racial segregation in both Africa and America that complicate the idea of progress and ultimately move the narrative toward a final definition of kinship based on race.

After their falling out over Reynolds Stanley, Sophia and Miss Eleanor Jane are reunited when the mayor's daughter finally learns from her family *why* Sophia came to work for them in the first place. Miss Eleanor Jane subsequently comes to work in Sophia's home, helping with the housework and taking care of Sophia's daughter Henrietta. Clearly an improvement in the domestic relationship between the two women, this new arrangement expresses Miss Eleanor Jane's new understanding of their domestic history together: to her family's question "Whoever heard of a white woman working for niggers?" Miss Eleanor Jane answers, "Whoever heard of somebody like Sophia working for trash?" For her part, Sophia's acceptance of Miss Eleanor Jane in her own home also signals progress, although when Celie asks pointedly if little Reynolds Stanley comes along with his mother, Sophia sidesteps the issue of her own feelings for the child by answering, "Henrietta say she don't mind him"(238).[15] Sophia's comment maintains the legitimacy of her own hard-earned attitudes toward the child, even as it reserves the possibility that different attitudes may be possible in future generations.

Sophia's employment in Celie's dry goods store also seems to signal an improvement in race relations, not only because it represents Sophia's final escape from her position as mammy but also because shops are used throughout *The Color Purple* to represent the status of economic and social integration between blacks and whites. Thus early in the novel Corrine, a Spelman graduate, is insulted when a white clerk calls her "Girl" (14) and intimidates her into buying some thread she doesn't want. Later the novel contrasts the histories of Celie's real Pa and Step-pa as store owners, histories that comment on the ability of African Americans to achieve economic integration into the American mainstream.[16] Celie's real father, in the tradition of the American success story, works hard, buys his own store, and hires two of his bothers to work it for him. Ironically, his model of industry and enterprise fails, since the store's very success leads "white merchants . . . [to] complain that this store was taking all the black business away from them" (148) Refusing to tolerate free competition from a black-owned and black-operated business, whites eventually burn the store and lynch Celie's Pa and his two brothers. The tragic history of Celie's real Pa thus compels readers to reinterpret Celie's family history in terms of the historical lack of access of African Americans to the "American Dream."

Believing that Celie's real Pa "didn't know how to git along," Alphonso, her step-pa, expresses a different path to economic integration:

> Take me, he say, I know how they is. The key to all of 'em is money. The trouble with our people is as soon as they got out of slavery they didn't want to give the white man nothing else. But the fact is, you got to give 'em something. Either your money, your land, your woman or your ass. So what I did was just right off offer to give 'em money. Before I planted a seed, I made sure this one and that one knowed one seed out of three was planted for *him*. Before I ground a grain of wheat, the same thing. And when I opened up your daddy's old store in town, I bought me my own white boy to run it. And what make it so good, he say, I bought him with whitefolks' money. (155)

Alphonso's decision to pay off whites and buy a white boy to work in the dry goods store establishes him in the tradition of the trickster who plays the system for his own benefit; however, the model of integration he represents is finally seen as accommodationist. Alphonso, in fact, is identified with white power from the beginning of the novel, where he is seen going off with a group of white men armed with guns (11–12). After he has made his fortune, Alphonso recalls the compromised African president described in Nettie's letter—like him Alphonso lives in a house that now looks like a "white person's house" (153), and like him he establishes paternalistic relationships with other blacks. Thus when Shug asks Alphonso's new wife, a "child" not "more than fifteen," why her parents allowed her to marry him, the girl replies: "They work for him. . . . Live on his land" (154). Alphonso's marriage thus makes explicit the degree to which his identification with white paternalism shapes his domestic relationships with other blacks.

In the context of these earlier histories, Sophia's coming to work in Celie's dry goods store has wider significance than just her finding suitable work outside the home. Indeed, for the first time in its history the store has an integrated workforce, since Celie keeps the "white man" who works there even as she hires Sophia to "wait on" blacks and "treat 'em nice" (245). In direct contrast to the white clerk who intimidated Corrine earlier, Sophia refuses to coerce customers and turns out to be especially good at "selling stuff" because "she don't care if you buy or not." Importantly, Sophia also resists the white clerk's attempts to define their relationship in the terms of plantation kinship: When he presumes to call her "auntie," she mocks him by asking "which colored man his mama sister marry" (237–238). While race relations in Celie's integrated store are obviously not ideal, Sophia's employment there is nonetheless both a personal and a communal triumph: Sophia finds employment that suits her as an individual, and the black community is treated with new respect in the marketplace.

Significantly, these small steps toward progress in race relations come not from some realization of the Olinka ideal or any recognition of identity *between* the races but from an evolving separatism and parallel growth in racial identity *within* the African and African American communities. The possibility of treating everyone like "one mother's children" is achieved within but not between racial groups by the end of *The Color Purple*. Instead, the conclusion leaves readers with images of an emerging Pan-Africanism in Africa and a nascent black nationalism in the American South.

In Africa separatism is represented by the *mbeles,* warriors who "live deep in the jungle, refusing to work for whites or be ruled by them" (193). Composed of men and women "from dozens of African tribes," the *mbeles* are particularly significant because they comprise a remnant group defined not by traditional village bloodlines but by their common experience of racial oppression and their shared commitment to active resistance, which takes the form of "missions of sabotage against the white plantations" (234). In the *mbeles, The Color Purple* accurately depicts the historical origin of many African "tribes" or nations in the reorganization of older societies decimated by colonization. Their plans for the white man's "destruction—or at least for his removal from *their continent*" (217; italics added)—also reflect a nascent pan-Africanism among the disenfranchised. Including among their number "one colored man ... from Alabama," the *mbeles* represent a form of kinship that is defined by racial rather than national identity.

In America, a parallel growth in black identity is suggested by Celie's final letter in *The Color Purple*. Indeed, the spirit of celebratory kinship with which the novel closes is achieved by Celie's group specifically in isolation from whites, as Harpo explains: "White people busy celebrating they independence from England July 4th ... so most black folks don't have to work. Us can spend the day celebrating each other" (242). By juxtaposing "white people" and "black folks," Harpo distinguishes his kinship group from the kinship of whites, defined by privilege and national identity. Importantly, the "folks" that Harpo refers to now include Celie's African daughter-in-law, Tashi. Also significantly, that group does *not* include Miss Eleanor Jane, no matter how strained her relationship with her own family or how successful her reunion with Sophia. Tashi's easy integration into the black community effaces her earlier fears that coming to America would rob her of all kinship ties, leaving her with "no country, no people, no mother and no husband and brother" (235). Instead, Tashi's quick acceptance by the Southern women, who make a fuss over her and "stuff her" with food (244), suggests once again that feelings of black identity make it easy for people to treat others as "one mother's children."[17]

But if the conclusion to *The Color Purple* suggests that feelings of racial identity can transcend national boundaries, the novel provides no such reassurances that the boundaries between races can be successfully negotiated. That sober conclusion is confirmed by the outcome of two other attempts at integration. The first is that of Shug's son, a missionary on an Indian reservation in the American West. The American Indians refuse to accept her son, Shug explains, because "everybody not a Indian they got no use for" (237).[18] The failure of Shug's son to become integrated into the American Indian community contrasts with Mary Agnes's successful integration with the mixed peoples of Cuba, but her experience there also emphasizes the importance of racial identity to kinship definitions. Indeed, it is because she is a person of color that Mary Agnes is recognized as kin: Even though some of the Cuban people are as light as Mary Agnes while others are "real dark," Shug explains, they are "all in the same family though. Try to pass for white, somebody mention your grandma" (211). Thus in Cuba—as well as in Africa and North America—feelings of racial identity among marginalized peoples become the basis for definitions of kinship by novel's end.

Finally, it is not surprising that, in elaborating her domestic trope for race relations, Walker is able to foreground the personal experience of her narrators while simultaneously offering an extended critique of racial integration. As Walker's integrated families remind us, the black family has seldom existed as a private, middle-class space protected from the interference of the state; therefore, the African American household is particularly inscribed with social meanings available for narration. Rather than opposing public and private spheres, Walker's narrative underscores their interpenetration. If her narrative does reveal an opposition, it is not between public and private discourse but between the universalist ethos of the Olinka ideal for race relations and the historical experience of African Americans as reflected in the narrative's analysis of specific integrated family groupings. For if the Olinka ideal questions the true nature of kinship in the novel's integrated families, these families also serve to criticize the Olinka myth for tracing the origins of racial discrimination back to some imaginary sin of black people, rather than to real, historical discrimination by whites.

It may be, however, that the growing sense of racial separatism at the conclusion to the *The Color Purple* is not necessarily at odds with the Olinka ideal for race relations. Past discrimination itself may dictate that improved relations between the races must begin with the destruction of false relations—the discovery of kinship among the disenfranchised the necessary first step, perhaps, toward recognizing all others as part of the same family. Like the Olinka Adam myth, the conclusion to Walker's novel raises the question of the future of race relations, but also like that myth, the novel offers no certain predictions. One thing is certain, however. Critics who believe that *The*

Color Purple sacrifices its ability to critique the public world of blacks in favor of dramatizing the personal experience of its narrators not only run the risk of reducing the narrative's technical complexity, but also of overlooking the work's sustained critique of racial integration levied from *within* the domestic sphere. Through its embedded narrative line and carefully elaborated kinship trope for race relations, *The Color Purple* offers a critique of race that explores the possibility of treating all people as "one mother's children"—while remaining unremittingly sensitive to the distance that often separates even the best of human ideals from real historical conditions.

NOTES

1. By characterizing the novel's point of view as "domestic," I mean no criticism, as my paper will Notes make clear. My approach to *The Color Purple* is in sympathy with recent revaluations of the domestic sphere in literature. See, for example, Barbara Christian, who charts in her discussion of George Simms (20) the well-known nineteenth-century denigration of sentimental fiction by male writers; and Jane Tompkins, who has argued that earlier interpretations of sentimental fiction were shaped by critics who taught "generations of students to equate popularity with debasement, emotionality with ineffectiveness, religiosity with fakery, domesticity with triviality—and all of these, implicitly, with womanly inferiority" (123). Closer at hand, Alison Light has attributed critics' "fear" of the happy ending in *The Color Purple* to similar attitudes toward sentimentality in fiction; Light points to an "'androcentricity' implicit and produced" in the "making" of public and private spheres (92) and notes that "terms like 'sentimental' and 'idealistic' are not themselves transparent descriptions of knowledge or response" but "carry with them cultural prescriptions and assumptions and have themselves to be historicized" (93). See also Susan K. Hams and Claudia Tate.

2. Called Walker's "best but most problematic" novel by Bernard Bell (263), *The Color Purple* has generated controversy since its publication in 1982 and especially since the appearance of the 1985 film of the same title. It should be noted that academic discussions of Celie's point of view in *The Color Purple* are paralleled in interesting ways by a controversy in the popular media over the representation of black men in novel and film. In "Sifting Through the Controversy: Reading *The Color Purple*," Jacqueline Bobo concludes that arguments in the public media focus on two values that sometimes seem in conflict: the need for positive images of black people in the media and the recognition of "the authority of black women writers to set the agenda for image-making in fiction and film" (334).

3. By placing my first reference to race in quotation marks I am following the practice of Gates and others in *"Race," Writing, and Difference*. The quotation marks indicate that "race" does not refer to some essential nature or fixed difference between people. Gates's collection illustrates a variety of critical approaches to what he calls "the complex interplay among race, writing, and difference" (15).

4. hooks also objects specifically to Walker's linking of the slave narrative form to that of the sentimental novel, an association that she believes "strips the slave narrative of its revolutionary ideological intent and content" by linking it to "Eurocentral bourgeois literary traditions" ("Writing" 465). But hooks's criticism is

problematic in light of the classical slave narrative tradition itself. Female authors of slave narratives often drew heavily upon the tradition of the sentimental novel to tell their stories. Note, for example, the case of what today is probably he best known woman's narrative, Harriet Jacobs's *Incidents in the Life of a Slave Girl.* Until recently Jacobs's autobiographical narrative was thought to *be* a sentimental novel. Jean Fagan Yellin details the textual history of the narrative in her edition of *Incidents.* See also Sekora's discussion of the genre of the slave narrative as a "mixed form" that syncretizes several literary traditions. While disagreeing with hooks about the genre of slave narratives in general and with her assessment of Walker's use of that tradition in particular, I want to acknowledge my debt to her work elsewhere on plantation family structures (as discussed in n14, below).

5. Unlike George Stade and bell hooks, Lauren Berlant and Elliott Butler-Evans seek not to criticize Walker's handling of the epistolary form but to uncover one effect that they believe follows from her chosen approach. Butler-Evans believes that the "restriction of focus to Celie's consciousness enables the novel to erase the public history and permits Celie to tell her own story" (166–167). Similarly, Berlant discusses Walker's "strategy of inversion, represented in its elevation of female experience over great patriarchal events" (847). Both critics detect an opposition or separation of discourses in the text, but their analyses differ in important ways. While sympathetic to Butler-Evans's method of analyzing the "politics of narration" (17) and especially to his analysis of sexual oppression, I believe his focus on the gender issues at the center of Walker's narrative leads him to underestimate both the extent and the importance of the novel's representation of race. Berlant's sophisticated argument cannot be summarized here, but if she means to limit—as I believe she does—her analysis of "nation" to Celie's understanding of the term, then our analyses may not be so much in conflict as they first appear. My own interest is in analyzing the narrative's embedded text on racial integration rather than in defining any particular character's understanding of race or nation. In other words, I believe that the implied reader of Walker's text is provided a political vantagepoint wider than that of any particular character in the novel, including its primary narrator, Celie.

6. Gates has analyzed the extent to which *The Color Purple* signifies upon Zora Neale Hurston's *Their Eyes Were Watching God* (*Signifying* 239–258). Note that, because of its layered narrative line, Walker's text is capable of another form of "doubleness"—an ability to signify upon itself.

7. While my purpose here is to focus primarily upon the representation of racial integration rather than gender, I should also note that this domestic ideal is expressed specifically in terms of matrilineal bonds. The recognition of all people as "one mother's children" is in keeping, of course, with the construction of gender elsewhere in the novel. Woman's love, understood as growing out of the experience of identity between mother and child (rather than out of the perception of difference between the sexes) is represented throughout *The Color Purple* as love that looks beyond differences in how people "look or act." As Celie tells Shug when the singer prepares to leave her, "I'm a woman. I love you. . . . Whatever happen, whatever you do. I love you" (221). For a theoretical alternative to Oedipal theories of maturation, see Chodorow.

8. While the boy's close proximity in age to Adam and Olivia accounts for some of his demeanor, his behavior raises issues of race and class nevertheless.

9. Note that Nettie's use of fairy-tale rhetoric to parody Doris undercuts the gender issues available in the white woman's narration and emphasizes instead issues of race and class.

10. Linda Abbandonato and others have pointed to Levi-Strauss's interpretation of the exchange of women as a "system of bonding men" (1109). Similarly, historian Gerda Lerner argues in *The Creation of Patriarchy* that the control of kinship—and especially of women's sexual and reproductive powers—leads to the historical development of patriarchal political structures, as power moves from the home and into law. Ironically, Doris leaves England to avoid becoming a wife, only to become an honorary husband in Africa. Doris's money has enabled her to escape becoming an object of exchange but not to escape the patriarchal system of exchange itself, which is seen to reach across continents.

11. Thus, in an article on "alienation and integration," Frank Shelton analyzes four kinds of alienation and integration in the novel-but not racial alienation or integration, probably because he believes that one component of such an analysis is largely missing from the text: "White people," he asserts, are "called a miracle of affliction" and then are "virtually ignored (382). Rather than being ignored, white people actually function in the latter half of the novel to underscore the presence of race and class hegemony in domestic space and to problematize the family ideal for racial integration.

12. My discussion of the black mammy builds upon the work of Hazel Carby, Barbara Christian, Trudier Harris, and bell hooks (*Ain't I a Woman*), all of whom have written on literary representations of the African American woman in the plantation household.

13. For other analyses of Squeak's rape, see Christine Froula's reading of Squeak's "self-naming" in light of the sexual violence in the novel (639), and Berlant's discussion of the rape as "the diacritical mark that organizes Squeak's insertion into the 'womanist' order" (844).

14. In doing so, Walker's novel joins the longstanding feminist critique of separate-spheres ideology as a false division used for power's self-maintenance. See Gayatri Chakravorty Spivak's comment that "the deconstruction of the opposition between the private and public" is "implicit in all feminist activity" (201).

15. Note that Celie's pointed question to Sophia about Miss Eleanor Jane's baby demonstrates her own understanding of the race issues involved in Sophia's relationship with the white baby.

16. See Berlant's reading of Celie's family history, which argues that Celie's "fairy-tale rhetoric emphasizes the personal over the institutional or political components of social relations" such that "the nonbiologized abstraction of class relations virtually disappears from the text" (841–842). According to Berlant, Celie never understands the economic or class issues implied by her family history.

17. The conclusion also suggests that feelings of kinship can transcend gender differences, even when these differences include prior wrongs as great as Albert's abuse of Celie. The novel resolves tensions between the sexes—but not those between the races—optimistically, with partners, husbands, wives, and estates well sorted out by the novel's end.

18. Shug's son may work for the same organization as Nettie, since we learn early on that the "American and African Missionary Society" has also "ministered to the Indians out west" (109). In any case, the American Indians' treatment of Shug's son underscores their own understanding of the colonial function of missionaries. By calling Shug's son the "black white man," the American Indians also complicate racial definitions of kinship by suggesting that the definition of race itself is ultimately located in social hegemony.

144 Linda Selzer

WORKS CITED

Abbandonato, Linda. "A View From Elsewhere: Subversive Sexuality and the Rewriting of the Heroine's Story in *The Color Purple*." *PMLA* 106 (1991): pp. 1106–1115.

Bell, Bernard. *The Afro-American Novel and Its Tradition*. Amherst: University of Massachusetts Press, 1987.

Berlant, Lauren. "Race, Gender, and Nation in *The Color Purple*." *Critical Inquiry* 14 (1988): pp. 831–859.

Bobo, Jacqueline. "Sifting through the Controversy: Reading *The Color Purple*." *Callaloo* 12 (1989): pp. 332–342.

Butler-Evans, Elliott. *Race, Gender, and Desire: Narrative Strategies in the Fiction of Toni Cade Bambara, Toni Morrison, and Alice Walker*. Philadelphia: Temple University Press, 1989.

Carby, Hazel. *Reconstructing Womanhood: The Emergence of the Afro-American Woman Novelist*. New York: Oxford University Press, 1987.

Chodorow, Nancy. *The Reproduction of Mothering: Psychoanalysis and The Sociology of Gender*. Berkeley: University of California Press, 1978.

Christian, Barbara. *Black Women Novelists: The Development of a Tradition, 1892–1976*. Westport: Greenwood, 1980.

Froula, Christine, "The Daughter's Seduction: Sexual Violence and Feminist Theory." *Signs* 2 (1986): pp. 621–644.

Gates, Henry Louis, Jr., ed. *"Race," Writing, and Difference*. Chicago: University of Chicago Press, 1986.

———. *The Signifying Monkey: A Theory of African-American Literary Criticism*. New York: Oxford University Press, 1988.

Harris, Susan K. *19th-Century American Women's Novels: Interpretive Strategies*. New York: Cambridge University Press, 1990.

Harris, Trudier. *From Mammies to Militants: Domestics in Black American Literature*. Philadelphia: Temple University Press, 1982.

hooks, bell. *Ain't I a Woman: Black Women and Feminism*. Boston: South End, 1981.

———. "Writing the Subject: Reading *The Color Purple*." *Reading Black, Reading Feminist*. Edited by Henry Louis Gates, Jr. (New York: Meridian, 1990): pp. 454–470.

Jacobs, Harriet. *Incidents in the Life of a Slave Girl. Told by Herself*. Edited by Jean Fagan Yellin. Cambridge: Havard University Press, 1987.

Lerner, Gerda. *The Creation of Patriarchy*. New York: Oxford University Press, 1986.

Light, Alison. "The Fear of the Happy Ending." *Plotting Change*. Edited by Linda Anderson. (London: Edward Arnold, 1993): pp. 85–96.

Sekora, John. "Is the Slave Narrative a Species of Autobiography?" *Studies in Autobiography*. Edited by James Olney. (New York: Oxford University Press, 1988): pp. 99–111.

Shelton, Frank W. "Alienation and Integration in Alice Walker's *The Color Purple*." *CLA Journal* 28 (1985): pp. 382–392.

Spivak, Gayatri Chakravorly. "Explanation and Culture: Marginalia." *Humanities and Society* 2 (1974): pp. 201–221.

Stade, George. "Womanist Fiction and Male Characters," *Partisan Review* 52 (1985): pp. 264–270.

Tate, Claudia. *Domestic Allegories of Political Desire: The Black Heroine's Text at the Turn of the Century*. New York: Oxford University Press, 1992.

Tompkins, Jane. *Sensational Designs: The Cultural Work of American Fiction*. New York: Oxford University Press, 1985.

Walker, Alice. *The Color Purple*. New York: Harcourt, 1982.

MARTHA J. CUTTER

Philomela Speaks: Alice Walker's Revisioning of Rape Archetypes in The Color Purple

The ancient story of Philomela has resonated in the imaginations of women writers for several thousand years. The presence of this myth in contemporary texts by African American women writers marks the persistence of a powerful archetypal narrative explicitly connecting rape (a violent inscription of the female body), silencing, and the complete erasure of feminine subjectivity.[1] For in most versions of this myth Philomela is not only raped—she is also silenced. In Ovid's recounting, for example, Philomela is raped by her brother-in-law, Tereus, who then tears out her tongue. Philomela is finally transformed into a nightingale, doomed to chirp out the name of her rapist for eternity: *tereu, tereu.* The mythic narrative of Philomela therefore explicitly intertwines rape, silencing, and the destruction of feminine subjectivity.

Contemporary African American women's fiction contains allusions to this archetypal rape narrative. In Toni Morrison's *The Bluest Eye,* for example, Pecola Breedlove's rape by her father Cholly causes a fragmentation of her psyche. Pecola's attempts to tell of her rape are nullified by her disbelieving mother, and by the novel's conclusion her voice is only exercised in internal colloquies with an imaginary friend. She flutters along the edges of society, a "winged but grounded bird" (158). Similarly, in Gloria Naylor's *The Women of Brewster Place,* after Lorraine is gagged and brutally gang raped, she becomes

MELUS, Volume 25, Numbers 3/4 (Fall/Winter 2000): pp. 161–180.

both insane and unable to speak of her rape. Finally, she is left with only one word, a word that echoes back to Philomela's *"tereu, tereu,"* the word she attempted to use to stop her attackers: "Please. Please" (173).[2] Rape is thus a central trope in these texts for the mechanisms whereby a patriarchal society writes oppressive dictates on women's bodies and minds, destroying both subjectivity and voice. Or, as Madonne Miner puts it, "Men, potential rapists, assume presence, language, and reason as their particular province. Women, potential victims, fall prey to absence, silence, and madness" (181).

For writers such as Naylor and Morrison, the myth of Philomela graphically illustrates the way a patriarchal society censors and erases women's voices. More damaging, perhaps, Philomela's story also indicates that if women find other methods of communicating, these alternatives lead only to more violence and an even deeper silence. After her rape Philomela is imprisoned in a tower of stone, but she manages to weave a tapestry (or in some accounts a robe) depicting Tereus's actions. She sends this artwork to her sister Procne, who "reads" this text and understands its import. Buried within this myth of patriarchal subjugation, then, there is a subtext that focuses on how women can "speak" across and against the limits of patriarchal discourse. However, the myth's final message seems to be that women's alternative texts fail to transform in any lasting way the social or linguistic forces of patriarchal domination. Procne's response to her sister is to first consider killing Tereus, whom she calls, as translated by Humphries, "the *author* of our evils" (149, emphasis added). Instead she kills her young son Itys, roasts and grills Itys's flesh, and serves this "feast" to her husband. When Tereus apprehends what has happened, he attempts to destroy both Philomela and Procne, but the gods intervene, transforming all three characters into birds.

The structural pattern of the myth (and its warning to women) seems clear; as Patricia Joplin explains, the myth fixes "in eternity the pattern of violation-revenge-violation. . . . The women, in yielding to violence, become just like the men. . . . The sacrifice of the innocent victim, Itys, continues, without altering it, the motion of reciprocal violence" (48–49). More importantly, the myth also instantiates an endless cycle of linguistic violence against women: violence (i.e., rape) leads to silence (the tongue is torn out); attempts to break this silence through assertions of an alternative feminine voice (the tapestry) lead only to more violence (the killing of Itys), and finally, to a more complete and final silence (the death of the characters and the loss of their human voices). The myth suggests that an assertion of alternative feminine voice merely imprisons women all the more exhaustively in pejorative mastertexts that make men, as Procne says, the "author of our evils."

Like the novels of Morrison and Naylor, Alice Walker's *The Color Purple* invokes this archetypal rape narrative, but Walker is most interested in re-envisioning this myth through an alternative methodology of language. As

Linda Abbandonato argues in her reading of the *The Color Purple*, it is important to consider how a woman can "define herself differently, disengage her self from the cultural scripts of sexuality and gender that produce her as feminine subject" (1107). Abbandonato argues that *The Color Purple* rewrites canonical male texts, but she does not discuss Walker's rewriting of the story of Philomela. Similarly, although critics such as Trudier Harris, Keith Byerman, Wendy Wall, Mae Henderson, and King-Kok Cheung have discussed Celie's acquisition of private and public languages, none of these critics has examined Walker's reconfiguration of linguistic elements of the myth of Philomela. Unlike the original mythic text, as well as the novels of Morrison and Naylor, Walker's text gives Philomela a voice that successfully resists the violent patriarchal inscription of male will onto a silent female body.

Yet Walker does more than simply allow Philomela to speak within the confines of patriarchal discourse.[3] Walker's novel revises the myth of Philomela by creating a heroine's text that reconfigures the rhetorical situation of sender-receiver-message and articulates Celie's movement away from an existence as a victim in a patriarchal plot toward a linguistic and narratological presence as the author/subject of her own story. Walker's novel also rewrites the myth through its creation of an alternative discourse that allows for the expression of both masculine and feminine subjectivity—a language of the sewn that withdraws from the violence of patriarchal domination, of patriarchal discourse.[4] Celie's skills as a seamstress both retrieve and refigure the myth of Philomela, for unlike Philomela's tapestry/text, Celie's sewing functions as an alternative methodology of language that moves her away from violence and victimization and into self-empowerment and subjectivity. The novel also deliberately conflates the pen and the needle, thereby deconstructing the binary oppositions between the masculine and the feminine, the spoken and the silenced, the lexical and the graphic. Walker's reconfiguration of the myth of Philomela thus overturns the master discourse *and* the master narrative of patriarchal society. In Walker's hands Philomela's speech becomes the instrument for a radical metamorphosis of the individual as well as a subversive deconstruction of the power structures that undergird both patriarchal language and the patriarchal world itself.

Susan Griffin argues that "more than rape itself, the fear of rape permeates our lives. . . . and the best defense against this is not to be, to deny being in the body, as a self; . . . to avert your gaze, make yourself, as a presence in this world, less felt" (83). Certainly, when Celie speaks of turning herself into wood when she is beaten or raped ("I say to myself Celie, you a tree" [30]), the response described by Griffin is apparent; to avoid pain Celie denies her body and her presence. Walker's story begins in the familiar mythic way: Celie is told after her rape by her (presumed) father: *"You better not never tell nobody but God. It'd kill your mammy"* (11). Celie is silenced by an external source, and like Morrison's and Naylor's protagonists, she experiences the nullification of subjectivity and internal voice allied with rape by the myth of Philomela. Celie's story starts with the fact that the one identity she has always known is no longer accessible: "I am fourteen years old. ~~I am~~ I have always been a good girl" (11). No longer a "good girl," Celie has no present tense subjectivity, no present tense "I am."

Like Pecola Breedlove of Morrison's *The Bluest Eye*, who ends the novel "flail[ing] her arms like a bird in an eternal, grotesquely futile effort to fly" (158), Celie appears to have been driven into semiotic collapse by the rape. Walker's text also uses bird and blood imagery to connect Celie with her mythic prototype, Philomela as well as to revise the mythic prototext. In *Metamorphoses*, Ovid describes how Procne and Philomela are transformed, a change that silences them as humans but does not erase their bloody deeds: "One flew to the woods, the other to the roof-top, / And even so the red marks of the murder / Stayed on their breasts; the feathers were blood-colored" (151). Throughout *The Color Purple*, Celie is associated with both birds and blood. Celie tells Albert that she loves birds (223), and Albert comments, "you use to remind me of a bird. Way back when you first come to live with me. . . . And the least little thing happen, you looked about to fly away" (223). Later in the novel, when Celie returns to confront her "Pa" (Alphonso) about his actions, she comments three times on how loudly the birds are singing around his house (164, 165, 167). The singing birds of the later scene recall Celie's earlier victimization, the way she was raped, bloodied, impregnated, and deprived of voice by Alphonso's statement that "she tell lies" (18).

Paradoxically, the birds of this scene are also a positive symbol to Celie of how nature persists in displaying its beauty despite the despoiling patterns of humanity. Similarly, Walker later transforms the blood symbolism of the early rape scene ("Seem like it all come back to me. . . . How the blood drip down my leg and mess up my stocking" [108–109]) into something more positive, revising the symbolism of blood in the mythic text. When Shug abandons Celie, Celie describes her heart as "blooming blood" (229). Here, although blood is painful, it is also generative: it blooms. Blood comes from Celie during her rape. It also covers her in other key scenes in the novel, such as her first meeting with Mr. _____'s (Albert's) family: "I spend my wedding day running from the oldest boy. . . . He pick up a rock and laid my head open. The blood run all down tween my breasts" (21). Like Philomela, whose breast feathers are stained "blood-colored" with the "red marks of the murder" after she is transformed into a bird (Ovid 151), Celie's breasts are stained with blood. However, Celie eventually transforms the blood of this attack into blooming blood, into a red that is creative and regenerative. A more mature Celie uses the color red as a positive element in her sewing, transforming it from a color of pain to a color of joy. She sews purple and red pants for Sofia (194), orange and red pants for Squeak (191), and blue and red pants for Shug (191). She paints her own room purple and red (248). The blood that marks Celie becomes a positive symbol of her artistic creativity, rather than (as in the myth) a negative symbol of how she is damned in perpetuity by her deed.[5]

Unlike the archetypal narrative, then, Walker's novel uses bird and blood imagery to suggest Celie's metamorphosis not from human to subhuman, but from victim to artist-heroine. The novel also differs from the mythic prototext, as well as from the novels of Morrison and Naylor, in that it begins (rather than ends) with Celie's rape, and in that the rape becomes not an instrument of silencing, but the catalyst to Celie's search for voice. After Celie is told to be silent about the rape, she confides the details in her journal, structured at first as letters to God. In these letters Celie begins to create a resistant narratological version of events that ultimately preserves her subjectivity and voice:

> He never had a kine word to say to me. Just say You gonna do what your mammy wouldn't. First he put his thing up gainst my hip and sort of wiggle it around. Then he grab hold of my titties. Then he push his thing inside my pussy. When that hurt, I cry. He start to choke me, saying You better shut up and git used to it. But I don't never git used to it. (11)

The horror of this experience is evident, but it is also apparent that Celie narrates these events to *resist* her father. Susan Brownmiller comments that "Rape by an authority figure can befuddle a victim. . . . Authority figures emanate an aura of rightness; their actions cannot easily be challenged. What else can the victim be but 'wrong'? (271). However, even the patent statement that "I don't never git used to it" demonstrates that Celie knows her Pa's actions are improper and that she refuses to live by his imperatives; she refuses to be the passive sheet upon which the father writes unalterable messages. By writing about her rape, Celie also externalizes her experiences so that they do not destroy her. Celie feels sorry for her mama because "Trying to believe his [the father's] story kilt her" (15). Taking one's place within a patriarchal text leads to the obliteration of feminine subjectivity. That Celie resists the father's narratives through her own writing means that she survives.

Celie's narration of these actions in her diary also enables the later moments in the novel when she speaks of her rape to Shug Avery: "While I trim his hair he look at me funny. He a little nervous too, but I don't know why, till he grab hold of me and cram me up tween his legs. . . . It hurt me, you know, I say. I was just going on fourteen. I never even thought bout men having nothing down there so big" (108). Ellen Rooney comments that scenes of sexual violence "may be privileged sites for investigating the construction of female subjectivity because they articulate questions of desire, power, and agency with a special urgency and explicitly foreground the opposition between subject and object" (92). Walker twice narrates Celie's violation in order to show how "Pa" attempts to deny Celie's subjectivity as well as how Celie creates her own spoken and written version of events which emphasizes her cognizance and functions as a counterpoint to her own earlier erasure of body and identity. Walker thus revises the archetypal paradigm depicting rape as an event that encapsulates women in patriarchal plots as the site of silence, absence, and madness. In Walker's text rape leads not to erasure, but rather to the start of a prolonged struggle toward subjectivity and voice.[6]

Celie's movement out of silence occurs despite repeated rape by her husband, who in his demeanor and behavior exactly parallels her father. Multiple or repeated rape is an important element of the violation detailed in the archetypal myth of Philomela as well as in texts by contemporary African American women. In the mythic text, after Tereus cuts out Philomela's tongue he rapes her again, perhaps more than once: "And even then—/ It seems too much to believe—even then, Tereus / Took her, and took her again, the injured body / Still giving satisfaction to his lust" (Ovid 147). In *The Women of Brewster Place*, Lorraine is repeatedly raped by six teenagers, while her "paralyzed vocal cords" cannot function because of the dirty paper bag that has been shoved in her mouth (170). In *The Bluest Eye*, Pecola's internal monologue reveals that her father, Cholly, raped her at least twice (155, 156), but her mother does not believe that either incident occurred (155).

Celie, too, is repeatedly raped by her "Pa," who impregnates her twice and then gives away her children. Celie is also raped, both actually and symbolically, by her husband, Mr. _____ (or Albert). Celie is quick to note the parallels between her husband and her father: "Mr. _____ say. . . . All women good for—he don't finish. He just tuck his chin over the paper like he do. Remind me of Pa" (30). And Celie's letters repeatedly emphasize that sex with Albert is the equivalent of rape: "He git up on you, heist your nightgown round your waist, plunge in. Most times I pretend I ain't there. He never know the difference. Never ast me how I feel, nothing. Just do his business, get off, go to sleep" (79; see also 109). In the imagery of Walker's text father and husband are conflated: both are rapists who deny that women can be anything other than objects of male abuse. This conflation echoes back to the myth of Philomela, for in Ovid's telling of the myth, when Tereus sees Philomela kissing her father, Tereus thinks that "He would like to be / Her father, at that moment; and if he were / He would be as wicked a father as he is a husband" (144–145). Furthermore, as in the myth of Philomela, in Walker's novel two women's sororal status does not stop the father/husband from wanting to have sexual intercourse with both sisters. Pa rapes Celie and then casts lascivious eyes at Nettie (13); Albert has intercourse with Celie but also attempts to rape Nettie (119). Given these parallels to the repeated rape paradigm in the myth of Philomela, Celie's resistance is all the more noteworthy.

Celie's resistant voice is enabled by her creation of an alternative conception of her audience and by a reconfiguration of the rhetorical triangle of sender-receiver-message. Rape is once again the catalyst for Celie's resistance. Albert's physical attempt to rape Nettie fails, but he finds a discursive way of "raping" both women when he refuses to deliver any of Nettie's letters to Celie. And indeed, this discursive rape is far more effective than his actual rape, as Celie's response shows. When Celie learns that Albert has suppressed all of Nettie's letters, her consciousness becomes a blank (116), and she feels "cold" and almost "dead" (115), "sickish" and "numb" (134). Moreover, as sometimes occurs in an actual rape, Celie's sexual responses to her lover Shug are deadened by Albert's symbolic rape (136). More than at any other point in the text, Celie seems on the verge of slipping into madness when she discovers Albert's suppression of her sister's letters.

However, in a text where "[c]riss-crossed letters, letters written to an absence, letters received from the dead, hidden and confiscated letters, all of these point to the instability of language" (Wall 94), perhaps it is no surprise that Albert's simplistic gesture of locking up Nettie's voice in his trunk does not actually disrupt the "conversation" between Celie and Nettie.[7] Although Nettie has never received a letter from Celie, Nettie still feels as if she is communicating with her sister: "I imagine that you really do get my letters and that you are writing back: Dear Nettie, this is what life is like for me" (144). Similarly, Celie discovers that she can converse with Nettie despite receiving no response, and even despite the possibility of Nettie's physical death: "And I don't believe you dead. How can you be dead if I still feel you? Maybe, like God, you changed into something different that I'll have to speak to in a different way, but you not dead to me Nettie. And never will be" (229–230). In a more positive version of the interchange between Philomela and Procne, Celie's letters to Nettie create an imagined linguistic persona with whom she can speak "differently." By doing so, Celie finds an alternative conception of the communicative process that allows her to bypass Albert's invalidation of her discourse and enables her survival. In most rhetorical situations, after all, the sender expects that the receiver will actually receive the message and shapes the message accordingly. But Celie subversively reconfigures her audience so that an imagined, rather than actual, person is the receiver of the message, and this allows her to shape her message in such a way that it cannot be erased or silenced, in such a way that it can exist despite Albert's attempt to deny both the communication and the communicator.

Walker also rewrites elements of the mythic paradigm of Philomela to emphasize a textual tradition in which women do more than simply defend themselves against male silencing: in Walker's new textual tradition women become active and articulate heroines of their own stories. In the myth, when Philomela is denied traditional channels of self-expression she creates an alternative text:

> . . . no power of speech
> To help her tell her wrongs. . . .
> She had a loom to work with, and with *purple*
> On a white background, wove her story in,
> Her story in and out. . . . (148, my emphasis)

Walker's title may be an allusion to Philomela's text, woven in purple.[8] However, in Ovid's myth this alternative text leads only to Philomela's further victimization by Tereus and to her silence. Celie, too, finds an alternative text, a text directed at a non- patriarchal audience, for in the second half of the novel she stops writing to God—whom she perceives as "just like all the other mens I know. Trifling, forgitful and lowdown" (175)—and starts writing to Nettie.

While Philomela's alternative text leads to her destruction, Celie's alternative text, her letters to Nettie, leads to reconstruction, allowing Celie to craft an identity for herself as the heroine of her own story. Celie gets a house and a profession, and she describes both these events in heroic terms in her letters to Nettie. Both Procne and Philomela are taken away from their familial homes by Tereus. Similarly, both Nettie and Celie are driven away from their family's home by the individual they call "Pa." Unlike Procne and Philomela, both Celie and Nettie return. Celie's letter to Nettie describes her triumphant homecoming and ends with the statement that "Now you [Nettie] can come home cause you have a home to come to!" (217). Signing this letter "Your loving sister, Celie" (217), Celie asserts both her right to this home and to this text in which she is no longer a displaced wife trapped within a patriarchal plot. Although Celie seldom signs her letters, she also signs the letter in which she describes her new profession to Nettie. These two signatures, "Your loving Sister, Celie" (217), and "Your Sister, Celie, Folkspants, Unlimited" (192) indicate the contours of the heroic role Celie has shaped for herself, and contrast sharply with her earlier inability to say "I am." And only in the second half of the novel, when Celie stops writing to God and starts writing to Nettie, does she actively articulate an alternative identity for herself.

Celie's insistence on her desire for Shug also formulates an alternative to being objectified as an absence in a male plot. If, as Catharine MacKinnon argues, "A woman is a being who identifies and is identified as one whose sexuality exists for someone else, who is socially male" (533), then Celie's insistence on her desire for Shug is crucial. Celie recounts her strong sexual response to Shug Avery (53), and even goes so far as to envision voicing her passion: "All the men got they eyes glued to Shug's bosom. I got my eyes glued there too. . . . Shug, I say to her in my mind, Girl, you looks like a real good time, the Good Lord knows you do" (82). This internal voicing of desire becomes external in the letter in which Celie tells Nettie of her love for Shug (221). Celie's love for Shug and others is the fulcrum of her new brand of heroism, and her willingness to articulate it in letters to her sister indicates that she has crafted a textual tradition that allows for feminine heroism and desire.[9]

Beyond giving Celie a resistant voice that allows her to reconfigure the rhetorical situation, recreate her audience, and enunciate a heroine's text, Walker's text also creates an alternative methodology of language. In the world Walker depicts, language is often an instrument of coercion and dominance, and it is often used by men to silence women. At first Celie merely turns the tables on Albert, using language to suppress him:

> He laugh. Who you think you is? he say. You can't curse nobody. Look at you. You black, you pore, you ugly, you a woman. Goddam, he say, you nothing at all.
>
> Every lick you hit me you will suffer twice, I say. Then I say, You better stop talking.
>
> Shit, he say. I should have lock you up. Just let you out to work.
>
> The jail you plan for me is the one in which you will rot, I say. (187)

In the mythic pattern, Tereus doubly silences Philomela, first by pulling out her tongue and then by imprisoning her in a tower, just as Albert doubly silences Celie, denying her voice ("you can't curse nobody") and presence ("I should have lock you up"). But Celie silences and imprisons the oppressor within her own narrative: "the jail you plan for me is the one in which you will rot," "You better stop talking." Like Albert, Celie has learned how to use both physical and linguistic violence to erase others.

However, Walker is not content with showing Celie's use of "the master's tools" against the master. Celie must learn that language can be used to understand, rather than destroy, another's subjectivity. Celie's later comment about Albert that "He ain't Shug, but he begin to be somebody I can talk to" (241) is therefore revealing. Celie accepts that Albert is capable of using language in a constructive rather than destructive way, and she no longer denies his voice. In the end, Celie's and Albert's voices become agents for conversation rather than combat: "Now us [Albert and Celie] sit sewing and talking and smoking our pipes" (238).

In this passage, sewing and conversation are allied and inseparable, part of the alternative methodology of speech Walker is explicating. Indeed, in this novel sewing often functions as a language, communicating far more effectively than lexical signs. Celie sews curtains to welcome Sofia, and when Sofia is angry at Celie, she cuts down these same curtains and returns them (45). When they reconcile their differences, Celie and Sofia use the spoiled curtains as part of a quilt (47). Similarly, Celie's and Corrine's only conversation occurs in a store where Corrine buys material and thread to make a dress for her daughter. Nettie can only make Corrine remember this conversation by finding a quilt that has squares from the dress material Corrine purchased that day. Sewing is thus a key way individuals communicate with each other, signifying their friendship and interconnectedness. Commenting on Walker's ubiquitous imagery of cloth-working, M. Teresa Tavormina argues that in the novel "sewing is an act of union, of connecting pieces to make a useful whole. Furthermore, sewing with others is a comradely act, one that allows both speech and comfortable, supportive silence" (224). Yet sewing does more than enable conversation: sewing *is* conversation, a language that articulates relationships and connects and reconnects networks of individuals to create a community.

Moreover, Walker's novel suggests that sewing is precisely the language that can replace the patriarchal discourse of Mr. _____ that can revise the mythic pattern of silence/violence/silence. Several critics have argued that the novel's form is quilt-like, and Walker's own comments have given strength to this interpretation.[10] The structure of the novel can also be read as an embroidered tapestry such as the one Philomela creates; in Walker's text, Celie's pen is the shuttle/needle that creates a design out of separate narrative threads. Celie's letters to God sometimes weave in quotes or threads from Nettie's and Shug's letters; for example, a short letter by Celie includes Nettie's own words, removed from the letter they came in:

> Dear God,
> Now I know Nettie alive I begin to strut a little bit. Think, When she come home us leave here. . . But I think bout Nettie.
> It's hot, here, Celie, she write. Hotter than July. Hotter than August *and* July. Hot like cooking dinner on a big stove in a little kitchen in August and July. Hot. (138; see also 235 and 238)

Furthermore, rather than allowing Nettie's letters to remain as separate blocks of narrative "fabric," Celie weaves them into her tapestry by interspersing her own voice into them: "Dear Celie, *the first letter say,*" (119), "*Next one said*" (120), "*Next one fat, dated two months later, say*" (122). Celie's narrative voice, then, is not just another square in a quilt, equal to all the other squares. Rather, in the text as a whole narrative voices are interwoven, imbricated, threaded together, and interconnected by the needle/pen of the spinner, Celie herself.

Weaving, embroidering, and sewing are thus important analogies for the novel's form, but they are also important metaphors for the kind of conversation Walker envisions replacing patriarchal discourse. Of course, there is nothing inherently peaceful about a needle, as illustrated by one character's comment that unlike Celie his wife would have taken a needle and sewn Shug's nostrils together (60). And the pen, like the needle, has a phallic shape that can rip and rend, rather than mend and stitch. What is important for Walker, however, is the use to which the instrument is put. For example, when Celie makes pants for Nettie, her sewing is envisioned as a language of love and re-membering: "Nettie, I am making some pants for you to beat the heat in Africa.... Every stitch I sew will be a kiss" (192). Like Philomela's tapestry, Celie's sewing connects the two sisters.

But unlike Philomela's tapestry, Celie's sewn gift to her sister is an act of interconnection and rejuvenation. In Walker's telling of the myth, then, brutal retaliation is actually replaced by creativity and by sewing itself. When Celie wants to react to Albert's suppression of Nettie's letters with violence, Shug tells her to sew pants instead. Celie understands and accepts this: "everyday we going to read Nettie's letters and sew. A needle and not a razor in my hand, I think" (137). It is here that Walker's text swerves most radically from the myth of Philomela and from the mythic paradigm. Nettie's recovered letters are like Philomela's tapestry: they speak the oppression of women, they incite the sister (or all sisters) to violence. But Walker suggests that violence will only end in more silence. An alternative must be found, and this alternative is sewing and conversation, sewing *as* conversation. Sewing is a language that explicates an alternative to the violence of patriarchal discourse.

In the novel as a whole, Celie's pen stitches together the narrative fabric of the text, remaking individual relationships and roles, replacing the violence of patriarchal discourse with a language that re-members and remakes. Celie's pen becomes a needle, then. Yet Celie's needle also becomes a pen. Celie embroiders "little stars and flowers" in her daughter Olivia's diapers, but she also sews language: she sews her name for her daughter, "Olivia," into the diaper (22). The needle is, quite literally, a pen, stitching a name that fits the child, that connects mother and daughter, that is both linguistic (written in letters) and sewn (embroidered). Tavormina notes that "in *The Color Purple,* both cloth-working and language become media for self-definition, self-expression, and self- sharing," but she also claims they have "distinct but similar processes and products" (229). I would suggest, however, that Walker deliberately confuses the processes and products of cloth-working and language, of sewing and communication. Ann Bergren explains that Philomela *"huphenasa en peploi grammata":* she weaves pictures/writing since *"grammata"* can mean either (72). Like Philomela's tapestry, Celie's embroidery deconstructs the barriers between the pictorial and the lexical.

In the end, the thread and the word cannot be separated, and sewing not only helps Celie achieve self-expression, it becomes an alternative methodology of language that resists other more standard or formal discourses. When Celie's employee Darlene tries to convince Celie to speak "correctly," Celie responds "only a fool would want you to talk in a way that feel peculiar to your mind," but she also notes that she is "busy making pants for Sofia," and that she dreams of Sofia "jumping over the moon" in these pants (194). Sewing functions as an alternative methodology of speech that cannot be separated from Celie's acquisition of an alternative spoken and written language. Walker's language of the sewn denies binaries and hierarchies of the hegemonic world, such as those between oral and written language, between informal and formal diction, between art and language, and between discourse and "craft."

Nor is this alternative language of the sewn limited to women. By the end of the novel, Albert is sewing, too. Indeed, sewing facilitates a retrieval of an earlier maternal conversation in which Albert once participated: "When I was growing up, he said, I use to try to sew along with mama cause that's what she was always doing. But everybody laughed at me" (238). Through sewing, Albert becomes part of Celie's community; when Nettie returns from Africa, Celie introduces both Shug *and* Albert as "my peoples" (250). It is significant that Walker allows Albert, an image of Tereus, of the father/rapist, to participate in the conversation of sewing. His transformation and inclusion in Walker's new version of the myth of Philomela shows that indeed the violence of the cycle can be broken. In Walker's revision of the myth of Philomela, both the sisters *and* the rapist turn from the violence of patriarchal discourse and find alternative methodologies of language that speak their recapitulation of self rather than their deconstruction of self and other.

Through her depiction of Albert's metamorphosis and inclusion in the conversation of sewing, Walker also elucidates broader possibilities for social amelioration. Once rape has been renounced as an instrument of male domination, once the rapist has been transformed and included in a new social order where he can engage in "feminine" activities and be part of "feminine" language, society can move toward a more equitable relationship between the sexes. Peggy Sanday has shown that in rape-free societies, "there is no symbol system by which males define their gender identity as the antithesis of the feminine" (98), and "silencing the feminine is not necessary for becoming a proud and independent male" (94). In rape-free societies, there is "sexual equality and complementarity" (93) between the genders. It is precisely this equality between the genders and validation of the "feminine" that Walker alludes to when she includes Albert in the sewing circle (238), when she shows Harpo feeding and bathing his father (200), and when she shows Sofia making shingles (67). Critics such as Keith Byerman (66) and bell hooks (222) argue that Walker's feminization of Albert and Harpo reflects a movement away from historical and ideological conflicts. However, Sanday's research demonstrates that Walker's approach to social change is realistic. In Walker's text, the "feminine" is not silenced and it belongs entirely to neither gender. The "feminine" functions as a language that both men and women can speak, a language that offers the possibility of radical social transformation.

The novel therefore indicates that alternative methodologies of language (whether spoken by men or women) need not perpetuate the mythic cycle of feminine destruction encapsulated within patriarchal discourse and patriarchal narrative. Celie's letters allow her to reconfigure the rhetorical situation and create a resistant heroine's text in which she has a narratological existence as the author/subject of her own story. The novel as a whole also creates an alternative methodology of language that replaces the phallic and destructive patriarchal discourse of the pen, which tears and rends, with a feminine (but not female) discourse of the needle, which remends, re-members, and remakes. This discourse, the language of the sewn rather than the rent, in turn becomes the cornerstone for a reconstruction of gender roles that undermines patriarchal subjugation itself. And yet in the end, these two discourses (the discourse of the pen and of the needle) are subversively conflated, and it is finally and most incisively through this conflation and confusion that Walker's text achieves its most radical aims. After all, the pen has typically been an instrument of male empowerment, a phallic substitute instantiating men's control over women, while the needle has typically been associated with femininity, demarcating the contours and limits of women's sphere.

When Walker's text conflates needle and pen, then, it undermines the most basic binary structures of patriarchal society: male versus female, public versus private, empowered versus disempowered, spoken versus silent. For if the needle has become the pen and the pen has become the needle, if the feminine and the masculine cannot in fact be separated, if patriarchal discourse has been replaced by a discourse that admits of both masculine and feminine subject positions, what pedestal remains for the subjugation of women and other "minorities" within culture? Thus Walker's novel engages in a wholesale revision of the archetypal rape narrative of Philomela as well as the dominant master narrative of patriarchal culture itself: the silencing and objectifying of women and "others" as the basis for male subjectivity.

Notes

1. Hartman defines archetype as a narrative whose suggestiveness is not explained by its parts or its context; archetype is a text "greater than the whole of which it is a part, a text that demands a context yet is not reducible to it" (337–338). Hartman (337), Joplin (39), and Rowe (53) view the myth of Philomela as archetypal; however, Rowe and Joplin present more positive readings of this archetype than mine.

The myth of Philomela also corroborates what many recent feminist critics have argued: that rape is more than just an act of physical or sexual violence: it is an attempt to stamp out or destroy a woman's agency, and it is tied to perpetuation of gender inequality and denial of feminine subjectivity. See, for example, Brownmiller (287), Griffin (23), Sanday (85), and MacKinnon (532). For an important discussion of the treatment of rape as an archetype in contemporary women's writing, see Froula.

2. Similarly, in Angelou's autobiographical *I Know Why the Caged Bird Sings*, after the young protagonist speaks in court about her rape, she almost seems to bite off her own tongue: "I could feel the evilness flowing through my body and waiting, pent up, to rush off my tongue if I tried to open my mouth. I clamped my teeth shut, I'd hold it in" (72). However, unlike those of Morrison's and Naylor's texts, Angelou's protagonist does eventually find her voice; as Froula argues, "Angelou's powerful memoir, recovering the history that frames it, rescues the child's voice . . . by telling the prohibited story" (637). The only study of the treatment of rape in African American fiction as a whole is that of Kubitschek; she examines different texts than I do and concludes that African American literature is most likely to portray "the strength which enables the rape victim to survive and recover" (44).

3. I have found no published statements in which Walker comments on having read the myth of Philomela. However, Walker's novel *Meridian* (1976) seems to refer even more directly to this myth than *The Color Purple*. One section of *Meridian* tells of an enslaved African American woman with an extremely powerful voice. She tells stories all the children love, but one day her stories frighten the master's son to death. In punishment, the master cuts out her tongue. She buries her tongue next to a tiny tree, which eventually flourishes and grows, becoming a symbol of the master's inability to completely erase women's voice, women's tongue. I believe the resonance between this story and the myth of Philomela is too strong to be coincidental.

4. Here I am arguing that Walker does more than simply allow her heroine to speak within the confines of patriarchal discourse. I use "patriarchal discourse" to mean a language system that grants men the right to be articulate subjects, while portraying women as silent objects. Such a discursive system is embodied in the novel by various male characters who believe that they should rule over women (Albert, Harpo), that women are objects of barter and exchange (Pa, Albert), and that women's main function is to support male subjectivity (Pa, Albert, and Harpo). The idea that men have more power in language than women also is directly alluded to by comments such as Albert's to Celie that "You can't curse nobody. . . . You black, you pore, you ugly, you a woman" (187) and by Harpo's to Mary Agnes: "Shut up Squeak. . . . It bad luck for women to laugh at men" (182). Yet within the novel there are many language systems, and Celie struggles in her letters and sewing to find an alternative methodology of language in which her own subjectivity and voice are not denied. I am not arguing, then, that language is always patriarchal, or for that matter, white; rather, I am arguing that it often gets *configured* as such, and that Walker's text is in larger measure about reconfiguring it.

5. In general, Greek myths do not offer raped women many options, as Zeitlin explains: "Whatever the outcome of the particular tale, and to whatever different uses it may be put, the repertory of Greek myth leaves us in no doubt that the female body is vulnerable to sexual assault. Fleeing sexual violence only entails another kind of forcible change to the body [metamorphosis], while those who succumb, especially when gods are the desirers, become pregnant and produce a hero child" (122–123).

6. Squeak/Mary Agnes's rape and movement towards voice can also be compared to Celie's. Again, Walker may be rewriting the mythic text, for after her rape Squeak becomes vocal, insisting that Harpo call her by her real name. Her creativity also seems to be unleashed; six months later she begins to sing. I am not arguing that Walker thinks rape is somehow "good" for women, nor do I agree with bell hooks's statement that Walker's treatment of the rape of a black woman by a white man shows "a benevolent portrayal of the consequences of rape" (222). Rather, Walker suggests that given the ubiquity of rape in society, women need to learn how to move beyond its victimization into agency and voice. All but one of Walker's central female characters have a rape (or an attempted rape) perpetrated against them. Celie and Squeak are actually raped, Nettie suffers an attempted rape, and even the strong-willed Sofia implies that she has learned to fight mainly to ward off unwanted sexual assaults by her male relatives (46).

7. Wall argues that in the novel, "the fact that no letters are ever exchanged (so that a running dialogue can occur) indicates a contemporary, solipsistic view of the absence within communication or, rather, of the continuous model of sender to receiver" (94).

8. Cheung also believes the title may be an allusion to the story of Philomela (172, n. 6) but does not discuss Walker's revision of this myth. For other readings of the title, see Abbandonato (1113).

9. For a corroborating view, see Abbandonato's statement that "in breaking the taboo against homosexuality, Celie symbolically exits the masternarrative of female sexuality and abandons the position ascribed to her within the symbolic order" (1111–1112). But for an alternative view, see hooks's argument that "Sexual desire, initially evoked in the novel as a subversive transformative force . . . is suppressed and finally absent—a means to an end but not an end in itself (217). I would agree with hooks that desire itself is not, per se, subversive in this novel, but that Celie's willingness to *articulate* her desire both privately and publicly is subversive.

10. For critics who argue that the novel's structure is quilt-like, see Abbandonato (1109), Wall (96), and Tavormina (225). Walker herself comments that she "wanted to do something like a crazy quilt. . . . A crazy-quilt story is one that can jump back and forth in time, work on many different levels, and one that can include myth" (*Black Women Writers at Work* 176).

Works Cited

Abbandonato, Linda. "A View from 'Elsewhere': Subversive Sexuality and the Rewriting of the Heroine's Story in *The Color Purple.*" *PMLA* 106 (1991): pp. 1106–1115.

Angelou, Maya. *I Know Why the Caged Bird Sings.* New York: Bantam, 1969.

Bergren, Ann L.T. "Language and the Female in Early Greek Thought." *Arethusa* 16 (1983): pp. 69–95.

Brownmiller, Susan. *Against Our Will: Men, Women and Rape.* New York: Simon and Schuster, 1975.

Byerman, Keith. "Walker's Blues." *Alice Walker.* Ed. Harold Bloom. (New York: Chelsea, 1989): pp. 59–66.

Cheung, King-Kok. "Don't Tell': Imposed Silences in *The Color Purple* and *The Woman Warrior.*" *PMLA* 103 (1988): pp. 162–174.

Froula, Christine. "The Daughter's Seduction: Sexual Violence and Literary History." *Signs* 11(1986): pp. 621–644.

Griffin, Susan. *Rape: The Politics of Consciousness.* San Francisco: Harper & Row, 1986.

Harris, Trudier, "From Victimization to Free Enterprise: Alice Walker's *The Color Purple*." *Studies in American Fiction* 14 (1986): pp. 1–17.

Hartman, Geoffrey. "The Voice of the Shuttle: Language from the Point of View of Literature." *Beyond Formalism*. (New Haven: Yale University Press, 1970): pp. 337–355.

Henderson, Mae G. "*The Color Purple:* Revisions and Redefinitions." *Alice Walker*. Ed. Harold Bloom. (New York: Chelsea, 1989): pp. 67–80.

hooks, bell. "Writing the Subject: Reading *The Color Purple*." *Alice Walker*. Ed. Harold Bloom. (New York: Chelsea, 1989): pp. 215–228.

Joplin, Patricia Klindienst. "The Voice of the Shuttle is Ours." *Rape and Representation*. Ed. Lynn Higgins and Brenda R. Silver. (New York: Columbia University Press, 1991): pp. 35–64.

Kubitschek, Missy Dehn. "Subjugated Knowledge: Toward a Feminist Exploration of Rape in Afro-American Fiction." *Black Feminist Criticism and Critical Theory*. Ed. Joe Weixlmann and Houston A. Baker, Jr. (Greenwood, FL: Penkeville, 1988): pp. 43–56.

MacKinnon, Catharine A. "Feminism, Marxism, Method, and the State: An Agenda for Theory." *Signs* 7 (1982): pp. 515–544.

Miner, Madonne. "Lady No Longer Sings the Blues: Rape, Madness, and Silence in *The Bluest Eye*." *Conjuring: Black Women, Fiction, and Literary Tradition*. Ed. Marjorie Pryse and Hortense Spillers. Bloomington: Indiana University Press, 1985.

Morrison, Toni. *The Bluest Eye*. New York: Washington Square, 1970.

Naylor, Gloria. *The Women of Brewster Place*. New York: Penguin, 1980.

Ovid. *Metamorphoses*. Trans. Rolfe Humphries. Bloomington: Indiana University Press, 1955.

Rooney, Ellen. "A Little More than Persuading': Tess and the Subject of Sexual Violence." *Rape and Representation*. Ed. Lynn Higgins and Brenda R. Silver. (New York: Columbia University Press, 1991): pp. 87–114.

Rowe, Karen E. "To Spin a Yarn: The Female Voice in Folklore and Fairy Tale." *Fairy Tales and Society: Illusion, Allusion, and Paradigm*. Ed. Ruth B. Bottigheimer. (Philadelphia: University of Pennsylvania Press, 1986):pp. 53–74.

Sanday, Peggy Reeves. "Rape and the Silencing of the Feminine." *Rape*. Ed. Sylvana Tomaselli and Roy Porter. (Oxford: Basil Blackwell, 1986): pp. 84–101.

Tavormina, M. Teresa. "Dressing the Spirit: Clothworking and Language in *The Color Purple*." *The Journal of Narrative Technique* 16 (1986): pp. 220–230.

Walker, Alice. *The Color Purple*. New York: Washington Square, 1982. Interview in *Black Women Writers at Work*. Ed. Claudia Tate. (New York: Continuum, 1983): pp. 175–187.

———. *Meridian*. New York: Simon and Schuster, 1976.

Wall, Wendy. "Lettered Bodies and Corporeal Texts in *The Color Purple*." *Studies in American Fiction* 16 (1988): pp. 83–97.

Zeitlin, Froma. "Configurations of Rape in Greek Myth." *Rape*. Ed. Sylvana Tomaselli and Roy Porter. (Oxford: Basil Blackwell, 1986): pp. 122–151.

CATHERINE E. LEWIS

Sewing, Quilting, Knitting: Handicraft and Freedom in The Color Purple and A Women's Story

From Susan Glaspell's short story "A Jury of Her Peers" (1917) to the film *How to Make an American Quilt* (1995), the presence of women working, making, caring, fighting, loving, arguing, and cherishing one another as they sew, quilt, weave, knit, and create has become a frequent image in 20th-century literature and film.[1] In a century defined largely by its mechanical progress and quickly turned-out products, movies and fiction seem to have regressed by 20th-century definitions. Handicraft has been reclaimed and accentuated, apparently in recognition of its ability to bond or its use as a medium to pass along information of former generations; furthermore, it frequently becomes neutral ground where everyone who participates is free to speak without fear or inhibition.

Despite their separations by time, race, nationality, and genre, Alice Walker's novel *The Color Purple* (1982) and Peng Xiaolian's film *A Women's Story* (1985) are representative of the use of handicraft in stories by and, largely, for women. National boundaries and differences in politics and custom disappear as these particular stories account for the lives of their characters and explore the means by which the women in them navigate their roles in two vastly different communities. From characterization and plot to more tenuous or abstract sisterly connections through oppressed womanhood, the works intersect. In each, three central women (there are others who appear in each

Literature/Film Quarterly, Volume 29, Number 3 (2001): pp. 236–245. © 2001 Salisbury University. All Rights Reserved.

work) from rural areas must battle social and political barriers to develop individual identities. Superficial elements also correspond closely, such as time
of publication or production, with *The Color Purple* published in 1982 and *A
Women's Story* produced in 1985 but released in 1987. That such similar narratives would develop from two artists who were unfamiliar with one another's
work initially seems coincidental.[2] The latter and other similarities notwith-
standing, an analysis of *The Color Purple* in conjunction with *A Women's Story* is
inherently problematic because of their multi-leveled stratification. *The Color
Purple*, a novel, is the story of an African-American woman, Celie, covering
30 years of her life, from the early to middle twentieth century. The other
two prominent women, Shug and Sofia, are developed also, but their stories
are told from Celie's perspective: Celie is foregrounded. *A Women's Story* is a
film that spans perhaps two weeks to a month in the lives of three Chinese
women—Mother Laizi, Xiaofeng, and Jinxiang—in the mid-1980s. The film
addresses them equally; in its limited omniscience, the camera does not privilege one woman over another. Thus, the works are cross-media, cross-genre,
cross-point-of-view, cross-time, cross-racial, and cross-cultural.

Any combination of these variables makes any evaluation difficult: with
all of them the question arises as to why one should even attempt such an
analysis. Different people bring into their evaluations vastly different ideologies and social codes. E. Ann Kaplan warns that such a culture-to-culture
analysis is "fraught with danger. We are forced to read works produced by the
Other through the constraints of our own frameworks/theories/ideologies"
(43). With all of the layers of difference, these two works would hardly seem
to correlate, and any combined evaluation would seem to be contrived.

It is understandable to want to study artistic endeavor within its own
contexts: such evaluation adds to the work's autonomy and fulfills the reader's
or viewer's sense of placement for the work. But works have many contexts:
time, author, genre, among others. While *The Color Purple* and *A Women's Story*
may digress in stylistics and ethnicity, at the core of each is the study of the
changing roles of women in evolving societies; consequently, the works are
not products simply of coincidental parallel evolution—borne of struggling
political systems in their respective countries—but become, rather, products
of convergent evolution, which means they may evolve in many ways from
diverse sources, but at some point they intersect,[3,4] Such points of intersection are key to the analysis of the relationship between *The Color Purple* and *A
Women's Story*. Despite the possibilities for a "[dangerous]" correlated reading,
"cross-cultural film analyses can be illuminating." Kaplan concedes. [I would
expand her discussion to multi-media arts as well.] She believes, "Theorists
outside the producing culture might uncover different strands of the multiple
meaning than critics of the originating culture just because they bring different frameworks/theories/ideologies to the texts" (42).[5]

Part of the intrigue of the relationship of *The Color Purple* and *A Women's Story* is that from disparity they are texts bound in feminist ideologies, bindings that are arguably transcultural. Across time, genre, and race the works join in their testimonies of the struggles and spirits of women who must make spaces for themselves in patriarchal societies. More concretely, the works unite as they explore the resources women have with which to fight. From early 20th-century Southern United States black communities to late 20th-century Chinese communities, women find means of liberation within the roles allotted them: in domestic duties and bonds the women in these works relate to one another, find individual and group strength, and turn skills from those roles into avenues for independence. In *The Color Purple* and *A Women's Story* alike, beyond intercultural differences, the heroines demand that patriarchal sanctions collapse upon themselves when the women use hand-crafts to free themselves from restrictions and take strength from female influence.

In their works, Alice Walker and Peng Xiaolian have created fictions, albeit art that is informed by history and society: hence, as creative pieces, the works should not be assumed to typify their originating cultures. To assume such would be to foster gross stereotypes of each culture. The women in each work do suffer and struggle in varying ways and degrees. However, black and Chinese men are not alone as instigators of female suffering, so the works are not "representative" of their respective cultures as wholes. In *The Color Purple*, Celie and Sofia endure horrible physical abuses; in *A Women's Story*. Mother Laizi, Xiaofeng, and Jinxiang fight the rigors of an anti-female society. And the sources of the oppressions differ also: the history of American slavery is an undercurrent in *The Color Purple*, and the patriarchal socialism and the wake of the disastrous Cultural Revolution drive much of *A Women's Story*.[6] Part of the difficulty of the cross-cultural and cross-time analysis is that the women of *The Color Purple* are much more limited at the beginning of the work, and the protagonists in *A Women's Story* have more options available to them. What is important in both works to the women's long-standing resilience is what King-Kok Cheung identifies as "psychological imperative," or the will to continue in life, and how this impetus leads to the use of manual skills, particularly those of domestic or hand-craft labors, as liberation techniques (165). Significant parallels emerge out of gender and culture to unite the heroines in their struggles and quests for individuation.

"My angel daughter," said Aurora, "if society has decreed that ladies must be ladies, then that is our first duty; our second is to live. Do you not see why it is that this practical world does not permit ladies to make a living? Because if they could, none of them would ever consent to be married. Ha! women talk about marrying for love;

but society is too sharp to trust them, yet! It makes it *necessary* to marry. I will tell you the honest truth; some days when I get very, very hungry, and we have nothing but rice—all because we are ladies without male protectors—I think society could drive even me to marriage!—for your sake, though, darling; of course, only for your sake!" (*The Grandissimes* 255)

If the women of *The Color Purple* and *A Women's Story* realize similar results from their fettered lives, the creation of salable items to effect economic and psychological empowerment, then these results are due largely to the women experiencing comparable forms of bondage. Again, the restraint in *The Color Purple* is much more harsh physically than that seen in *A Women's Story*, but the motivations in each are similar. Male domination appears in a variety of forms in each work; sexual subordination, financial limitations, and emotional domination are included as male tools of restraint. The link between the two works is evident early in each as both open with the silencing of women.

When, in *The Color Purple*, Celie is raped by her stepfather Alphonso, he orders her to "not never tell nobody but God. It'd kill your mammy" (11). In this threat he imposes fear and guilt of possible maternal death on the young, superstitious, and psychologically naïve Celie. Alphonso silences Celie's voice. Later, when he and Albert barter for her, Alphonso again silences Celie, but this time it is her credibility, for he tells Albert, "[s]he tell lies" (18).[7] Repeatedly in the novel other women (never another man) admonish her to fight or speak up for herself or intervene for her with Albert; others act as her voice, for she has none. Albert's sister Kate tells him Celie needs a new dress; she cannot even declare her most basic needs, much less those that are psychologically intricate. Celie imagines Albert thinking of her as "It," objectifying herself in his mind as though she were a floor that needed a new rug. Later, Celie asks Shug to remain in their home because Albert beats Celie when Shug is not there, a confession that leads Shug to reject Albert eventually in favor of Celie.

The concern with voiced-ness occurs again when Sofia, who is quite outspoken, suffers horribly and extensively for "[s]assing the mayor's wife" (85). When she is arrested the officers beat her savagely, rendering her speechless: "When I [Celie] see Sofia I don't know why she still alive. They crack her skull, they crack her ribs. They tear her nose loose on one side. They blind her in one eye. She swole from head to foot. Her tongue the size of my arm, it stick out tween her teef like a piece of rubber. She can't talk" (87). Sofia must be punished at the mouth that offended, according to white legal and political dictates in the novel. When Celie, Albert, Harpo, and Shug are allowed to visit her and Celie asks her how she copes, Sofia answers in a way that reinforces the significance of voiceless female passivity in their community: "Every time they ast me to do something, Miss Celie, I act like I'm you. I jump right up and do just what they say" (88). Sofia condemns Celie's docility, intimating that despite the trouble, she would still rather have fought than be trod over anyway while remaining quiet. Her family and friends recognize the weight of Sofia's remarks and are essentially speechless themselves at her quiet intensity: "Mr. _____ suck in his breath. Harpo groan. Miss Shug cuss [a speech act of indefinite meaning] ... I can't fix my mouth to say how I feel" (88). Sofia continues her vituperation at the white patriarchy, and her visitors "don't say nothing" (89). Sofia is quiet to her jailers but retains her voice in her own group, an act that Celie cannot yet muster. Whether it is the white jailers or the black men in Celie's life, each embodies the patriarchy, silencing the women physically, legally, or ideologically.

In *A Women's Story*, the women have the physical ability to speak, but, like Celie, they are limited in power; they do not have a "say" or a "voice" as to how they conduct their lives. The initial scene pans into the home of Jinxiang, a young woman who must submit to a forced marriage with a deaf-mute. Further comparable to Celie is that a male, Jinxiang's brother, has arranged the marriage, without consideration for his sister's feelings, so she, too, is a commodity to be bartered. The brother gets the wife he chooses, the deaf-mute's sister, if the deaf-mute gets Jinxiang. Ironically, a man incapable of speech has more power or "say" than a woman with voice; his physical silence is more capable than her voice for her desire is silenced. Jinxiang's mother, a representative of the old or patriarchal nature of the society, is no female ally for her daughter. The mother tells Jinxiang to "be a good girl" (submit to the marriage for your brother's and family's sake), reminding her that "women often have no choice." The scene ends with Jinxiang's cries and protests while young *male* children run through the village mocking her.

The situations of the other two women are just as clouded by male patriarchy, but are less confrontational than shown in the scene with Jinxiang. Of the three women. Mother Laizi is the oldest and most traditional. She has a son, the male heir so vital in the community, and throughout the film, her concern and longings and efforts for economic security are for him and his future. Her voicelessness is indicated in her loss of identity. She is called "Mother Laizi" in the entirety of the film; her identity is bound up in a boy approximately eight years old, for her son is "Laizi." She is known only as his mother. This privileging of young males is also resonant with *The Color Purple* in that Celie, upon marriage to Albert, is prey to the actions of 12-year-old Harpo; he splits her head open with a rock when she arrives at Albert's home on their wedding day, and there is negligible reproach from Albert.

The third woman in *A Women's Story* is Xiaofeng, who is made to feel inferior in her community because she is, through no fault of her own, from a family of four girls and no boys. Xiaofeng and her mother and sisters are scorned and ridiculed. Without males, the family is ostracized and statusless. Xiaofeng is in love with a young man in the village, but because she has no standing, or a male to speak for her, other women laugh at the thought that she will marry whom she chooses. Xiaofeng's situation also correlates with *The Color Purple* since Sofia's family has many girls (although some males), and Albert tries to cast patriarchal aspersions on Sofia's character as he attempts to block her marriage to Harpo. Also, as society shuns Xiaofeng, Shug also is shunned. The preacher speaks against Shug, and no one speaks up for her. Religion is one more institution that silences women, for the minister's words, coming from the pulpit are sanctified, given credence.

In each work the author or director sets into the narrative framework women who are bound physically, legally, psychologically, and socially by male codes, codes often held up by other women. The central figures in the works are restricted by the lack of free expression and by men and the male institutions; these women are considered worthless unless codified by the presence of some male Other in their lives.

Commentary on creativity in Victorian England includes the idea that much artistic production was the result of rechanneled energies in the repressive times.[8] During the times of tension in the book and the film, creative energies are omnipresent. Much of this creativity takes place in domestic situations, particularly in *The Color Purple*. The impetus for Celie's writing is her rape by Alphonso. Alice Walker presents the book as the result of Celie's silence, confusion, and frustration. Celie takes Alphonso's idea literally, and as tensions rise in the family, Celie records herself. When she marries Albert, she continues to write, and much of her account is of creativity or arrangement; she designs what parts of her life she can, out of frustration about her separation from Nettie and about her abusive marriage to a virtual stranger. Whether combing hair, cooking or cleaning, necessary domestic endeavors provide Celie with routine when the psychological, social, and sexual parts of her life are anything but predictable.

One component of Celie's life that becomes more and more stable is her ability to relate to women. She finds her voice louder and more clearly with them first, and then she is able to eventually face the men in her life. Many of the scenes in *The Color Purple* where Celie learns to bond are those in which the women share in sewing or quilting.[9] Walker introduces the extensive bonds possible through hand-work when Sofia confronts Celie after she encourages Harpo to beat Sofia. The two women reconcile over cutting torn curtains into quilting squares (47). As Celie and Sofia continue to work on the quilt, it becomes an emblem of unity among the women. Judy Elsley declares, "Celie's quilt becomes a celebration of fragments, a recognition and reverence for pieces" (76). With each woman in Celie's female support-system contributing, the quilt, made in the "Sister's Choice" pattern, reverberates a sense of sorority. Celie and Sofia make the quilt of shared materials; Celie uses pieces of a yellow dress Shug donated to the effort. Elsley notes that at the heart of the Sister's Choice pattern is a nine-square patch, the design Corinne uses when making quilts of her and Olivia's old dresses (77). It is one of Corinne's quilts Nettie uses to exonerate herself and Samuel in Corinne's accusations of adultery and then to prove Adam and Olivia's maternity. Walker links six women in the quilting scene, strengthening the bonds among them all that have seen and will see each woman through much hardship.

Once the bonds are established, Celie grows in confidence. Again, however, male interference brings the need for a redirection of Celie's malevolent energies. When Shug tells Celie that Nettie has written her sister for years but that Albert has hidden the letters, Celie, for the first time, does not resign herself to God's will and the abstract dream of a heaven that waits and rewards; Celie records clearly her anger and bitterness instead of a resigned hope of a vague hereafter. Just as Sofia wants to kill white people after she is beaten and jailed, when she experiences the extreme of the abuse she hates most, being beaten, so does Celie express a desire to kill when she experiences the final hateful blow dealt her by Albert—willful and spiteful separation from Nettie's letters *for years*! Celie can withstand the perhaps impulsive beatings, but she does not tolerate Albert's premeditated deprivation of the letters:

He been keeping your letters, say Shug.

Naw, I say. Mr. _____ mean sometimes, but he not that mean.

She say, Humpf, he that mean.

But how come he do it? I ast. He know Nettie mean everything in the world to me. . . .

I watch him so close, I begin to feel a lightening in the head. Fore I know anything I'm standing hind his chair with his razor open.
. . .

All day long I act just like Sofia. I stutter. I mutter to myself. I stumble bout the house crazy for Mr. _____ blood. In my mind, he falling down dead every which a way. By the time night come, I can't speak. Every time I open my mouth nothing come out but a little burp. (115)

Mr. _____ has once again rendered her speechless. For Celie, this is the turning point in the novel.

With Shug's assistance, Celie embarks on a new outlet for her rage, and eventually turns that rage into her means of escaping Albert's domination:

> She [Shug] say, Times like this, lulls, us ought to do something different.
>
> Like what? I ast.
>
> Well, she say, looking me up and down, lets make you some pants.
>
> What I need pants for? I say. I ain't no man.
>
> Don't git uppity, she say. But you don't have a dress do nothing for you. You not made like no dress pattern, neither.
> I don't know, I say. Mr. _____ not going to let his wife wear pants.
>
> Why not? say Shug. You do all the work around here. It's a scandless, the way you look out there plowing in a dress. How your keep from falling over it or getting the plow caught in it is beyond me. . . .
>
> What us gon make 'em out of. I say.
>
> We have to git our hands on somebody's army uniform, say Shug. For practice. . . .
>
> And everyday we going to read Nettie's letters and sew.
>
> A needle and not a razor in my hand, I think. (136–137)

In this passage Celie's bond with Shug is cemented. Shug rescues the letters and repudiates Albert and his hold on Celie. Celie is flattered that Shug has noticed her in the field and begins to understand that she has Shug's unconditional affection. Shug further seals the circle of another set of the three women—Shug, Celie, and Nettie—when she wants to be a part of Celie's joy at reading the letters: there is no jealousy or attempt to soothe Celie's anger with a clichéd comment about the passage of time healing Celie, Shug returns Celie's altruistic love and shows Celie how to turn her sewing skills and anger into productive work.

Throughout *The Color Purple*. Celie puts others before herself, a habit that often works to her detriment. When she and Shug create Folkspants

Unlimited, though, that selflessness reaps rewards, for Celie makes custom-tailored pants to fit the bodies and personalities of the people who wear them. She chooses colors and styles based on her interpretations of the people who will wear the pants. Soon, orders come in from all over since Shug and the band wear the pants on their tours. Celie is even able to hire employees and support herself, due largely to Shug's helping her to focus her anger. Once she sees the potential of Folkspants, though, Celie combines her care for meticulous quality with her skill. She indicates this combination with the care and reverence she gives to making Nettie's pants, choosing the material to fit the African climate and hand-sewing them, so that "[e]very stitch [I] sew will be a kiss" (192).

A Women's Story unfolds similarly to *The Color Purple*. The three women leave their village because the fields and factory do not provide them with sufficient means on which to live. They take yarn that has been mass-produced in their village to sell in the more populous and prosperous city. While in the city the women fall prey to standard country versus city difficulties. They get lost. Mother Laizi is duped by a con artist. Jinxiang is lured by the exotic fashions of the city girls. Xiaofeng falls for a construction worker and spends the night with him, incurring the wrath of the traditional Mother Laizi. As they stay in the city, however, they begin to bond with one another as they face their trials.

From the first day of their journey they are essentially haunted by the recurring presence of a pregnant woman. Foreshadowing her own complete repudiation of societal expectations, Xiaofeng befriends the outcast woman who is removed from the train and who is pursued by the police. This almost spectral woman is a glaring reminder of the imposition of the Chinese state on a woman's body. The woman is pregnant for the second time during a time when women of childbearing age may have only one child; most desire that the child be a male, someone who cannot bear more children and who will be, supposedly, a more valuable worker. This is ironic in a country that asserts that it upholds socialist politics, ostensibly a situation that presumes that it practices gender equity. For an incredibly populated city, it is a bit contrived in the film that the women happen upon the pregnant woman three times. It is not clear from the film whether Peng Xiaolian wanted to comment on the cruelty of limits imposed upon those who desire to care for and love more than one child, or if she wanted to make clear the Chinese state's ideological preference for male children. But the last time the women see the mother, she is exhausted from the outdoor, unattended birth and weakly stumbles away, muttering that she got her boy. If Peng Xiaolian included the pregnant woman for either or both purposes, she certainly succeeded in showing the extent to which the government controls women and constrains them to produce males in order that the state may maintain its male-centered system. Women are little more than son-bearers.

To make her characters more able to compete in their society, Peng Xiaolian must, like Walker, have her women work within the system for a while in order to eventually have the means by which to transcend it. When trying to compete in the open sellers' market, the women have little success. There are other yarn sellers and the women must repeatedly try to undercut one another; when they work at odds with one another, there is little to be gained. Also, in the film, it is evident that part of what they must learn in the city is that most people buy clothing that is pre-manufactured, not yarn with which consumers would have to knit their own goods. When rains and trampling ruin much of their yarn, they must find ways to recoup their losses. Mother Laizi has lost one inventory to a thief; she cannot afford to lose again. The women finally start to see success when they work together. They dry the wet yarn, order more from their boss at the mill, and hit upon the idea to knit the yarn into usable goods. Working together, the women earn the money they sought when they left home. They knit at night and sell the sweaters and vests and other items in the daytime.

Moral critics may argue that Celie and the other women in each story accomplish what they do because they are patient, they endure, and they work hard. Considering what each has to contend with, such an argument seems flimsy. Much of the success in the two works depends on the women's abilities to function in male terms in their male-dominated world. At the crux of that functioning is economic independence. For Celie, Sofia, Shug, Jinxiang, Xiaofeng, and Mother Laizi, their bonds with one another and their new-found strengths result in part from helping one another to become more financially secure. Once they achieve that security, they are able to shed the chains imposed upon them by the men and male institutions in their lives. In her essay "The Unhappy Marriage of Marxism and Feminism: Towards a More Progressive Union," Heidi I. Hartmann documents other cases in which male-centered patriarchal employment systems unravel because of the restrictions against women. The men then blame the women in the work-force for problems that would not have existed had the males not bound the economic sources (21). Similar situations exist in *The Color Purple* and *A Women's Story*. Ironically, Celie eventually escapes Albert because of indignities heaped upon her. He brings his mistress into his home and expects his wife to care for her; this woman, Shug, then loves Celie in preference to Albert and helps Celie to direct her anger, fury that is a direct result of Albert's hiding Nettie's letters. Celie finds her voice in spite of Albert, and when she does, she uses it to speak against him. Shug says Celie will accompany her to Memphis; Albert forbids it and asks why, hurt that he is not going with Shug. Celie's pent-up wrath explodes at Albert:

I thought you was finally happy, he say. What wrong now?

You a lowdown dog is what's wrong, I say. It's time to leave you and enter into the Creation. And your dead body just the welcome mat I need.

Say what? he ast, Shock.
All round the table folkses mouths be dropping open.

You took my sister Nettie away from me, I say. And she the only person love me in the world. . . .

Sofia so surprise to hear me speak up she ain't chewed for ten minutes. (181)

After this Celie and Shug go to Memphis, and Celie's business increases to the point that she is self-supporting and an employer. Albert pushes far past the point of rebellion; he does not count on the strength the women find through each other.

Likewise, in *A Women's Story*, the women find strength from among themselves when their patriarchal society refuses to acknowledge their demands. Xiaofeng ignores her culture's demands of propriety when it refuses to help her and defiantly sleeps with a construction worker she meets in the city. Jinxiang also feels no obligation to a system that so callously offers her for exchange. While Peng Xiaolian's statement against the government is quite understated, she does offer an ending that corroborates the argument thus far.[10] At the end of the film the women return to the village. Mother Laizi is reunited with her son; Xiaofeng returns to the haven of her family. However, the film ends with Jinxiang's jilted husband walking toward her to take her home with a rope in his hands and a large, hired tough-guy with him. Xiaofeng and, surprisingly, Mother Laizi walk away from the other cowering women of the village to surround Jinxiang and encourage her to take him to court to get out of the marriage; they vow to support her. In the end, Peng Xiaolian offers the faint hope that these women, strengthened by one another and more financially competitive than at the outset of the film, will overcome the rigors of the state.

In "The Laugh of the Medusa" Hélène Cixous proclaims:

If she [woman] is whole, it's a whole composed of parts that are wholes, not single partial objects but a moving, limitlessly changing ensemble, a cosmos tirelessly traversed by Eros, an immense astral space not organized around any one sun that's any more of a star than the others. (217)

Cixous's argument assumes an ideal situation, one that certainly does not exist in the worlds of the women in *The Color Purple* and *A Women's Story*. But parts of her assertion are certainly applicable. As each woman strives to be "whole," she is more able to achieve wholeness because she is a sum of parts; she is made up of those around her; she takes from their strengths and gives of her own strength to help the other women in her life become whole also. Certainly Celie, Shug, and Sofia, and Mother Laizi, Xiaofeng, and Jinxiang are elements in Cixous's galaxy as they interact with one another. They do not eclipse one another; thus, they meet each of Cixous's requirements except that they are not yet whole. They are still striving for it, although they have advanced significantly toward wholeness by the ends of their works. Celie and Mother Laizi offer resiliency; Shug and Jinxiang are daring; Sofia and Xiaofeng are strong; in each work, the women, with their individual strengths and weaknesses, combine to create a unified whole being out of a tripartite union; they evolve from sisterly reciprocity that reinforces rather than diminishes them. Despite the cultural differences of the two works, they, too, take from one another and combine in a relationship perhaps not anticipated at their inceptions. The sets of women in each take the meager external resources available to them and combine them with the phenomenal internal assets accorded to each character. What results are two works that assert that neither the constraints of patriarchy nor the sisterhood that can transcend that patriarchy are bound by culture or time. Women's common experiences that have too long been undervalued, such as domestic and manual labor, can be used to overturn the systems that have imposed and labeled the tasks.

NOTES

1. See also Susan Glaspell's play *Trifles*, which tells the same story as "A Jury of Her Peers." Terry McMillan's "Quilting on the Rebound" (1991) in *Calling the Wind*, edited by Clarence Major, and Kaye Gibbons's *A Cure for Dreams* (1991) and *Charms for the Easy Life* (1992), among others.

2. *The Color Purple* was not published in Chinese translation until 1986; thus it is unlikely that Peng Xiaolian was familiar with the book, (source: *RLIN*).

3. E. Ann Kaplan, Esther C. M. Yau, and Yuejin Wang acknowledge the difficulties of evaluating Asian cinema through Western ideologies. saying that cross-cultural analyses can easily lapse into "sentimental leftism" (Wang 33), that tries to apply Western feminist interpretations to works that are imbued with more layers of social and political concerns than Westerners initially understand.

4. To assign to each work the image of a ray that continues forward and intersects the other ray at only one point is somewhat misleading, for these works may generate from far-ranging sources, but they intersect at many points. Commonalties in these works refute linear notions of intersection.

5. Kaplan's comments resonate with the writings of Roland Barthes's essay "From Work to Text," in which he asserts that "works" become "texts" as they meet with varied readings and interpretations, situations that infinitely defer meaning, in accordance with Barthes's fourth postulate in the essay (160).

6. In each work the imposing institutions are what Louis Althusser has termed "ideological state apparatuses"—ideologies bound in systems, perceived governing structures of religious, legal, political, social, or other regional institutions (242).

7. Bakhtin's concept of the effect of authorial influence is relevant in the study of Alphonso's effect on Celie. In his "Discourse in the Novel" Bakhtin says, "We have in mind first of all those instances of powerful influence exercised by another's discourse on a given author. When such influences are laid bare, the half-concealed life lived by another's discourse is revealed within the new context of the given author" (786). Alphonso inculcates in Celie's mind a sense of her own cipher-like quality. When Shug calls her ugly, Celie is not surprised or hurt; she simply acknowledges it as a fact. Alphonso beats her verbally as well as physically.

8. G. D. Klingopulos discusses this at length, exploring the hypothesis that tumultuous society often experiences a balance of order in its art (14–17). To under-score this possibility are the echoes of Victorian England in each of the works in question. When Celie finally retrieves Nettie's letters from Albert's hiding place, they are covered with "little fat queen of England stamps" (114). Also, the images of Western influence are shown in the teeming city in *WS*, reminding viewers of England's empirical presence in 19th century mainland China and 20th century Hong Kong.

9. The metaphorical implications in Walker's attention to quilting details have been the focus of a number of critical inquiries (see Cheung, Judy Elsley, Priscilla Leder, Mary Jane Lupton, and M. Teresa Tavormena, among others).

10. In an interview with Chris Berry, Peng Xiaolian relays the story of how she was bound as a filmmaker for a state-run studio. Each film is screened and reviewed by a board that demands the removal of footage it deems inappropriate.

Works Cited

Althusser, Louis. "Ideology and Ideological State Apparatuses." *Critical Theory Since 1965.* Ed. Hazard Adams and Leroy Searle. (Tallahassee: University of Florida Press, 1986): pp. 238–250.

Bakhtin, Mikhail. "Discourse in the Novel." *The Critical Tradition.* Ed. David H. Richter. (New York: St. Martin's, 1989): pp. 781–791.

Barthes, Roland. "From Work to Text." *Image, Music, Text.* Trans, Stephen Heath. (New York: Hill and Wang, 1977): pp. 155–162.

Berry, Chris. "An Interview with Peng Xiaolian." *Wide Angle* 11 (1989): pp. 26–31.

Cable, George Washington. *The Grandissimes.* 1879. Athens: University Georgia Press, 1988.

Cheung, King-Kok. "'Don't Tell': Imposed Silences in *The Color Purple* and *The Woman Warrior.*" *Reading the Literature of Asian America.* Ed. Shirley Geok-Lim and Amy Ling. (Philadelphia: Temple University Press, 1992): pp. 163–189.

Cixous, Hélène. "The Laugh of the Medusa." *Critical Theory Since 1965.* Ed. Hazard Adams and Leroy Searle. (Tallahassee: University of Florida Press, 1986): pp. 309–321.

Elsley, Judy. "'Nothing Can Be Sole or Whole that has Not Been Rent': Fragmentation in the Quilt and *The Color Purple.*" *Weber Studies* 9 (Spring/Summer 1992): pp. 71–81.

Hartmann, Heidi. "The Unhappy Marriage of Feminism and Marxism: Towards a More Progressive Union." *Women and Revolution.* Ed. Lydia Sargent. (Boston: South End, 1981): pp. 1–41.

Kaplan, E. Ann. "Problematizing Cross-Cultural Analysis: The Case of Women in Recent Chinese Cinema." *Wide Angle* 11 (1989): pp. 40–50.

Klingopulos, G. D. "Notes on the Victorian Scene." *The New Pelican Guide to English Literature: 6. From Dickens to Hardy.* Ed. Boris Ford. (Middlesex, England: Penguin, 1982): pp. 13–52.

Leder, Priscilla. "Alice Walker's American Quilt: *The Color Purple* and American Literary Tradition." *Journal of the American Studies Association of Texas* 20 (October 1989): pp. 79–93.

Lupton, Mary Jane. "Clothes and Closure in Three Novels by Black Women." *Black American Literature Forum* 20 (Winter 1986): pp. 409–421.

Peng, Xiaolian, dir. *A Women's Story.* Shanghai Film Studio, 1987.

Tavormena, M. Teresa. "Dressing the Spirit: Clothmaking and Language in *The Color Purple.*" *Journal of Narrative Technique* 16 (Fall 1986): pp. 220–230.

Walker, Alice. *The Color Purple.* New York: Washington Square, 1982.

Wang, Yuejin. "The Cinematic Other and the Cultural Self? Decentering the Cultural Identity on Cinema." *Wide Angle* 11 (1989): pp. 32–39.

Yau, Esther C. M. "Cultural and Economic Dislocations: Film's Phantasies of Chinese Women in the 1980s." *Wide Angle* 11 (1989): pp. 6–21.

Chronology

1944	Walker is born on February 9, in Eatonton, Georgia, the eighth and last child of Willie Lee and Minnie (Grant) Walker, both sharecroppers.
1961–1963	Walker attends Spelman College in Atlanta Georgia and becomes involved with the civil rights movement.
1964	Walker travels to Africa and begins writing the poems that will later appear as *Once*. She also transfers to Sarah Lawrence College in New York.
1965	Walker receives BA degree from Sarah Lawrence College.
1965–1968	Walker works in the welfare department in New York City and becomes deeply involved in the civil rights movement.
1967	Walker marries Melvyn Roseman Leventhal, a civil rights lawyer, and later has one daughter, Rebecca.
1968	Walker's book of poetry, *Once*, written in the aftermath of a traumatic abortion in college, is published. She becomes a writer-in-residence and teacher of black studies at Jackson State University, Mississippi. The following year she teaches at Tougalou College.
1970	Walker's first novel, *The Third Life of Grange Copeland*, is published.
1973	*In Love and Trouble: Stories of a Black Women*, is published as well as *Revolutionary Petunias*, a book of poetry.

1974	Walker publishes *Langston Hughes*, a biography for young people, and receives the National Institute of Arts and Letters Award for *In Love and Trouble*.
1976	*Meridian*, a second novel, is published. She and Leventhal divorce.
1977	Walker receives a Guggenheim Fellowship.
1979	*Good Night Willie Lee, I'll See You in the Morning*, a collection of poems, is published. Walker edits *I Love Myself When I Am Laughing . . . And Then Again When I Am Looking Mean and Impressive: A Zora Neale Hurston Reader*. She moves to California to begin work on *The Color Purple*.
1981	*You Can't Keep a Good Woman Down*, a book of stories, is published.
1982	*The Color Purple*, a novel, is published. Walker is named distinguished writer in Afro-American Studies at Berkeley. She teaches at Brandeis University as the Fannie Hurst Professor of Literature.
1983	Walker wins the Pulitzer Prize and the American Book Award for *The Color Purple* and publishes *In Search of Our Mother's Gardens: Womanist Prose*, a collection of essays.
1984	*Horses Make a Landscape Look More Beautiful*, a volume of poetry, is published.
1985	*The Color Purple* is adapted for film, directed by Steven Spielberg and stars Whoopi Goldberg as Celie.
1988	*Living by the Word: Selected Writings, 1973–1987* is published.
1989	*The Temple of My Familiar*, a novel, is published.
1991	*Her Blue Body, Everything We Knew: Earthling Poems 1965–1990 Complete* is published.
1992	*Possessing the Secret of Joy*, a novel, is published.
1993	*Warrior Marks: Female Genital Mutilation and the Sexual Blinding of Women* is published as a companion volume to the documentary *Warrior Marks*, directed by Pratibha Parmar and produced by Walker.
1996	*The Same River Twice: Honoring the Difficult*, a book of essays, is published.
1997	*Anything We Love Can Be Saved*, a collection of essays, is published.
1998	*By the Light of My Father's Smile*, a novel, is published.

2000	Walker's novel *The Way Forward Is with a Broken Heart* is published.
2002	*A Poem Traveled down My Arm: Poem and Drawings,* is published.
2003	*Absolute Trust in the Goodness of the Earth: New Poems,* Walker's first poetry collection in twelve years, is published.
2004	*Now Is the Time to Open Your Heart,* Walker's ninth novel, is published.
2008	Emory University acquires Alice Walker's entire archival papers.

Contributors

HAROLD BLOOM is Sterling Professor of the Humanities at Yale University. He is the author of 30 books, including *Shelley's Mythmaking* (1959), *The Visionary Company* (1961), *Blake's Apocalypse* (1963), *Yeats* (1970), *A Map of Misreading* (1975), *Kabbalah and Criticism* (1975), *Agon: Toward a Theory of Revisionism* (1982), *The American Religion* (1992), *The Western Canon* (1994), and *Omens of Millennium: The Gnosis of Angels, Dreams, and Resurrection* (1996). *The Anxiety of Influence* (1973) sets forth Professor Bloom's provocative theory of the literary relationships between the great writers and their predecessors. His most recent books include *Shakespeare: The Invention of the Human* (1998), a 1998 National Book Award finalist, *How to Read and Why* (2000), *Genius: A Mosaic of One Hundred Exemplary Creative Minds* (2002), *Hamlet: Poem Unlimited* (2003), *Where Shall Wisdom Be Found?* (2004), and *Jesus and Yahweh: The Names Divine* (2005). In 1999, Professor Bloom received the prestigious American Academy of Arts and Letters Gold Medal for Criticism. He has also received the International Prize of Catalonia, the Alfonso Reyes Prize of Mexico, and the Hans Christian Andersen Bicentennial Prize of Denmark.

DANIEL W. ROSS is professor of English at Columbus State University in Columbus, Georgia. He edited *The Critical Response to William Styron* (1995).

LAUREN BERLANT is George M. Pullman Professor of English at the University of Chicago. Among her books is what she calls a trilogy on national sentimentality. It comprises, in order: *The Anatomy of National Fan-*

tasy (1991); *The Female Complaint: the Unfinished Business of Sentimentality in American Culture*, will (2008); and *The Queen of America Goes to Washington City: Essays on Sex and Citizenship* (1997).

JACQUELINE BOBO is professor and chair of the Women's Studies Program at The University of California, Santa Barbara. She is editor of the *Black Studies Reader* (2004) and *Black Feminist Cultural Criticism* (2001) and author of *Black Women as Cultural Readers* (1995).

PRISCILLA L. WALTON is professor of English at Carleton University in Ottawa, Ontario. She is the author of *Our Cannibals, Ourselves* (2004) and *Detective Agency: Women Rewriting the Hard-boiled Tradition* (1999).

OM P. JUNEJA is a professor of English at Mysore University, Baroda. She is author of *Post-Colonial Novel: Narratives of Colonial Consciousness* (1995).

CHARLES L. PROUDFIT is emeritus professor of English at University of Colorado at Boulder

DIANE GABRIELSEN SCHOLL is professor of English at Luther College.

LINDA SELZER is assistant professor of English at the Pennsylvania State University, specializing in African American literature and culture. She is co-editor of *New Essays on the African American Novel: From Hurston and Ellison to Morrison and Whitehead* (2008).

MARTHA J. CUTTER is associate professor of English Kent State University. She is author of *Unruly Tongue: Language and Identity in American Women's Writing, 1850-1930* (1999) and *Lost and Found in Translation: Contemporary Ethnic American Writing and the Politics of Language Diversity* (2005).

CATHERINE E. LEWIS is an instructor at Louisiana State University.

Bibliography

Alps, Sandra. "Concepts of Self-Hood in *Their Eyes Were Watching God* and *The Color Purple*." *Pacific Review* 4 (Spring 1986): pp. 106–112.

Awkward, Michael. *Inspiring Influence: Tradition, Revision and Afro-American Women's Novels*. New York: Columbia University Press, 1991.

Babb, Valerie. "*The Color Purple:* Writing to Undo What Writing Has Done." *Phylon* 47 (June 1986): pp. 107–116.

Banks, Erma Davis, and Keith Byerman. *Alice Walker: An Annotated Bibliography 1968–1986*. New York: Garland, 1989.

Bloom, Harold, ed. *Alice Walker*. New York: Chelsea House, 1989.

Bobo, Jacqueline. "*The Color Purple:* Black Women as Cultural Readers," edited by Brooker, Will and Jermyn, Deborah. *The Audience Studies Reader*. London, England: Routledge, 2003.

Butler-Evans, Elliot. *Race, Gender, and Desire: Narrative Strategies in the Fiction of Toni Cade Bambara, Toni Morrison and Alice Walker*. Philadelphia: Temple University Press, 1989.

Byerman, Keith. "Desire and Alice Walker: the Quest for a Womanist Narrative." *Callaloo* 12 (Spring 1989): pp. 343–345.

Chambers, Kimberly. "Right on Time: History and Religion in Alice Walker's *The Color Purple*." *CLA Journal* 31 (September 1987): pp. 44–62.

Cheung, King-Kok. "'Don't Tell': Imposed Silences in *The Color Purple* and *The Woman Warrior*." *PMLA* 103 (March 1988): pp. 162–174.

Christian, Barbara. "The Contrary Black Women of Alice Walker." *Black Scholar* 12 (March–April 1981): pp. 21–30, 70–71.

————."Alice Walker: The Black Woman Artist as Wayward." In *Black Women Writers (1950–1980): A Critical Evaluation,* edited by Mari Evans. Garden City, NY: Anchor-Doubleday, 1984.

Coleman, Viralene J. "Miss Celie's Song." *Publications of the Arkansas Philological Association* 11 (Spring 1985): pp. 27–34.

Collins, Gina Michelle. "*The Color Purple:* What Feminism Can Learn From a Southern Tradition." In *Southern Literature and Literary Theory,* edited by Jefferson Humphries. Athens: University of Georgia Press, 1990.

Cutter, Martha J. "Philomela Speaks: Alice Walker's Revisioning of Rape Archetypes in *The Color Purple.*" *MELUS,* 25:3–4 (2000 Fall–Winter), pp. 161–180.

Davis, Jane. "*The Color Purple:* A Spiritual Descendant of Hurston's *Their Eyes Were Watching God.*" *Griot* 6 (Summer 1987): pp. 317–331.

Dieke, Ikenna, ed. *Critical Essays on Alice Walker.* Westport, CT: Greenwood, 1999.

Dozier, Judy. "Who You Callin a Lady?: Resisting Sexual Definition in *The Color Purple.*" *Griot: Official Journal of the Southern Conference on Afro-American Studies, Inc.,* 21:2 (2002 Fall), pp. 8–16.

Dreifus, Claudia. "Alice Walker: Writing to Save My Life" (interview). *The Progressive* 53 (August 1989): pp. 29–32.

Duckworth, Victoria. "The Redemptive Impulse: Wise Blood and *The Color Purple.*" *The Flannery O'Connor Bulletin* 15 (1986): pp. 51–56.

DuPlessis, Rachel Blau. *Writing Beyond the Ending: Narrative Strategies of Twentieth-Century Women Writers.* Bloomington: Indiana University Press, 1985.

Early, Gerald. "*The Color Purple* as Everybody's Protest Art." *Antioch Review* 44 (Summer 1986): pp. 261–275.

Eddy, Charmaine. "Marking the Body: The Material Dislocation of Gender in Alice Walker's *The Color Purple.*" *ARIEL: A Review of International English Literature,* 34:2–3 (2003 April–July): pp. 37–70.

El Saffer, Ruth. "Alice Walker's *The Color Purple.*" *International Fiction Review* 12 (Winter 1985): pp. 11–17.

Fannin, Alice. "A Sense of Wonder: The Pattern for Psychic Survival in *Their Eyes Were Watching God* and *The Color Purple.*" *The Zora Neale Hurston Forum* 1 (Fall 1986).

Fifer, Elizabeth. "The Dialect and Letter of *The Color Purple.*" In *Contemporary American Women Writers: Narrative Strategies,* edited by Catherine Rainwater and William J. Scheick. Lexington: University Press of Kentucky, 1985.

Freeman, Alama S. "Zora Neale Hurston and Alice Walker: A Spiritual Kinship." *SAGE* 2 (Spring 1985): pp. 37–40.

Hankinson, Stacie Lynn. "From Monotheism to Pantheism: Liberation from Patriarchy in Alice Walker's *The Color Purple.*" *Midwest Quarterly: A Journal of Contemporary Thought,* 38:3 (1997 Spring): pp. 320–328.

Heglar, Charles J. "Named and Namelessness: Alice Walker's Pattern of Surnames in *The Color Purple.*" *ANQ: A Quarterly Journal of Short Articles, Notes, and Reviews,* 13:1 (2000 Winter): pp. 39–41.

Heirs, John T. "Creation theology in Alice Walker's *The Color Purple.*" *Notes on Contemporary Literature* 14 (September 1984): pp. 2–3.

Henderson, Mae G. "*The Color Purple:* Revisions and Redefinitions." *SAGE* 2 (Spring 1985): pp. 14–18.

Hite, Molly. *The Other Side of the Story: Structures and Strategies of Contemporary Feminist Narrative.* Ithaca, N.Y.: Cornell University Press, 1989.

Hudson-Weem, Clenora. "The Tripartite Plight of African-American Women as Reflected in the Novels of Hurston and Walker." *Journal of Black Studies* 20 (Dec. 1989): pp. 192–207.

Inge, Tonette Bond, ed. *Southern Women Writers: The New Generation.* Tuscaloosa: University of Alabama Press, 1990.

Irwin, Edward E. "Freedoms as Value in Three Popular Southern Novels." *Proteus* 6 (Spring 1989): pp. 37–41.

Jump, Harriet Devine, ed. *Diverse Voices: Essays on Twentieth-Century Writers in English.* New York: St. Martin's Press, 1991.

Juneja, Om P. "The Purple Colour of Walker Women: Their Journey from Slavery to Liberation." *The Literary Criterion* 25 (1990): pp. 66–76.

Kelly, Lori Duin. "Theology and Androgony: The Role of Religion in *The Color Purple.*" *Notes on Contemporary Literature* 18 (March 1988): pp. 7–8.

Lysik, Marta. "'You Have Seen How a [Wo]Man Was Made a Slave; You Shall See How a Slave Was Made a [Wo]Man': Alice Walker's *The Color Purple* as a Neo-Slave Narrative." *American Studies,* 21 (2004): pp. 17–34.

Manora, Yolanda M. "'Us': Southern Black Communal Subjectivity and Male Emergence in Alice Walker's *The Color Purple.*" *Southern Studies: An Interdisciplinary Journal of the South,* 13:3–4 (2006 Fall–Winter): pp. 77–99.

McDowell, Deborah E. *"The Changing Same": Black Women's Literature, Criticism, and Theory.* Bloomington: Indiana University Press, 1995.

Pickney, Darryl. "Black Victims, Black Villains." *The New York Review of Books* (January 29, 1987): pp. 17–20.

Pifer, Lynn and Slusser, Tricia. "'Looking at the Back of Your Head': Mirroring Scenes in Alice Walker's *The Color Purple* and *Possessing the Secret of Joy.*" *MELUS,* 23:4 (1998 Winter): pp. 47–57.

Proudfit, Charles L. "Celie's Search for Identity: A Psychoanalytic Developmental Reading of Alice Walker's *The Color Purple.*" *Contemporary Literature* 32 (Spring 1991): pp. 112–137.

Robinson, Daniel. "Problems in the Form: Alice Walker's *The Color Purple.*" *Notes on Contemporary Literature* 16 (January 1986): p. 2.

Ross, Daniel M. "Celie in the Looking Glass: The Desire for Selfhood in *The Color Purple.*" *Modern Fiction Studies* 34 (Spring 1988): pp. 69–84.

Saunders, James Robert. "Womanism as the Key to Understanding Zora Neale Hurston's *Their Eyes Were Watching God* and Alice Walker's *The Color Purple.*" *The Hollins Critic* 25 (October 1988): pp. 1–11.

Scholl, Diane Gabrielsen. "With Ears to Hear and Eyes to See: Alice Walker's *The Color Purple.*" *Christianity and Literature* 40 (Spring 1991): pp. 255–266.

Shelton, F. W. "Alienation and Integration in Alice Walker's *The Color Purple.*" *CLA Journal* 28 (June 1985): pp. 382–392.

Stade, George. "Womanist Fiction and Male Characters." *Partisan Review* 52 (1985): pp. 265–270.

Tapia, Elena. "Symmetry as Conceptual Metaphor in Walker's *The Color Purple.*" *International Journal of English Studies,* 3:1 (2003), pp. 29-44.

Tavormina, M. Teresa. "Dressing the Spirit: Clothworking and Language in *The Color Purple.*" *Journal of Narrative Technique* 16 (Fall 1986): pp. 220–230.

Terry, Jill. "The Same River Twice: Signifying *The Color Purple.*" *Critical Survey,* 12:3 (2000): pp. 59–76.

Thomas, Jackie. "Reverend Samuel: The Missionary Minister in *The Color Purple.*" *Griot: Official Journal of the Southern Conference on Afro-American Studies, Inc.,* 16:2 (1997 Fall): pp. 15–18.

Thyreen, Jeannine. "Alice Walker's *The Color Purple:* Redefining God and (Re)Claiming the Spirit Within." *Christianity and Literature,* 49:1 (1999 Autumn): pp. 49–66.

Tucker, Lindsey. "Alice Walker's *The Color Purple:* Emergent Woman, Emergent Text." *Black American Literature Forum* 22 (Spring 1988): pp. 81–95.

Walsh, Margaret. "The Enchanted World of *The Color Purple.*" *The Southern Quarterly* 25 (Winter 1987): pp. 89–101.

Wasserman, Jerry. "Queen Bee, King Bee: *The Color Purple* and the Blues." *Canadian Review of American Studies/Revue Canadienne d'Etudes Américaines,* 30:3 (2000): pp. 301–316.

Williams, Carolyn. "'Trying to Do Without God': The Revision of Epistolary Address in *The Color Purple.*" In *Writing the Female Voice: Essays on Epistolary Literature,* edited by Elizabeth Goldsmith. Boston: Northeastern University Press, 1989.

Acknowledgments

"Celie in the Looking Glass: The Desire for Selfhood in *The Color Purple*," by Daniel W. Ross. *Modern Fiction Studies*, Volume 34, Number 1 (Spring 1988): pp. 69–84. © The Johns Hopkins University Press. Reprinted with permission of the Johns Hopkins University Press.

"Race, Gender, and Nation in *The Color Purple*," by Lauren Berlant. *Critical Inquiry*, Volume 14, Issue 4 (Summer 1988): pp. 831–859. Copyright © 1988 University of Chicago Press. Reprinted with permission.

"Sifting Through the Controversy: Reading *The Color Purple*," by Jacqueline Bobo. *Callaloo: A Journal of African American and African Arts and Letters*, Volume 12, Issue 2, Number 39, (1989 Spring): pp. 332–342. © The Johns Hopkins University Press. Reprinted with permission of the Johns Hopkins University Press.

"'What She Got to Sing About?': Comedy and *The Color Purple*," by Priscilla L. Walton. *ARIEL: A Review of International English Literature*, Volume 21, Number 2 (April 1990): pp. 59–74. © 1990 University of Calgary, Alberta. Reprinted by permission of the Board of Governors, University of Calgary, Alberta

"The Purple Colour of Walker Women: Their Journey from Slavery to Liberation," by Om P. Juneja. *The Literary Criterion*, Volume 26, Number 3 (1990): pp. 66–76. © Mysore Printing and Publications. All rights reserved.

"Celie's Search for Identity: A Psychoanalytic Developmental Reading of Alice Walker's *The Color Purple*," by Charles L. Proudfit. *Contemporary Literature*, Volume 32, Number 1 (Spring 1991): pp. 12–37. ©1991 by the Board of Regents of the University of Wisconsin System. Reprinted by permission of the publisher.

"With Ears to Hear and Eyes to See: Alice Walker's Parable *The Color Purple*," by Diane Gabrielsen Scholl. *Christianity and Literature*, Volume 40, Number 3 (Spring 1991): pp. 255–266. © 1991 Pepperdine University. Reprinted by permission of the publisher.

"Race and Domesticity in *The Color Purple*," by Linda Selzer. *African American Review*, Volume 29, Number 1 (Spring 1995): pp. 67–82. © 1995 Linda Selzer. Reprinted by permission of the author.

"Philomela Speaks: Alice Walker's Revisioning of Rape Archetypes in *The Color Purple*," by Martha J. Cutter. *MELUS*, Volume 25, Numbers 3/4 (Fall/Winter 2000): pp. 161–180. © 2000 MELUS. Reprinted courtesy of *MELUS: The Journal of the Society for the Study of the Multi-Ethnic Literature of the United States*.

"Sewing, Quilting, Knitting: Handicraft and Freedom in *The Color Purple* and *A Women's Story*," by Catherine E. Lewis, *Literature/Film Quarterly*, Volume 29, Number 3 (2001): pp. 236–245. © 2001 Salisbury University. All Rights Reserved. Reprinted by permission of the publisher.

Index